Financial Statement Fraud

Founded in 1807, John Wiley & Sons is the oldest independent publishing company in the United States. With offices in North America, Europe, Asia, and Australia, Wiley is globally committed to developing and marketing print and electronic products and services for our customers' professional and personal knowledge and understanding.

The Wiley Corporate F&A series provides information, tools, and insights to corporate professionals responsible for issues affecting the profitability of their company, from accounting and finance to internal controls and performance management.

Financial Statement Fraud

Strategies for Detection and Investigation

GERARD M. ZACK
CFE, CPA, CIA, CCEP

WILEY
John Wiley & Sons, Inc.

Cover image: John Wiley & Sons, Inc.
Cover design: @ Kajal Patel/iStockphoto

Published by John Wiley & Sons, Inc., Hoboken, New Jersey.

Published simultaneously in Canada.

Library of Congress Cataloging-in-Publication Data:

Zack, Gerard M.
Financial statement fraud : strategies for detection and investigation / Gerard M. Zack.
p. cm.
Includes bibliographical references and index.
ISBN 978-1-118-30155-5 (cloth); ISBN 978-1-118-41977-9 (ebk);
ISBN 978-1-118-43405-5 (ebk); ISBN 978-1-118-42147-5 (ebk)
1. Misleading financial statements. 2. Fraud. I. Title.
HF5681.B2Z2343 2013
658.4'73 — dc23 2012028599

10 9 8 7 6 5 4 3 2 1

This book is dedicated to my wife, April. Your encouragement, support, and love made this book possible and make my life so rich. I am very lucky to have you as my partner in life. I love you.

Contents

Foreword

FINANCIAL STATEMENT FRAUD certainly is not new, although there are few times in history when it has received more public scorn. Some would claim that its genesis is in the corporate structure. The first entity to issue shares to the public was the Dutch East India Company, which was granted a government monopoly over the Asian trade in 1602. In the same year, the Amsterdam Stock Exchange was founded. It quickly grew to an organization of 50,000 civilian employees with 40 warships, 20,000 sailors, and 10,000 soldiers. And soon, tiny Holland ruled the world of commerce.

But, as Lord Acton so famously said, power corrupts. By 1637, corporations had become so powerful in the Netherlands that stock market speculation led to a frenzy that nearly destroyed the entire credit system. At the time, audits were almost unheard of. They didn't gain prominence until nearly two centuries later, after the infamous American stock market crash of 1929. Until then, the price of shares was largely determined by insiders engaging in "pump and dump" schemes; the value of stock would be pumped through shameless and aggressive promotion, only to be dumped before the bottom fell out. In response to the massive frauds uncovered during the Great Depression, the U.S. passed the Securities Act of 1933. Among other provisions, it required for the first time that publicly traded companies be independently audited. That, in turn, gave real impetus to the CPA profession.

However, audits did not turn out to be a panacea. Crooked business executives have managed to consistently skirt internal controls designed to stop their financial chicanery. The last half of the twentieth century was littered with increasingly bold frauds that have become close to legendary: Crazy Eddie's, Enron, and WorldCom, to name a few. There are several disparate reasons for this mushrooming crime trend.

First, the nature of investing has completely changed over the last 50 years. Historically, stocks were purchased because buyers thought they understood the company. They believed in its products or services and that the value of their investments would increase over time. But then came institutional investors; and in the last decade, computerized trading. The effect of this shift, according to many, has been to create a stock market of speculators where share price is the only king. That, in turn, places enormous pressure on corporate executives to deliver good numbers, whether or not they are true. However, don't believe for a moment that financial statement fraud is limited to publicly traded companies; it occurs regularly in private-sector entities whose victims are typically lenders.

A second reason for an increase in financial statement fraud may have to do with the kind of executives now running companies. They have been described as greedy. But that is an incomplete answer; greed is a natural human trait and its extent cannot be empirically measured. Recent studies do suggest, however, that higher-status people are more unethical and behave in ways that serve their own self-interests. Moreover, affluence may foster a sense of entitlement; the rules are for others, not them. This could have created a bolder, more aggressive white-collar criminal.

The third reason is that auditors and accountants have been ill-equipped to detect financial statement fraud. Indeed, the profession has had a long and tortured history concerning its fraud-related responsibilities. Although the public has always felt fraud detection was a major aspect of the audit, CPAs believed otherwise. As a result, fulfilling this important duty was largely ignored until the mid-1980s. Then a plethora of audit failures leading to multimillion-dollar legal judgments against major accounting firms got the profession's attention. Still, not much changed until the beginning of the twenty-first century. That's when anti-fraud training began to be implemented for accounting students at the college and university level.

Education is by far the most important defensive weapon against frauds of all kinds. It is nearly impossible to defraud elderly victims in telemarketing scams if they have been taught to hear the signs; it becomes more difficult to fool the auditor who has the knowledge to recognize fraud schemes. In the latter instance, one would be hard pressed to find a better resource than Gerard Zack's *Financial Statement Fraud: Strategies for Detection and Investigation.*

Logically organized and wonderfully detailed with real examples, the book begins with revenue-based schemes. They are among the most common financial statement frauds but can be surprisingly difficult to detect—unless you know what to look for. Zack thoroughly covers fictitious and inflated sales; timing schemes such as bill and hold, channel stuffing, and fraudulent use of reserves; and misclassification shemes. The book then addresses asset-based schemes and unreported liabilities, which can be the Achilles' heel of the auditor. Particularly useful is an entire chapter on fraudulent disclosures and omissions.

The author doesn't stop there. He gives solid advice on how to uncover financial statement fraud schemes before they become catastrophic. By illustrating a variety of analytical techniques, Mr. Zack has simplified what could ordinarily be a complex topic. But more than that, he knows how to tell a story. Make no mistake: Fighting fraud is a war, one that honest commerce must win. *Financial Statement Fraud: Strategies for Detection and Investigation* certainly belongs in the arsenal.

Dr. Joseph T. Wells, CFE, CPA
Founder and Chairman, Association
of Certified Fraud Examiners

Preface

ABOUT THIS BOOK

According to the *Report to the Nations on Occupational Fraud and Abuse: 2012 Global Fraud Study*, prepared and published by the Association of Certified Fraud Examiners (ACFE), financial statement fraud is the least common of the three categories of frauds studied. Asset misappropriations are by far the most common, present in 86.7 percent of the cases studied. Corruption schemes (e.g., bribes, kickbacks, undisclosed conflicts of interest, etc.) represent 33.4 percent of the cases. Only 7.6 percent of the cases are financial statement fraud schemes (the total is more than 100 percent since some cases were classified in more than one category).

This level of frequency has not changed too much over the years. In the ACFE's 2010 study, financial statement fraud was involved in just 4.8 percent of the cases, while in 2008, this statistic was 10.3 percent.

However, while it might be the least frequently encountered, financial statement fraud is by far the most costly. In the 2012 report, the ACFE states that the median loss in financial statement fraud cases was $1 million. Median losses in asset misappropriation cases were only $120,000, while the figure rises to $250,000 in cases involving corruption.

Yet the measurement of losses from financial statement fraud is also the most difficult. There is the obvious loss in value of a company when its stock price drops. And there are other measurable losses. But, the indirect losses that result when financial statement fraud occurs are significant and almost impossible to measure. Not only are jobs lost, but for the employees who remain, morale, and therefore productivity, often plummets. In some cases, there may even be a loss of support from customers, partners, and even vendors who wish to disassociate themselves from the guilty company.

Writing a book about financial statement fraud is a bit dangerous. There are many angles that can be taken to the subject, many sub-topics within the overall topic. For this book, I have chosen to focus on the following:

1. Descriptions of the most common or emerging schemes involving the preparation and issuance of fraudulent financial statements.
2. References to the pertinent U.S. and international accounting standards that were violated in the preparation of the fraudulent financial statements, since it is critical to prove that the statements violate the principles that they purport to conform to in order to prove fraud.
3. A wide range of detection tools, from the simplest of ratios to complex analyses and tests, as well as fraud indicators.
4. A discussion of auditor liability, presented as a tool for investigators in assessing whether an auditor has liability for failing to detect fraud, as well as for auditors, as a tool for minimizing their risk of failure to detect fraudulent financial reporting.
5. Significant use of actual cases to illustrate many of the fraud schemes explained throughout the book.

This book is not designed to cover the basics of financial reporting and accounting. It assumes the reader already knows what the basic financial statements are and what purpose each serves, as well as basic accounting concepts, such as accrual basis accounting. Instead, I will jump right into the fraud schemes and the accounting principles that each violates.

Most of the cases used to illustrate the fraud schemes involve publicly traded companies, since public records for these cases are much more extensive than any with cases involving privately held businesses. But the schemes themselves vary less than one might think from public company to small business. The only difference may be that some public companies are just more complex and diverse in their operations, opening themselves up to a broader range of fraud schemes.

There is a companion website that accompanies this book. What can be found on the companion website are copies of the SEC's Accounting and Audit Enforcement Releases (AAERs), complaints that were filed, and certain other documents associated with most of the cases cited in the book. A handful of cases are used that were based on press reporting, with little issuance of official documents from enforcement agencies. But, the vast majority of the cases used in this book are supported with official releases and other publicly available reports or complaints.

GLOSSARY OF ABBREVIATIONS USED THROUGHOUT THIS BOOK

Several terms are used extensively throughout this book.

AAER Accounting and Audit Enforcement Release

These are documents published by the SEC, sometimes accompanied by a copy of a complaint filed in court, describing a variety of possible violations of SEC regulations, including allegations of misstatements in the financial statements of a publicly traded company. Many of the misstatements are explicitly described as being caused by fraud, while others are not directly attributed to acts of fraud. Regardless, AAERs serve as excellent tools to illustrate how fraudulent financial reporting can occur.

AICPA American Institute of Certified Public Accountants

The AICPA is the organization that promulgates auditing standards in the U.S. applicable to audits of non–publicly traded entities (referred to as "non-issuers"). Prior to the creation of the PCAOB, the AICPA's auditing standards covered audits of public companies as well.

ASC Accounting Standards Codification

The ASC represents the uniform codification of all sources of U.S. GAAP, combining into a single code the guidance previously issued from a variety of sources, such as Statements of Financial Accounting Standards, Emerging Issues Task Force, FASB Interpretations, and others. The ASC is maintained by FASB.

FASB Financial Accounting Standards Board

This is the organization that promulgates and maintains U.S. GAAP in the form of the ASC.

GAAP Generally Accepted Accounting Principles

As it is referred to in this book, GAAP refers to the set of accounting principles applicable in the United States. These principles are codified in the ASC, maintained by FASB. There are also numerous country-specific GAAPs outside of the United States.

IAS International Accounting Standard

International Accounting Standards are numbered consecutively (IAS 27, IAS 28, etc.) and each addresses a specific accounting or financial reporting topic under IFRS. New IASs are no longer issued; however, revisions to existing ones are. New sources of IFRS are now titled IFRS 11, IFRS 12, IFRS 13, and so on.

IASB International Accounting Standards Board

The IASB is the organization that promulgates and maintains the International Financial Reporting Standards applicable in more than 100 countries.

IFRS International Financial Reporting Standards

IFRS is the term used to describe the complete body of international standards applicable to the preparation of financial statements. IFRS has been adopted in more than 100 countries. The IFRS as a whole encompasses a variety of original standards, such as IASs, SICs, IFRICs (IFRS Interpretations Committee Updates), and new standards referred to simply as IFRS 11, IFRS 12, and so on.

PCAOB Public Company Accounting Oversight Board

The PCAOB was established in 2002 to oversee auditors of publicly traded companies in the United States and to issue auditing standards applicable to those audits. When it was created, the PCAOB adopted the auditing standards previously issued by the AICPA, but has since issued its own auditing standards, some of which mirror those issued by the AICPA but are customized for audits of public companies. The PCAOB performs inspections of auditors of public companies and issues public reports on the results of those inspections.

SEC Securities and Exchange Commission

The SEC is the government agency that oversees publicly traded companies in the United States and their audits. The SEC has the authority to issue regulations associated with public companies and the markets on which they are traded.

SIC Standing Interpretations Committee

The SIC is a body that promulgates IFRS on certain limited-scope topics. As the committee issues new guidance, it is numbered consecutively, such as SIC 11, SIC 12, and so on.

Acknowledgments

THANKS TO DR. JOSEPH T. WELLS, founder of the Association of Certified Fraud Examiners, who continues to serve as such an inspiration to me and to countless others who fight the fight against fraud every day.

I'd also like to thank the great team at John Wiley & Sons, who make an author's job so much easier. In particular: Tim Burgard, Acquisitions Editor, Stacey Rivera, Development Editor, and Chris Gage, Production Editor.

Finally, I'd like to thank Dominyka Sakalauskaitė, a talented Ph.D. student at Aarhus University, who assisted in researching some of the financial statement fraud cases.

PART ONE

Revenue-Based Schemes

SIXTY-ONE PERCENT of the financial statement frauds studied in connection with the 2010 report, *Fraudulent Financial Reporting 1998–2007, An Analysis of U.S. Public Companies*, from the Committee of Sponsoring Organizations of the Treadway Commission (COSO) involved misstatements of revenue, making this the single most common category of financial statement fraud. This statistic has been rather consistent over time. In an analysis of SEC AAERs issued from 1982 to 2005, it was reported by Dechow, Ge, Larson, and Sloan that 54 percent of 676 misstatements involved incorrect reporting of revenue.

Since accounting inherently involves two sides to every transaction, when a revenue account is misstated, some other account is likely to be misstated as well. The schemes covered in this part of the book, however, are driven by a desire by the perpetrators to misstate revenue. The other accounts that are affected may be assets, liabilities, expenses, or even other revenue accounts. But, the motive behind the schemes described in this part is to misstate one or more revenue accounts.

CHAPTER ONE

Introduction to Revenue-Based Financial Reporting Fraud Schemes

REVENUE RECOGNITION PRINCIPLES

U.S. GAAP describes revenues as inflows or other enhancements of an entity's assets or settlements of its liabilities (or a combination of both) from delivering or providing goods, rendering services, or other activities that constitute the entity's ongoing major or central operations. Under IFRS, revenue is defined in IAS 18, *Revenue*, as "The gross inflow of economic benefits during the period arising in the course of the ordinary activities of an entity when those inflows result in increases in equity, other than increases relating to contributions from equity participants."

The primary accounting standard governing revenue recognition under IFRS is IAS 18, a comprehensive standard covering numerous considerations. In addition, rules have been published dealing with certain specific types of revenue (e.g., IAS 11 on construction contracts, SIC 31 on barter transactions, etc.).

Under U.S. GAAP, there is currently not a comprehensive revenue standard that is analogous to IAS 18. Instead, there is very broad guidance found in ASC 605, supplemented by standards dealing with specific types of revenue (e.g., revenue from software at ASC 985-605-25) or specific industries (e.g., the music industry at ASC 928-605-25).

As of the writing of this book, however, FASB and IASB are involved in a joint project that will result in changed revenue recognition principles under both U.S. GAAP and IFRS. An exposure draft of a new standard, *Revenue from Contracts with Customers*, was published by FASB in January 2012, with a comment period that ended in March 2012. FASB and IASB had previously jointly issued an exposure draft in November 2011.

For obvious reasons, this book is based on accounting rules currently applicable under U.S. GAAP and IFRS, as well as cases that have been brought forward pertaining to alleged violations of those rules. The proposed new accounting principles will be briefly explained in the next section.

Under ASC 605, revenue should be recognized when it is earned and either realized or realizable. Reference is then made to more comprehensive guidance published by the SEC. The SEC's Staff Accounting Bulletin (SAB) Topic 13 identifies the following criteria that should all be met in order to demonstrate that revenue is realized or realizable and has been earned:

- Persuasive evidence of an arrangement exists
- Delivery of the goods has occurred or the services have been rendered
- The price is fixed or determinable
- Collectibility is reasonably assured

Under IAS 18, revenue from the sale of goods should only be recognized if all five of the following criteria have been met:

1. All significant risks and rewards associated with ownership of the goods have been transferred.
2. The seller does not retain any ownership-like managerial involvement or control over the goods that were sold.
3. The amount of revenue can be measured reliably.
4. It is probable that the economic benefits associated with the transaction will flow to the seller.
5. Transaction costs can be measured reliably.

With respect to recognition of revenue from the provision of services, only the third, fourth, and fifth criteria from the preceding list should be applied. However, in addition, the stage of completion of the project at the end of the reporting period must be able to be measured reliably.

CHANGES PROPOSED BY FASB AND IASB

The goals of FASB and IASB in proposing a new approach to revenue recognition are to:

1. Remove inconsistencies in existing requirements and improve comparability of revenue recognized under U.S. GAAP and IFRS (hopefully, some of the differences explained in this book will go away once the new standard takes effect)
2. Provide a more robust framework for addressing revenue recognition issues, a framework that can be applied to a wide variety of different revenue arrangements
3. Reduce the number of different revenue recognition rules currently in effect, thereby simplifying research and application of accounting principles

Since the new rules are still in exposure draft format as of the writing of this book, a detailed explanation of them seems pointless. However, a few key points from the draft warrant mentioning.

The core principle of the new standard is that revenue should be recognized to depict the transfer of goods or services to customers in an amount that reflects the consideration to which the entity expects to be entitled in exchange for those goods or services. Five steps would be undertaken to apply this principle:

1. Identify the contract(s) with the customer
2. Identify the separate performance obligations
3. Determine the transaction price
4. Allocate the transaction price
5. Recognize revenue when a performance obligation is satisfied

These steps borrow, with some modification, some of the existing revenue recognition concepts, such as the multiple-element revenue arrangement rules introduced in Chapter 2. And the existing basic requirements associated with persuasive evidence, delivery, a determinable price, and collectibility are by no means eliminated. Rather, they are updated and clarified in a manner designed to apply to a wide variety of revenue arrangements.

OVERVIEW OF REVENUE-BASED SCHEMES

Revenue schemes focus on manipulating revenue. This normally means falsely increasing reported revenue, but in some cases the reverse can be true. Revenue schemes are classified into the following categories:

- Timing schemes
- Fictitious or inflated revenue
- Misclassification schemes
- Gross-up schemes

Think of these categories as the when, why, where, and how of revenue recognition.

Timing schemes shift revenue that belongs in one accounting period to another. Over the course of two or more periods, combined, the fraud self-eliminates. However, since each accounting period stands on its own and must conform to relevant accounting principles, timing schemes represent a form of financial statement fraud. Most commonly, revenue is recognized too soon in the financial statements. This is known as premature revenue recognition.

The rationalization behind prematurely recognizing revenue is simple. The company is borrowing future revenues for today, holding out hope that it can make up for this difference in the next period. This is often done when a company begins to lag behind revenue expectations. The mentality of individuals perpetrating timing schemes is that they feel they will always figure out a way to make the next period successful. They feel that they just need to get through the current period and all will be okay.

Fictitious and inflated revenue both involve fabricating additional revenue to improve profits, decrease losses, or simply appear larger. Fictitious revenue refers to amounts that have been recognized that have no basis whatsoever. Either the customer is fake, the transaction is fake, or both. Inflated revenue, however, starts from a legitimate transaction with a real customer. But, the value of the transaction has been inflated in some manner.

Misclassification schemes do not affect the bottom line of the reporting entity. However, these schemes can have a material impact on certain important financial measures by classifying a transaction improperly, resulting in the transaction appearing on the wrong line of the financial statements.

The final category, gross-up schemes, is designed to accomplish one objective—to make the company appear larger. As with misclassification schemes, the bottom line is not impacted. Rather, revenue and costs or expenses are overstated in equal amounts. This technique is utilized when growth or a specific revenue goal is desired and the company is falling short.

The remaining chapters of Part I will explain how each of these four types of revenue-based schemes are perpetrated.

CHAPTER TWO

Timing Schemes

ALTERATION OF RECORDS

A sales transaction is often supported by several types of records: contracts, sales orders, sales journals, shipping documents, and many others. Physically changing information in any of these may be all that is necessary to perpetrate a revenue recognition fraud scheme. Two examples of record alteration in connection with timing schemes are:

1. **Backdating of agreements**. This method is as simple as it sounds. Sales or revenue arrangements that are finalized in one accounting period are falsely dated as though they were executed in the preceding period. This technique may or may not require the knowledge of the customer. Backdating of shipping documents is a variation on this technique and can be used to accomplish the same goal.
2. **Keeping the accounting records open past the end of the period**. Similar to the backdating of an agreement, this technique allows for sales of the subsequent period to be recorded as though they occurred in the preceding period. Years ago, when many businesses maintained their accounting records manually, this was accomplished simply by entering

an inaccurate (earlier) date for a transaction in the sales journal. In an automated environment, keeping accounting records open beyond the end of a period can be accomplished either by entering an incorrect date, or overriding a computer-generated date during the input stage of a transaction or by making changes to the computer program itself.

An example of the latter occurred in the case of Sensormatic Electronics Corporation in 1994 and 1995. According to the SEC, as described in AAER 1017, on the last day of the quarter, Sensormatic would bring down the computer system that recorded and dated shipments to customers. As a result, the computer date would continue to reflect the last day of the quarter, resulting in the false recording of shipments made after the end of the quarter as though they were shipped before the end of the quarter.

Another example of keeping the books open beyond the end of the quarter involved Computer Associates International, Inc. (CA). In its complaint, the SEC charged CA with premature revenue recognition on software contracts from 1998 through 2000. The CA scheme was very simple. The company kept the books open for several days after the end of each quarter, allowing contracts executed by customers or CA after the end of the quarter to be recognized as though they were executed within the quarter just ended. CA would often conceal this practice by "using licensing contracts that falsely bore preprinted signature dates for the last day of the quarter that had just expired, rather than the subsequent dates on which the contracts actually were executed." This enabled CA to meet analysts' expectations. In the first quarter after ceasing this practice, CA missed its earnings estimate and its stock price fell by 43 percent in one day.

Finally, the case of Del Global Technologies Corp. involved a complete second set of sales and accounts receivable records, one supported with fake invoices or shipping documents, to support the early recognition of revenue from 1997 through 2000. Del Global is described more fully in the next section, on shipping schemes.

SHIPPING SCHEMES

The shipping department can be utilized to prematurely recognize revenue. By doing so, shipping documents become available as support for a sale that should not really be recognized until the next period.

One such method is to ship goods prior to a sale being fully consummated. This may occur when a sale is in the latter stages of negotiation and the company anticipates completion soon. The shipping department is then directed to ship the goods on one of the last days of the accounting period in order to recognize a sale.

Another variation on the preceding scheme is for shipment to intentionally be done in a manner that results in a lengthy period in transit, ensuring that the customer does not receive the goods prior to signing the sales agreement (or prior to a previously agreed-upon date). For example, a company may ship goods at the end of one accounting period, recording the sale in that period, but utilize a delayed shipment scheme so that the goods do not arrive at the customer's location until well into the next period, which is when the customer has requested delivery. In the Sensormatic Electronics Corporation case (see preceding section and SEC AAER 1017) the company instructed carriers to delay delivery of goods in order to meet customers' expectations that goods would arrive in the subsequent quarter. These requested delays resulted in deliveries beyond normal transit times, ranging from just a few days to as much as a few weeks.

In some cases, shipments might even be made to some intermediary warehouse prior to delivery to the customer, thus arranging for a delay. Taking this approach one step further, in the Sensormatic case, goods were shipped to another warehouse that was leased by Sensormatic, but sales were recorded for these shipments as though they had been sent to the customer. The actual shipments to the customers, in accordance with the customers' orders, were not made until the next accounting period, sometimes several months later.

In addition to providing relevant examples of timing schemes, the Sensormatic case also illustrates how financial reporting fraud can, and often does, involve more than one method. This is a valuable lesson for auditors and investigators. When one fraud scheme has been uncovered, keep looking. There are likely others.

Another example of a shipping scheme is the case of Del Global Technologies Corp. ("Del Global"), introduced in the preceding section. In 2004, the SEC charged Del Global with a massive accounting fraud involving numerous methods of inflating earnings (see AAER 2027). One of those methods involved recognizing revenue in connection with shipments of products to third-party warehouses. In many cases, these shipments occurred months before the customers had agreed to take delivery of or assume the risks of ownership of the products. In one case cited by the SEC in its complaint, the products remained in the third-party warehouse two years after shipment and recognition of revenue. Senior Del Global officers instructed others to engage in this practice, despite complaints from personnel that it was inappropriate.

Del Global engaged in a variety of schemes to conceal this and other frauds from its auditors, and this will be discussed further in Chapter 20. In connection with this particular scheme, however, subsequent to shipping products and fraudulently recognizing the revenue, Del Global would issue customer credit memos and then reissue sales invoices in order to "refresh" the accounts receivable sub-ledger, making these accounts appear more current than they really were.

You'll read more about Del Global later, as this case is useful for illustrating several types of financial statement frauds.

In each of the preceding cases, when an agreement states that delivery is to be made in a subsequent period (or the agreement is not even entered into until the next period), the accounting principles described earlier would preclude recognition of the sale in the earlier period.

Shipping incorrect goods when goods ordered by a customer are not in stock, knowing that in the subsequent period the customer will return the incorrect items, is yet another shipping scheme that can result in premature revenue recognition. It enables the company to maintain supporting documentation for a sales order received as well as a shipment from the warehouse, albeit an incorrect one. The itemized shipping documents may indicate that the correct items were shipped when, in fact, incorrect goods were delivered to the customer. In the subsequent accounting period, when the company has an adequate inventory of the correct goods, the incorrect goods are received back from the customer and the correct goods are then delivered.

PERCENTAGE OF COMPLETION SCHEMES

Long-term contracts, such as construction projects, are ordinarily accounted for using the percentage of completion method.

Under U.S. GAAP, the percentage of completion method is used for most construction contracts. Contracts that do not meet the criteria for percentage of completion are accounted for using the completed contract method, whereby all revenue is recognized upon the completion of the contract. Under IFRS, percentage of completion accounting must be used for all construction contracts (i.e., the completed contract method is prohibited).

One additional difference between U.S. GAAP and IFRS is that under U.S. GAAP the percentage of completion method is limited to construction contracts. This method may not be utilized for nonconstruction service contracts, which means these contracts must use some form of proportional performance model for revenue recognition. IFRS, on the other hand, requires use of the percentage of completion method for service contracts unless progress toward completion cannot be measured reliably, in which case a zero-profit methodology must be used until the contract is completed.

Under the percentage of completion method of accounting, total revenue associated with a project is multiplied by the estimated percentage of completion to determine the revenue to be recognized through the end of an accounting period. The percentage of completion is usually measured by dividing the actual costs incurred to date by the estimated total costs of the project. Thus, cumulative revenue to be recognized is equal to the result of the following formula:

Total revenue × Costs incurred to date/Estimated total costs of the project

Premature revenue recognition can occur by manipulating either the numerator or denominator of the fraction used to measure percentage of completion. Most commonly, the estimate of the remaining costs necessary to complete a project may be underestimated, resulting in the denominator being understated and, therefore, a higher percentage completion to be applied to total revenue.

However, the numerator of the fraction may also be falsely stated. By overstating the costs incurred to date, the percentage of completion can also be inflated. Overstating actual costs incurred to date can be accomplished using several techniques, including:

1. Prepaying vendors and subcontractors for goods and services not yet provided and failing to set up such prepayments as assets, and instead, expensing the expenditures. (This can be made even more difficult to detect if vendors and subcontractors are in on the act by agreeing to invoice for undelivered goods and services early, making the invoices appear as though delivery had occurred; some vendors might not even think of this as facilitating a fraud—they view it as simply getting paid early for work they will do later!)
2. Disguising payments made to related parties as project-related costs.
3. Creating fictitious entities made to look like vendors and subcontractors and then making or accruing payments to these shell companies.
4. Creating ghost employees and falsifying records to make it appear that these ghosts have been working on the project and getting paid.
5. Misclassifying legitimate costs that have been incurred on other projects or activities to the project for which percentage of completion is to be inflated.
6. Double-booking costs incurred by reflecting expenditures as costs of two different projects, or as a cost of a project and an operating expense of the company.

Utilizing actual and estimated costs to complete is not the only acceptable method of measuring percentage of completion. A physical measure of the proportion of the work completed, or a units-of-work approach, may be used if this provides a more reliable measure.

It should be noted that progress payments made by a customer rarely represent accurate measures of the percentage of completion on a project.

A 2008 class action suit filed by investors in Integral Systems, Inc. illustrates a different risk involving percentage of completion accounting. One of the issues addressed in the suit pertained to a contract held by Integral, the Next Generation Global Positioning System (GPS OCX) contract. Integral had recognized $2.4 million of license revenue in connection with this contract, which was a subcontract with Northrup Grumman. This contract fell under Integral's accounting policy requiring application of the percentage of completion method to its software license contracts. In December 2008, Integral restated its financial statements for the first three quarters of fiscal 2008, noting that $2.0 million of the $2.4 million should have been recognized in future periods under proper application of the percentage of completion method.

In explaining the restatement, an Integral official noted that it was "debatable" whether Integral was "making significant modifications or merely adding functionality beyond the software's core capabilities." Merely adding some additional functionality after the recognition of the $2.4 million in revenue would indicate that most or all of the $2.4 million was properly recognized. However, if Integral still had to make significant modifications to the software, recognition of revenue as though the contract had been completed would be inappropriate, and that appears to be the conclusion in the restatement.

One of the most comprehensive and illustrative cases pertaining to percentage of completion accounting involves Golden Bear Golf, Inc. and its wholly owned subsidiary, Paragon Construction International, Inc. (Paragon). In a 2002 complaint filed by the SEC, it was alleged that Paragon accelerated revenue recognition and hid losses that should have been recognized under percentage of completion contracts. This was accomplished in a number of manners:

1. Intentionally underestimating the costs to complete certain contracts, resulting in early recognition of income (or avoidance of recognizing losses).
2. Changing project managers' estimates of progress on certain contracts. For example, one project manager estimated progress on the "Twin Eagles" project at 3 percent, but Paragon accrued 14 percent of contract revenue, resulting in an overstatement in revenue of $698,000. On another project,

called the "Keene's Pointe" project, the manager estimated 2 percent completion, but Paragon accrued revenue at 12 percent, resulting in $704,000 of extra revenue.

3. Entering into contracts for amounts that were less than Paragon's estimated costs as a result of underbidding to beat the competition, meaning these contracts should have been accounted for as losses from the very beginning.

At one point, Paragon even switched from the cost approach of estimating percentage of completion. Since understating estimated costs to complete became more difficult to conceal on certain projects, Paragon changed to the "earned value" approach to estimating percentage of completion. Under this method, a judgment of the physical progress on a project was used to estimate the percentage completed. The additional judgment involved in this approach allowed Paragon officials to overestimate the progress on certain contracts.

In its announcement that former Paragon executives had pled guilty to criminal charges and had settled the SEC's enforcement action filed against them, the SEC noted that the loss to shareholders in connection with this scheme was in excess of $49 million.

IMPROPER ESTIMATES OF REVENUE RECOGNITION PERIOD

The percentage of completion method of accounting only applies to certain types of long-term contracts, as explained in the preceding section. There are numerous other revenue arrangements in which some factor other than costs must be identified as a basis for measuring the portion of revenue that is attributable to a specific accounting period. Whenever an initial sales price includes an amount allocable for subsequent services, that amount should be deferred and recognized as revenue over the period during which the service is rendered. With some arrangements, this requires that an estimate be made by management in order to allocate revenue among accounting periods.

Take, for example, a transaction in which a one-time initiation fee is paid by a customer. That initiation fee entitles the customer to certain benefits for an unlimited time period, potentially extending up to the person's death. The accounting question in this transaction is: Over how many years should the company allocate the initiation fee?

In some cases, customers' remaining life expectancies are used as the basis for these estimates, based on average ages of customers at the time the fees are paid.

In other cases, however, using life expectancies is not appropriate. For example, Bally's Total Fitness Holding Corporation was charged with accounting fraud by the SEC in a 2008 civil complaint. The SEC asserted that Bally's engaged in material financial reporting violations from 1997 through 2003. As an example of just how material this scheme was, the SEC alleged that the 2001 annual Form 10-K filed by Bally's was misstated to the tune of nearly $2 billion! The financial statement filed by Bally's reported year-end net worth (shareholders' equity) of $513 million. The SEC noted that "In truth, Bally's year-end 2001 net worth—once all of the accounting improprieties were corrected—was *negative* $1.3 *billion*. Simply put, Bally's overstated its year-end 2001 net worth by $1.8 billion."

The Bally's improprieties covered a variety of revenue recognition issues, of which only two are relevant here. Bally's operated fitness centers. Three forms of revenue are pertinent to the accounting improprieties: (1) an initiation fee paid upon first joining, (2) monthly membership dues, and (3) a reactivation fee paid when reactivating someone whose membership had lapsed.

Initiation fees could be paid up front or financed over time, usually 36 months. Revenue recognition principles require that these fees be recognized as income over the expected life of the membership. Therefore, a liability for deferred revenue would be recorded and then amortized into income over an estimated period of membership, not just over the initial financing period (36 months) or initial period of membership. Instead, Bally's recognized initiation fee revenue over periods that were shorter than the estimated membership life, in most instances even less than the initial period of membership. This resulted in premature recognition of revenue. In 2004, Bally's acknowledged that its method of deferring and recognizing revenue for initiation fees did not conform to U.S. GAAP.

Bally's also improperly accounted for reactivation fees. Once lapsed members had not paid monthly dues for six months or more, they were eligible for reactivation by paying a fee. This fee was lower than the initiation fee described in the preceding paragraph. To reactivate a membership, an individual would sign a new contract. Under revenue recognition principles, recognition of any revenue from reactivation fees would be prohibited until the binding contract had been executed. However, Bally's prematurely recorded reactivation fee revenue based on its internal estimates of future reactivations. This revenue was based on projected reactivations up to three years into the future. While these projections were based on evaluations of historical reactivation rates, there is no basis under U.S. GAAP for recognizing any of this revenue until a reactivation occurs. Once again, in 2003 and 2004, Bally's changed this method of accounting, acknowledging that its previous filings did not conform to GAAP.

MULTIPLE-ELEMENT REVENUE RECOGNITION SCHEMES

One of the most common marketing techniques used by businesses is the bundling of multiple products and services together, resulting in a single purchase price that is less than the sum of the purchase prices of the individual items when purchased separately. When all of the deliverables are satisfied concurrently, there is little risk of a revenue timing fraud. For example, if the purchase price of a book is $25, but can be combined with another $25 book for a total price of $45, the allocation of the sales price between the two books has no impact on the seller's financial statements as long as both books are delivered at the same time.

However, when certain elements of an arrangement are satisfied in one period while others are not satisfied until a future period, the issue of how much revenue to recognize in each period takes on greater importance. And the risk of fraud is introduced.

U.S. GAAP includes very specific guidance on this type of transaction, described at ASC 605-25. This guidance changed starting with 2011 fiscal year-ends, so both the pre-2011 and post-2010 rules will be explained here. IFRS does not have a direct counterpart to the specific rules included in U.S. GAAP. IAS 18 requires that revenue should be recognized as an element of a transaction if that element has commercial substance on its own. Otherwise, separate elements should be linked together and accounted for as a single transaction. But, IAS 18 does not describe any specific criteria to be applied in making this determination.

Under pre-2011 U.S. GAAP, revenue arrangements with multiple deliverables should be divided into their separate units of accounting if all three of the following conditions are present:

1. The delivered item(s) has value to the customer on a standalone basis. An item has standalone value if it is sold separately by any vendor or the customer could resell the delivered item(s) on a standalone basis (the ability to resell does not require the existence of an observable market).

2. There is objective and reliable evidence of the fair value of the undelivered item(s).
3. If the arrangement includes a general right of return relative to the delivered item(s), delivery or performance of the undelivered item(s) is considered probable and substantially in the control of the vendor.

When a multiple deliverable revenue arrangement meets these three criteria, revenue should be allocated among the separate units based on their relative fair value. Then, an appropriate revenue recognition method should be determined for each unit. The amount allocated to an element is limited to the lesser of the amount otherwise allocable (based on fair value) or the noncontingent portion of the arrangement.

Accounting Standards Update (ASU) No. 2009-13, published in October 2009, makes significant amendments to the preceding guidance (which originally came from Emerging Issues Task Force 00-21), effective for revenue arrangements entered into or materially modified in fiscal years beginning on or after June 15, 2010 (i.e., generally, fiscal years ended June 30, 2011, and later). Under ASU No. 2009-13 (now codified as ASC 605-25), in revenue arrangements with multiple deliverables, the delivered item(s) should be considered separate units of accounting if the following two conditions are present:

1. The delivered item(s) has value to the customer on a standalone basis. An item has standalone value if it is sold separately by any vendor or the customer could resell the delivered item(s) on a standalone basis (the ability to resell does not require the existence of an observable market).
2. If the arrangement includes a general right of return relative to the delivered item(s), delivery or performance of the undelivered item(s) is considered probable and substantially in the control of the vendor.

The difference between the new and old criteria is merely the elimination of the second pre-2011 criterion, which required a fair value assessment of each unit. Instead, the new accounting standard is based on the "relative selling price" method.

Arrangement consideration must be allocated at the inception of the arrangement to all deliverables on the basis of their relative selling price (the relative selling price method), unless one of the deliverables otherwise must be accounted for at fair value based on some other accounting standard.

In applying the selling price method to the allocation of revenue, the selling price for each deliverable should be determined using a prescribed hierarchy:

1. Vendor-specific objective evidence of selling price should be used first, if it exists (i.e., if the company sells each unit separately, those prices should be utilized—see below).
2. If vendor-specific evidence is not available (i.e., the company does not sell each unit separately) third-party evidence may be used (e.g., relative selling prices of other companies that offer the units separately).
3. If no third-party evidence is available, then the vendor's best estimate is to be used.

Vendor-specific objective evidence of selling price is limited to either of the following:

1. The price charged for a deliverable when it is sold separately.
2. For a deliverable not yet being sold separately, the price established by management with the relevant authority (it must be probable that the price, once established, will not change before the separate introduction of the deliverable into the marketplace).

The opportunities for fraudulent financial reporting regarding multiple-element revenue recognition fall into two categories:

1. Misapplication of the criteria for being eligible to segregate a transaction into multiple elements (e.g., claiming that a transaction satisfies the criteria when, in fact, it does not).
2. Improperly allocating revenue among the multiple elements that are segregated in a qualifying multiple-element transaction. In an effort to improve profits, a company may overallocate revenue to elements that are recognized first, while underallocating revenue to elements that may be deferred into future periods.

One of the most well-publicized cases involving multiple-element revenue recognition involved Xerox Corporation. In a 2002 complaint, the SEC charged Xerox with misapplying the multiple-element revenue recognition rules to its bundled transactions involving copier leases from 1997 to 2000. Under these arrangements, customers paid a single monthly amount, called "Total Cost of Ownership" (TCO), in exchange for photocopier equipment, service, supplies, and financing provided by Xerox. The fair value of the equipment provided at the beginning of the term qualified for revenue recognition upon delivery and acceptance by the customer, under the "sales-type" lease accounting rules. All other elements—the service, supplies, and financing—were to be recognized as revenue over the life of the agreement. The SEC alleged that Xerox reallocated the TCO revenue so that more of it was attributed to the up-front delivery of equipment, resulting in the shift of "revenues and earnings from future periods, knowing that such reallocations would negatively affect those future periods." Xerox claimed it was impractical to estimate the fair value of the equipment. Therefore, they backed into the fair value by subtracting the fair value of the other elements from the total TCO. These other elements (to be deferred and recognized as revenue later) were the ones that Xerox decreased its estimated fair value of, leaving a larger fair value to apply to the up-front provision of equipment. In particular, the SEC was critical of the reduction by Xerox (multiple times) of the discount rate used to measure the portion of TCO associated with financing revenue. By lowering the rate to unsupported and unrealistic levels ("unsupported by either objective evidence or economic reality"), too small of a portion of TCO was allocated to financing income. The result of Xerox's reallocation was to pull forward "nearly $3.1 billion in equipment revenue and pre-tax earnings of $717 million from 1997 through 2000." The reallocation of TCO revenue was one of many accounting changes made by Xerox in order to meet financial reporting expectations, and the SEC noted that "Certain of these activities clearly violated GAAP."

Another improper application of the pre-2011 multiple-element revenue recognition rules involved Qwest Communications International, Inc. (Qwest), the telecommunications, long distance telephone, and Internet services giant. One of Qwest's important sources of revenue during the period in question, from 1999 to 2002, involved the sale of indefeasible rights of use, known as IRUs. An IRU is an irrevocable right to use a specific fiber strand or specific amount of fiber capacity for a specific period of time.

Qwest treated its IRU sales as having multiple elements, as follows:

1. Right of way
2. Conduit
3. Fiber
4. Equipment
5. Facilities
6. Operations and maintenance

Revenue was recognized up front on three of these elements—fiber, equipment, and facilities. This early recognition represented approximately 80 percent of the total revenue associated with each IRU sales transaction. The other elements, representing just 20 percent of the total, were recognized as revenue over the course of the lease term.

The SEC argued that Qwest's IRU sales did not meet the criteria for utilizing multiple-element accounting. This charge was based on the fact that each of the elements did not represent a separate earnings process. As a result, none of the revenue should have been recognized up front. Rather, all revenue should have been recognized ratably over the term of the lease.

The SEC went on to argue that even if the other elements required for multiple-element accounting were met, Qwest failed to have vendor-specific evidence supporting its allocation of 80 percent of the revenue to the elements recognized up front. When Qwest restated its financial statements, it acknowledged that it did not have sufficient evidence on which to objectively determine the appropriate allocation among the six elements identified.

Multiple-element revenue recognition rules have also been in place in connection with revenue from software, in the AICPA Statement of Position 97-2, although the guidelines in that document are very similar to the rules explained earlier. This standard was the focus of a restatement of the financial statements of SmartForce PLC, a developer of electronic learning courseware, software and referenceware products which subsequently merged into SkillSoft PLC. Some of these products were treated as multiple element arrangements and SmartForce allocated revenue among each element, recognizing certain elements immediately upon a sale and deferring other elements. In the restatement of the company's 8-K/A filed with the SEC, SmartForce explained that it did not have the requisite vendor-specific evidence regarding the value to be assigned to each element:

> SmartForce did not have vendor-specific objective evidence of the fair value of its products and services as defined in American Institute of Certified Public Accountants ("AICPA") Statement of Position ("SOP") 97-2, "Software Revenue Recognition," as amended by SOP 98-4 and SOP 98-9 ("SOP 97-2, as amended"), to permit separate revenue recognition for individual elements included in multiple-element transactions. As a result, these financial statements reflect a deferral of certain revenue that previously was recognized at the time of delivery. Because in most cases the undelivered element related to services provided over time, revenue is generally recognized over the term for which the services are provided.

This restatement is among a variety of issues that resulted in a class action suit being filed in 2003 on behalf of stockholders. In addition, in 2007, the SEC settled actions against former executives of SmartForce, noting that revenue was overstated by $113.6 million during the 3½-year period ended in mid-2002.

It is too early for there to be any cases to report on under the new U.S. GAAP provisions announced in ASU No. 2009-13, although there have been some vocal critics of the rules and the early adopters. But, by including third-party evidence as well as management's best estimate among the acceptable methods of determining relative selling price, the opportunities for fraud are equally expansive. Readers should note that under the new rules, companies must disclose in the notes to the financial statements which of the three approaches to determining relative selling price was used. The greatest scrutiny should be applied to the third approach, that involving management's best estimate.

CUSTOMER LOYALTY PROGRAMS

Customer loyalty programs represent another opportunity for financial statement fraud. These programs involve the accumulation of customer benefits as a customer purchases goods or services from a company. For example, as a customer purchases goods, points or other credits accumulate, enabling the customer to obtain future goods at no charge or at a discount, based on the amount of credits that have accumulated.

IFRS provides very specific guidance on this issue in the form of IFRIC 13, *Customer Loyalty Programmes*. There is no such specific guidance under U.S. GAAP. However, the guidance described in the preceding section on multiple deliverables can be applied.

Under IFRIC 13, for any of the following benefits, a liability should be recorded at the time of a sale in order to recognize the obligation that a company has incurred to a customer:

- Awards that entitle the holder to discounted goods or services
- Award credits that entitle the holder to discounted goods or services provided by another entity
- Arrangements in which third-party organizations provide a service of redeeming awards against a variety of goods or services

The method of recording a liability for future obligations associated with customer loyalty programs is to allocate a portion of the initial sale to the obligation and establish it as deferred revenue. When customers exercise their credits, the liability is relieved. At any point in time, the liability should be measured at the fair value, not the cost, of all outstanding future obligations that are expected to be redeemed. Fair value is often equal to the amount of discount that a customer is entitled to for future purchases. However, it may also be the value of other products or services to which a customer is entitled.

As a result of this accounting treatment, there are the following opportunities for financial statement fraud in the form of underreporting a company's liability (and, therefore, overstating recognized revenue):

- Failing to recognize any liability for future obligations
- Underestimating the liability by measuring it at cost, rather than fair value
- Underestimating the liability by improperly measuring fair value
- Overestimating the portion of award credits that customers will not redeem (underestimating the redemption rate)

Another example of a customer loyalty program that results in a requirement to record a liability is an airline frequent flier program. Take the following example from a footnote in the 2005 financial statements of American Airlines:

> **Frequent Flyer Program** The estimated incremental cost of providing free travel awards is accrued when such award levels are reached. American also accrues a frequent flyer liability for the mileage credits that are expected to be used for travel on participating airlines based on historical usage patterns and contractual rates. American sells mileage credits and related services to companies participating in its frequent flyer program. The portion of the revenue related to the sale of mileage credits, representing the revenue for air transportation sold, is valued at current market rates and is deferred and amortized over 28 months, which approximates the expected period over which the mileage credits are used. The remaining portion of the revenue, representing the marketing products sold and administrative costs associated with operating the AAdvantage program, is recognized upon sale as a component of passenger revenues, as the related services have been provided. The Company's total liability for future AAdvantage award redemptions for free, discounted, or upgraded travel on American, AMR Eagle, or participating airlines, as well as unrecognized revenue from selling AAdvantage miles, was approximately $1.5 billion and $1.4 billion (and is recorded as a component of air traffic liability on the accompanying consolidated balance sheets) at December 31, 2005 and 2004, respectively.

After one reading of this note, it is easy to see that accruing a liability for something that seems so simple can become quite complicated very quickly.

The American Airlines note also illustrates a difference between U.S. GAAP and IFRS. As noted earlier, unlike IFRS, U.S. GAAP does not contain specific guidance directed toward customer loyalty programs, other than guidance indicating that a liability exists. How to measure that liability is not clearly stated.

As a result, two approaches have emerged. Some companies consider customer loyalty programs as a multiple-element revenue recognition issue (explained in the preceding section). Accordingly, these companies measure a customer loyalty program liability based on the fair value of the credits, and the liability is offset by a reduction in revenue. Other companies, such as American Airlines in the financial statements cited here, utilize an incremental cost approach. Under this approach, an expense is accrued (rather than a reduction in revenue) to recognize the liability.

Obviously, it is important to read the notes to the financial statements carefully to understand how a company is accounting for its customer loyalty programs.

Additional materials to review for clues regarding details of a company's customer loyalty programs include websites, sales brochures, and other sales and marketing materials.

CHANNEL STUFFING

Channel stuffing is included here even though it may not always represent fraud. Channel stuffing occurs when an unusually large sale is made to an existing customer, normally a distributor. For example, a customer may normally place monthly orders for products from a company. However, shortly before year-end, a salesperson for the company persuades the customer to order a six-month supply, an unusual order for this customer.

On the surface, this may indicate nothing more than a salesperson doing a good job of convincing a customer to accelerate his or her ordering. Perhaps the salesperson merely needed a little extra push to make his sales goal for the month.

However, channel stuffing should always raise two separate red flags. First, the mere fact that such an unusual sale took place, especially if the sale enables a company to barely achieve its stated goals or analysts' expectations for a period, should be viewed as a sign that a possible motive to perpetrate financial statement fraud exists. The company may be so desperate to make its numbers, that it is taking unusual action to do so. Even if the channel stuffing sales are legitimate, could their existence be a sign that something else might be going on?

This leads to the more likely question: Are these channel stuffing sales even legitimate sales in the first place? Do they meet the criteria for recognition?

Often, such large and unusual sales to distributors are accompanied by special terms designed to encourage the customer to enter into the transaction. These special terms can result in the transaction not meeting the accounting standards' requirements for revenue recognition. Examples of special terms include the following:

- Customers have no firm obligation to pay for the products or very lenient credit terms
- Very lenient return or exchange policies, enabling the distributor to easily return goods and receive a full refund
- Providing guarantees of profits to the distributors
- Unusual discounts and rebates

Some payment terms granted to customers in channel stuffing transactions are so lenient that the transaction is in essence a sale on consignment. The distributor has virtually no obligation to pay for the products until the products have been sold.

ASC 605-10-S99, which includes guidance provided by the SEC from SAB Topic 13, identifies certain characteristics that, if present, would preclude the recognition of revenue. Among these characteristics (any one of which would preclude revenue recognition) are the following:

- The customer has a right of return plus no obligation to pay at the time of the sale or at specified future dates, or the obligation to pay is contractually or implicitly excused until the customer resells the product (in essence, making the transaction into a consignment sale).
- The seller is required to repurchase the product at specified prices and those prices are adjusted to cover fluctuations in costs incurred by the buyer in purchasing and holding the product (the equivalent of reimbursing the customer not just for the amount paid by the customer, but also for other costs the customer incurred, including financing costs).

There are other examples in ASC 605-10-S99 as well. However, these two represent the most commonly seen in side agreements, sometimes in writing but often not, between sellers and buyers.

There are numerous examples of channel stuffing cases, including those discussed in the following sections.

Bristol-Myers Squibb

In 2004, the SEC filed an enforcement action against Bristol-Myers Squibb (BMS), alleging that throughout 2000 and 2001 BMS stuffed its distribution channels with excess inventory at the end of every quarter in amounts sufficient to meet targets by making pharmaceutical sales to wholesalers ahead of demand. This resulted in the improper recognition of $1.5 billion USD in revenue from such sales to its two largest wholesalers. BMS agreed to pay a $100 million penalty as well as $50 million into a fund for the benefit of stockholders. In 2005, BMS agreed to pay another $300 million to avoid prosecution.

McAfee, Inc.

In 2006, the SEC filed charges against McAfee, stating that the company's net revenues were inflated by $562 million from 1998 to 2000 as a result of using a "variety of undisclosed ploys" to aggressively oversell its products to distributors. These ploys included attractive sales incentives such as price discounts and rebates. McAfee also paid distributors millions of dollars in exchange for their agreement to hold the excess inventory, rather than returning it for a refund. In some instances, McAfee utilized an undisclosed wholly owned subsidiary to repurchase inventory that had been oversold to distributors.

Krispy Kreme Doughnuts

A complaint filed in December 2004 quotes a former sales manager at Krispy Kreme as stating that he shipped double orders to customers on the final Friday and Saturday of 2004 in order to meet Wall Street projections, knowing that the doughnuts would be returned for credit the following week, once 2005 was under way.

ClearOne Communications, Inc.

An SEC complaint charged ClearOne with stuffing its distribution channels while entering into secret agreements with its distributors beginning in 2001. These secret agreements allowed the distributors to hold off on paying ClearOne until they sold the merchandise, in effect making the arrangements into consignment sales. In some cases, ClearOne's relationships with its distributors resulted in the distributors sending blank purchase orders to ClearOne at the end of a quarter, allowing ClearOne to fill in whatever quantities it needed to meet its quarterly targets. The amounts filled in would be shipped, but with the understanding that the distributors would not have to pay for the merchandise.

Lantronix, Inc.

In AAER 2485, the SEC charged Lantronix in 2006 with inflating its earnings by shipping excessive quantities of products to distributors and granting either full stock rotation rights or return rights. Stock rotation rights refer to the right to exchange any portion of an order, or even the entire order, for any other product. Return rights allowed distributors to return any unsold items for full credit.

BILL AND HOLD SCHEMES

A bill and hold transaction is one in which a customer places an order for goods, but requests that the seller hold the goods for delivery at a future date. The question with a bill and hold transaction is when to record the revenue—at the time the order is placed, at the time of delivery, or somewhere in between.

ASC 605-10-S99 provides the following criteria (from SAB Topic 13) that must be met in order to recognize revenue in connection with bill and hold transactions:

1. The risks of ownership must have passed to the buyer
2. The customer must have made a fixed commitment to purchase the goods (preferably in writing)
3. The buyer, not the seller, must request that the transaction be on a bill and hold basis
4. There must be a fixed schedule for delivery of the goods and such delivery must be reasonable and consistent with the buyer's business purpose
5. The seller must not have retained any specific performance obligations such that the earning process is not complete.
6. The ordered goods must have been segregated from the seller's inventory and must not be available for filling orders of other customers
7. The goods must be complete and ready for delivery

As a result, revenue from bill and hold transactions may be recognized prior to delivery to a customer, as long as the preceding criteria are met. Each of these criteria, therefore, poses a unique fraud risk.

One example of a misstatement caused by improper bill and hold accounting involved Diebold, Inc., a company that manufactures and sells automated teller machines (ATMs), bank security systems, and electronic voting machines. In a civil complaint filed in 2010, the SEC asserted that Diebold engaged in accounting fraud from 2002 to 2007 by accounting for certain transactions as bill and hold transactions that failed to meet the ASC 605-10-S99 criteria. The transactions in question involved products that were manufactured and shipped to a Diebold warehouse, at which point revenue was recorded. This would be permitted if the preceding criteria were met. However, only some of the criteria were met.

Diebold required its customers to sign a standard memorandum of agreement that contained a clause stating that the customer had requested Diebold to hold products for the customer's convenience (thereby meeting the second and third criteria). Once the products were manufactured and shipped to a Diebold warehouse, the final three criteria may have been met. However, these transactions "generally did not have fixed delivery schedules" (the requirement of criterion number four). In addition, in some instances, required software had not yet been installed in the ATMs that had been manufactured and shipped to the Diebold warehouse for storage, indicating that the fifth criterion had not been met either.

In an even bolder example, Raytheon Company violated the seventh criterion, requiring that a product be complete and ready for delivery, in order to meet earnings expectations. According to a complaint filed by the SEC, Raytheon Aircraft Company improperly accounted for transactions as bill and hold transactions from 1997 through 1999, resulting in an overstatement in sales of $80 million for 1997 and $110 million for 1998. In the complaint, the SEC charged that at the end of each quarter, especially the final quarter of the fiscal year, Raytheon executives would identify "unfinished planes in the production process that could be 'pulled forward' for a 'financial delivery' to 'bridge' certain 'gaps' or 'shortfalls' in RAC's performance targets." The planes were not yet fully manufactured, yet Raytheon recognized them as sales. "Financial delivery"? A typical customer would probably have argued that delivery meant something else, although the complaint goes on to say that "significant incentives were being given to customers in order to induce them to accept a 'sale' before quarter- or year-end, all of which disqualified the aircraft for sales treatment under GAAP." Always be wary of side deals or other special terms and conditions!

Other bill and hold cases and their citations include:

- Serologicals Corporation, Inc. (AAER 1551)
- Candie's, Inc. (AAER 1770)
- PictureTel Corp. (AAER 1536)

SALES WITH RIGHT OF RETURN

When a sale occurs, but a customer has the right to return the product, an accounting issue arises. Should the entire amount of the sale be recognized in income at the time of the sale?

U.S. GAAP for recognition of sales when a right of return exists is covered in ASC 605-15-25. There are two crucial elements to the accounting of these transactions:

1. Determining whether and when a sale can be recorded.
2. Accounting for the obligation associated with possible future returns.

Under ASC 605-15-25, sales in which a buyer has the right to return a product may only be recognized at the time of the sale if all six of the following criteria are met:

1. The price is fixed or determinable on the date of the sale.
2. The buyer has either paid the seller or is obligated to pay the seller and this obligation is not contingent on the buyer reselling the product (i.e., such as in consignment arrangements).
3. The buyer's obligation to pay would not be affected by theft, destruction, or damage of the product.
4. If the buyer has purchased the product for resale, the buyer has economic substance apart from that provided by the seller (for example, the buyer does not have physical facilities or employees).
5. The seller has no significant obligation to directly bring about the resale of the product by the buyer.
6. The amount of future returns can be reasonably estimated (note that the right of a customer to exchange an item for another of the same kind, quality, and price is not considered a right of return).

Extremely lenient rights of return can be a sign of a disguised consignment arrangement. See Chapter 3 for a discussion of consignment sales.

In AAER 2265, the SEC charged Schick Technologies, Inc. (STI) in 2005 with improperly recording revenue in connection with sales involving a right of return. In one example, STI engaged in the practice of shipping merchandise to customers under a loaner program, under which the customer accepted the products on a trial basis with no obligation to purchase the product. Since the customer had not yet accepted the products, STI improperly recognized revenue in connection with these arrangements. In addition, the SEC alleged that STI failed to establish sufficient sales return reserves in connection with recorded sales involving the right of return.

IFRS does not explicitly address returns in the same extensive manner as U.S. GAAP. However, recall from the explanation on revenue recognition in Chapter 1 that one of IAS 18's required conditions for recognition of a sale is that all significant risks and rewards associated with ownership of the goods must have been transferred. In connection with this criterion, IAS 18 notes that if a buyer has the right to rescind a transaction under defined conditions and the seller cannot reasonably estimate the likelihood of such rescission, the sale should not be recognized.

Recording a reserve for estimated future returns represents the second aspect of these transactions that has the potential for fraud. When sales transactions meet the ASC 605-15-25 criteria, a reserve should be established to account for estimated future returns. Estimating returns is normally based primarily on past history. But other factors may contribute to the difficulty of this estimate, such as:

- A lack of historical experience with similar products, especially when estimating returns associated with new products
- External factors, such as competition, technological advances, or obsolescence
- Longer time periods over which some products may be returned

IMPROPER PUSHING OF CURRENT REVENUE TO FUTURE PERIODS

All of the revenue timing schemes described so far have involved premature revenue recognition. That is, they are perpetrated in order to make the current period appear to have been more successful than it really has been. However, sometimes the opposite incentive exists. Perhaps the current period has been successful beyond expectations and concerns exist about the company's ability to match or improve upon this success in subsequent periods. What, then, can a company do to ensure a steady rate of growth?

The risks of fraud under such circumstances include the opposite of some of those described earlier in this section, such as:

- Physical alteration of shipping documents to make it appear that an order was filled later than it really was (or simply delaying the actual shipment of goods until the next period).
- Manipulation of the percentage of completion on long-term contracts to make it appear that less of the contract revenue has been earned (by either overestimating costs to be incurred in order to complete the work or by underrecognizing costs actually incurred in the contract at year-end).

Deferral of revenue to future periods that should be recognized in the current period may pose one additional problem for the crooked company. What to do if the revenue has not only been earned, but the customer has already paid the company? The most commonly utilized schemes in these cases involve hiding the earned income in a phony reserve account (which could either be a contra-asset account or a liability) or recording the income as deferred revenue (a liability) or even as a loan.

Other techniques used to aid in pushing revenue to future periods include:

- Delayed invoicing of customers
- Arranging for delayed payments from customers
- Altering sales documents to make it appear that the sale took place in a subsequent period

The case of Beazer Homes USA, Inc. is a great example of the improper use of reserves to push current income into future periods. In AAER 2884, the SEC accused Beazer of an improper earnings management scheme that was carried out from 2000 to 2007. According to the SEC, from 2000 to 2005, Beazer experienced strong financial growth and performance. During this time, Beazer understated its profits through the use of accruals, or "reserves." Then, when its performance began to decline in 2006 and 2007, Beazer began reversing these reserves in order to improve its reported results.

The reserves used by Beazer in this scheme were known as "house to complete" reserves. As a homebuilder, Beazer would recognize revenue and profit upon the close of a sale of a home. However, consistent with industry practices, Beazer would record a house-to-complete reserve against this profit, to cover any known and unknown expenses that Beazer might incur on sold homes after the close. Such costs can be rather common and involve things like outstanding invoices for work completed but not billed prior to closing, cost overruns, and minor repairs or touchups. Normally, any unused portion of a house to complete reserve left after four to nine months would be eliminated and taken into income. However, from 2000 to 2005, Beazer overreserved these house cost to complete expenses.

USE OF RESERVES AS A RAINY DAY FUND

The method used by Beazer of pushing current revenue into future periods is more common than it may sound. Many companies have been accused of establishing reserves as liabilities on the balance sheet. In the purported interest of being "conservative" with revenue recognition, these reserves are often not scrutinized nearly as carefully as they should be. They may represent a financial fraud in the form of creating a cookie jar or rainy day fund that can be dipped into when future periods fall short of revenue expectations.

Not many companies can claim to have more effectively (and fraudulently) abused reserve accounts better than Cardinal Health, Inc. Cardinal, who will appear later in this book in connection with bogus related party transactions, maintained no less than 60 different reserve accounts. According to charges made by the SEC, between 2000 and 2004 Cardinal inflated its earnings by more than $65 million as a result of improperly releasing amounts into income from these reserve accounts.

What is sometimes lost in the discussion of reserve schemes like Cardinal's is that the initial creation of the reserve may have been fraudulent, as well as the subsequent use of the reserve to boost revenue.

As explained in Chapter 10, liabilities for contingencies should be recorded when it is both probable that a liability has been incurred and the amount of the liability can be reasonably estimated. Conversely, once the likelihood of a liability becomes less than probable or it is no longer reasonably estimable, the reserve should be removed from the books. Maintaining general reserves that are not associated with any specific contingent liability cannot be supported under U.S. GAAP or IFRS.

In Cardinal's case, some of its reserves, which could have been justified in their initial establishment, were later flagged as an "available item not used"—meaning the reserve should have been reversed, but it was kept on the books as a liability, that is, as a cushion that could be used as needed. When that need arose, such as in 2002, the reserve was dipped into. In one e-mail exchange of December 13, 2002, cited by the SEC in its complaint, two members of Cardinal's management team discussed reversing a $2 million reserve in order "to help make the quarter," noting that "[w]e built it for a rainy day . . . and it looks like it is pouring!"

CHAPTER THREE

Fictitious and Inflated Revenue

FICTITIOUS REVENUE SCHEMES

Fictitious revenue schemes artificially inflate a company's profits by recording phony revenues for goods or services that are never delivered. These schemes are distinguished from timing difference schemes in that with fictitious revenues, the revenue should not be recognized in any period. This is normally accomplished in one of two manners:

1. Recording journal entries for sales without attributing the sales to specific customers (e.g., "top-side" entries)
2. Recording sales attributable to fictitious customers

A third technique, recording of phony sales to legitimate customers, can be utilized but is less common.

The mechanics of fictitious revenue schemes will be illustrated through descriptions of three cases:

1. Satyam Computer Services Ltd.
2. Symmetry Medical Sheffield
3. LocatePlus Holdings Corporation

Satyam Computer Services Ltd.

One of largest reported fictitious revenue cases occurred with Satyam Computer Services Ltd., which later became Mahindra Satyam Ltd. Satyam was incorporated in India and was recognized as one of that country's largest information technology services companies. It employed more than 40,000 people in offices throughout the world.

From at least 2003 through September 2008, false and inflated sales invoices were created outside the normal accounting processes by which revenues were recorded. This resulted in fraudulently reported revenues of more than $1 billion. During this period, more than 6,600 false sales invoices were generated and recorded in Satyam's invoice management system. Some of these invoices were false sales to real customers, while others involved fictitious customers altogether. This was accomplished by providing special log-in access to certain employees. This enabled these employees to enter the fraudulent sales invoices without the knowledge of the heads of Satyam's business units, who would have otherwise recognized that the services reflected on the invoices had not been provided to customers. The phony sales nonetheless rolled up to the company-wide financial statements and were reported as revenue, as data from the invoice management system was exported into the corporate financial system.

As with so many financial reporting frauds, the scheme grew over time. In a complaint filed by the SEC, the fictitious revenue reported by Satyam was $46 million in fiscal year 2004 (which ended March 31, 2004), almost $69 million in 2005, $149 million in 2006, $151 million in 2007, and more than $430 million in 2008. Another $275 million in fraudulent revenue was recorded in the first six months of the fiscal year 2009 (i.e., the period from April 1 through September 30, 2008).

Satyam's false revenue inflated the company's profits, but also impacted several other areas of its financial statements. When the chair of Satyam's board admitted the fraud in January 2009, he stated that cash was overstated by approximately $1 billion, while other assets were overstated by lesser amounts and certain liabilities were understated. Senior management tried desperately to acquire real assets to fill in the gaps created by the fraud. But the fraud continued to escalate. In connection with the growing nature of the fraud, the chair stated that it "was like riding a tiger, not knowing how to get off without being eaten."

An investigation by India's Central Bureau of Investigation concluded that 10 individuals involved defrauded the company (and its investors, of course) of $2.5 billion.

Symmetry Medical Sheffield

In January 2012, four former executives and accountants of the British company Symmetry Medical Sheffield LTD, formerly known as Thornton Precision Components (TPC), were charged for their roles in a massive fictitious revenue scheme that took place between 2004 and 2007. TPC accounted for a significant portion of the consolidated revenues of its parent company, U.S.-based Symmetry Medical, Inc., a manufacturer of prosthetics, medical implants and instruments, and other specialized products for the aerospace industry. Symmetry Medical acquired TPC in 2003 and had its IPO in December 2004.

A timing scheme to recognize revenue early had already been in place at TPC as early as 1999. However, things got really interesting in 2004, when the strategy shifted from premature revenue recognition to fictitious revenues. Beginning in 2004, one of TPC's executives would assess how much TPC fell short of its sales targets on a monthly and quarterly basis. When shortfalls existed, a top-side journal entry would be made debiting accounts receivable and crediting sales. These were internally referred to as "provisional" sales. In an attempt to conceal the fictitious revenue, this individual then sent a record of the provisional sales to another person, who calculated and recorded the fictitious cost of goods sold associated with the fictitious sales. This helped TPC's gross margin remain comparable, at least temporarily.

The top-side sales entries made TPC's accounts receivable subsidiary ledger out of balance with the general ledger (which had the higher figure for receivables). To hide this from all parties not involved in the scheme (including the external and internal auditors), a fictitious sub-ledger was created in the form of an Excel spreadsheet. This spreadsheet only reflected total accounts receivable and aging by customer and not the details by sale and invoice number normally included in a sub-ledger. The spreadsheet was created from a downloaded copy of a summary version of the real sub-ledger which was exported into Excel, and the fictitious receivables were then added to the schedule so that it agreed to the general ledger balance.

These fictitious sales had a material impact on the financial statements of TPC. At the close of fiscal year 2005, £4,122,000 (38 percent) of the total reported accounts receivable of £10,717,000 was fictitious. For 2006, £6,031,000 (48 percent) of the reported £12,440,000 was fictitious.

Although the perpetrators of this fraud recorded cost of goods sold to align with the fictitious sales, the scheme also involved a separate effort to inflate inventory balances and, therefore, understate cost of goods sold. This was accomplished using a similar approach to the fictitious accounts receivable—top-side journal entries supported by a falsified inventory subledger containing inserted lines of fictitious work-in-process inventory, all prepared after the physical count. At the end of fiscal year 2005, only £3,531,000 (36 percent) of TPC's reported inventory of £9,753,000 actually existed. Cost of goods sold for 2005 was understated (and, therefore, gross profit was overstated) by £2,505,000 as a result of the inventory inflation scheme. At the end of 2006, just £3,692,000 (33 percent) of the reported inventory balance of £10,973,000 was real, and cost of goods sold was understated by £1,058,000.

The incentive behind the TPC schemes was nothing new—pure greed. The perpetrators received bonuses based on the purported performance of TPC, and they profited handsomely from their sale of parent company Symmetry stock.

LocatePlus Holdings Corporation

In 2010, the SEC charged LocatePlus Holdings Corporation, a seller of personal information used for investigative searches, with inflating its revenue during 2005 and 2006 through the creation of a fictitious customer known as Omni Data Services, Inc. ("Omni Data"). In order to make the transactions appear legitimate, Omni Data paid LocatePlus for the sales. However, these payments were actually funded with cash routed through entities under the control of LocatePlus executives. This practice is sometimes known as a "round-trip transaction."

For example, in one transaction, LocatePlus made a $650,000 payment to an entity, which then transferred $600,000 to Omni Data, and Omni Data then paid the $600,000 back to LocatePlus as purported payment for services. In another transaction, at least $250,000 of the proceeds of unregistered stock sales were transferred to Omni Data, which then transferred those funds to LocatePlus, again as payment for purported services. The improper Omni Data payments were fraudulently included as revenue in LocatePlus's financial statements.

In total, approximately $2 million was funneled to OmniData in support of phony sales transactions. The effects on LocatePlus's financial statements were material. Phony sales to Omni Data represented 31 percent of LocatePlus's 2005 reported revenue and 22 percent of 2006 reported revenue.

In addition to its charges that LocatePlus fraudulently reported revenue from this fictitious customer, the SEC also charged LocatePlus with failing to disclose the fictitious customer as a related party! Now that's just pouring salt in the wound.

SALES TO RELATED PARTIES

Speaking of related parties, sales to related parties are especially susceptible to manipulation. The very fact that these are not arm's-length transactions means that they pose an increased risk of fraudulent financial reporting.

In some cases, the effect of any inflated profits from sales to related parties may be eliminated in consolidation, when the related parties involved are under the control of an entity that prepares consolidated financial statements. However, when the related party is not included in the consolidated financial statements of the seller, financial reporting fraud can result.

One such case involved Lernout & Hauspie Speech Products N.V. (L&H), a Belgian company that at the time of the case was a developer, licensor, and provider of speech and language technologies. Between 1996 and 1999, L&H recorded more than $60 million in false revenue from transactions with two entities, Dictation Consortium N.V. and Brussels Translation Group N.V. Dictation was disclosed as a related party. One day after its creation, Dictation entered into a $5 million agreement with L&H to license certain technology. Three months later, a second agreement was signed, this one providing for Dictation to pay $25 million to L&H to develop software using the technology licensed to Dictation in the first agreement. This agreement also gave L&H the option to buy back the rights to the license and any software developed. During 1996, 1997, and 1998, L&H recognized $26.7 million in revenue from these agreements. But, in May 1998, before L&H had developed any marketable product for Dictation, L&H purchased Dictation for $43.3 million. In essence, L&H purchased the product of its own research and development at a premium of about $16 million.

The $26.7 million of "revenue" recognized by L&H from 1996 to 1998 should have been accounted for as a loan, not as revenue, according to a complaint filed in 2002. L&H carried out a similar strategy with Brussels Translation Group N.V.

But L&H wasn't done yet. They also reported approximately $175 million in fraudulent revenue from their Korean operations (L&H Korea). L&H Korea sales personnel were instructed to agree to "whatever terms and conditions were necessary to induce customers to sign purchase orders." In many cases, either written or verbal side deals made the initial purchase order unenforceable. As a result of recording this phony revenue, L&H had no expectation of collecting on the recorded accounts receivable. To prevent these aging receivables from raising questions, L&H entered into a series of transactions to factor the receivables with four Korean banks, purportedly on a nonrecourse basis. In fact, side deals with these banks required L&H to maintain blocked deposits to cover the amounts of the supposedly factored receivables. These transactions with the banks amounted to nothing more than fully secured loans, not the factoring of receivables.

Following up on the first part of these transactions, the phony sales to its customers, L&H Korea also arranged for third parties to "purchase" the licensing agreements from the original customers. The transferees then would obtain loans to pay L&H Korea through the original customers. However, these loans were collateralized by—you guessed it—L&H Korea assets!

FASB ASC 850, *Related Party Disclosures*, requires the disclosure of related party transactions. "Related Parties" is defined to include the following:

- Affiliates of an entity. An affiliate is a party that, directly or indirectly through one or more intermediaries, controls, is controlled by, or is under common control with the entity. For purposes of this rule, "control" means the possession, direct or indirect, of the power to direct or cause the direction of the management and policies of an entity through ownership, by contract, or otherwise.
- Entities for which investments are accounted for by the equity method by the reporting entity.
- Trusts for the benefit of employees, such as pension and profit-sharing trusts that are managed by or under the trusteeship of management.
- Principal owners of an entity. Principal owners are owners of record or known beneficial owners of more than 10 percent of the voting interests of an entity.
- Management of an entity. Management includes persons who are responsible for achieving the objectives of the entity and who have the authority to establish policies and make decisions by which those objectives are to be pursued. Management normally includes members of the board of directors, the chief executive officer, chief operating officer, vice presidents in charge of principal business functions (such as sales, administration, or finance), and other persons who perform similar policymaking functions. Persons without formal titles may also be members of management.
- Members of the immediate families of principal owners of the entity and its management. Immediate family includes family members whom a principal owner or a member of management might control or influence or by whom they might be controlled or influenced because of the family relationship.

- Other parties with which the entity may deal if one party controls or can significantly influence the management or operating policies of the other to an extent that one of the transacting parties might be prevented from fully pursuing its own separate interests.
- Other parties that can significantly influence the management or operating policies of the transacting parties or that have an ownership interest in one of the transacting parties and can significantly influence the other to the extent that one or more of the transacting parties might be prevented from fully pursuing its own separate interests.

The *Wall Street Journal* reported in 2003 that 75 percent of the 400 largest U.S. public companies disclosed at least one related party transaction. The vast majority of these transactions are likely to be legitimate transactions between two entities that are connected through one or more of the relationships described above.

Revenue from related parties should always be scrutinized carefully. Increasing levels of revenue from related party transactions have been correlated with an increased risk of financial reporting fraud—more on this later.

The IFRS coverage of related party transactions is found in IAS 24, as amended in 2009. Under IFRS, a person or a close member of a person's family is considered to be related to the reporting entity under any of the following circumstances:

- The person has control or joint control over the reporting entity
- The person has significant influence over the reporting entity
- The person is a member of the key management personnel of the reporting entity or of a parent of the reporting entity

An entity is considered to be related to the reporting entity if any of the following criteria are met:

1. The entity and the reporting entity are members of the same group (i.e., each parent and subsidiary are related to the others).
2. One entity is an associate or joint venture of the other entity (or an associate or joint venture of a member of a group of which the other entity is a member).
3. Both entities are joint ventures of the same third party.
4. One entity is a joint venture of a third entity and the other entity is an associate of the third entity.

5. The entity is a postemployment benefit plan for the benefit of employees of either the reporting entity or an entity related to the reporting entity (if the reporting entity is itself a plan, the sponsoring employers are also considered to be related to the reporting entity).
6. The entity is controlled or jointly controlled by a person identified above.
7. A person identified in 1 above has significant influence over the entity or is a member of the key management personnel of the entity (or of a parent of the entity).

The term "significant influence," used here, is defined similarly to its U.S. GAAP counterpart—it represents the power to participate in the financial and operating policy decisions of an entity, as differentiated from control. Significant influence may arise from ownership, but also via a contract or other agreement, as well as from a statute.

While the Lernout & Hauspie Speech Products N.V. case provides an excellent illustration of fraudulent financial reporting pertaining to related party transactions, there are, unfortunately, many other examples. Some additional examples of financial reporting fraud involving sales of goods or services to related parties include:

- **NetEase.com, Inc.** In 2006, the SEC charged NetEase with inflating its reported results through a series of transactions with related parties (see AAERs 2382, 2383, and 2384). Most of the questionable transactions pertained to related arrangements involving two separate related parties and were executed in order to close the gap between actual and expected financial results. For example, in one arrangement, NetEase sold advertising services to one related party, while purchasing offsetting services from another related company. In another example, NetEase sold advertising to one of its stockholders while purchasing an offsetting amount of financial advisory services from the same stockholder. No services were performed or received in connection with these arrangements.
- **Itex Corporation.** In 2000 and 2002 (see AAERs 1224, 1229, and 1510), the SEC alleged that between 40 and 60 percent of Itex's revenue came from suspect or outright sham barter arrangements between Itex and various offshore entities related to or controlled by the founder of Itex. As noted in Chapter 5, barter transactions can involve goods or services that may be difficult to value. That is exactly what occurred here, with Itex recognizing revenue in connection with bartered artwork and prepaid advertising, as well as completely bogus assets, including leases on vacant property and unpatented and undeveloped mineral claims.

- **SoftPoint.** In three AAERs from 1995 (see AAERs 666, 706, and 709), the SEC charged SoftPoint with reporting, as well as failing to disclose as related party transactions, fictitious sales to three foreign companies owned or under the control of SoftPoint's president.
- **Ciro, Inc.** In a 1994 complaint (see AAER 612), the SEC charged Ciro with falsely reporting as revenue amounts received as capital infusions from Ciro's chairman of the board and its president and CEO.

Each of these cases involved some form of fictitious revenue resulting from purported sales to related parties. While the focus in this section is on the use of related party transactions to inflate revenue, related transactions can be a source of several types of fraudulent financial reporting. In their excellent paper, "The Role of Related Party Transactions in Fraudulent Financial Reporting," Henry, Gordon, Reed, and Louwers identify financial reporting frauds involving related parties in all of the following areas:

1. Sales of goods or services to a related party
2. Purchases of goods or services from a related party
3. Sales of assets to a related party
4. Purchases of assets from a related party
5. Borrowing from a related party
6. Lending to a related party
7. Investments in equity in a related party
8. Selling of ownership interests to a related party

The authors studied 48 cases in which the SEC alleged fraudulent reporting associated with related party transactions and found examples in each of the preceding eight categories.

Related party transactions fall under a disclosure obligation, which serves as a notice for all readers of the financial statements. These disclosure requirements are described in Chapter 14 in connection with disclosure frauds.

In addition, as explained in Chapter 17, increasing proportions of sales with related parties has been shown to have a high correlation with fraudulent financial reporting.

INFLATED REVENUE SCHEMES

Inflated revenue schemes utilize actual sales transactions with legitimate customers, but inflate the transactions in amounts, thus overstating earnings.

These transactions may be more difficult to detect than completely fictitious customers. Often, fictitious customers stand out among other customers when a detailed customer master file is examined. Fictitious customers often appear to have certain key data omitted, such as street addresses, telephone numbers, and so on. These signs make it a bit easier to identify the need for investigation.

With inflated revenue schemes, however, the customer is real. The inflation of the revenue can come from either of the following:

1. Phony transactions
2. Inflated amounts as part of a legitimate transaction (e.g., fictitious line items added to a transaction, inflated quantities, inflated sales prices, etc.)

The NutraCea case provides a good illustration of one technique used to inflate revenue.

In January 2011, the SEC charged NutraCea, a manufacturer of health food products, and some of its former executives with engaging in a revenue inflation scheme during fiscal year 2007 (see SEC AAER 3234). One of NutraCea's customers was Bi-Coastal Pharmaceutical Corp. During the second quarter of 2007, NutraCea inflated its reported sales to Bi-Coastal by $2.6 million, representing approximately 35 percent of the quarter's total sales revenue. Not coincidentally, NutraCea had incurred a $2.6 million shortfall in revenue for the first quarter of 2007 after having a disagreement with its auditor over the recognition of certain sales in that quarter. According to the SEC's complaint, NutraCea's CEO instructed Bi-Coastal's president to falsify his family's financial statements to reflect a higher net worth in order to support the higher false sales to Bi-Coastal. In fact, Bi-Coastal's supposed $1 million down payment on the $2.6 million sale was provided as a loan by NutraCea's former chief operating officer. Bi-Coastal then submitted $2.6 million in purchase orders, based on NutraCea's CEO's instructions, with no intention of ever honoring these orders. NutraCea's CEO even informed Bi-Coastal's president that he had several other possible customers for these same products and that Bi-Coastal would never even have to take possession of the products. When NutraCea's controller attempted to discuss her suspicions with the CFO that the $1 million down payment came from a loan from the former COO, NutraCea's CFO "covered his ears and said, 'No, no, no, no, no, no, no, no, no. I don't want to hear it.'"

CONSIGNMENT OR FINANCING ARRANGEMENTS

In many cases, inventory on the shelves in retail stores does not really even belong to the retailer. It has been delivered to the retailer by a manufacturer or wholesale distributor, but under special terms that differ from a typical sales transaction. When inventory is held on consignment, the party holding the inventory (usually a retailer) does not really own the inventory. Instead, the inventory belongs on the financial statements of the manufacturer or wholesaler, who is also prohibited from recording income from a "sale" to the retailer until such time as the retailer sells the product, usually to an end user.

SAB 104 (SEC codification Topic 13) identifies the following characteristics of a consignment or financing arrangement in which revenue recognition is prohibited even if title to the product has passed to the buyer:

1. The buyer has the right to return the product, in addition to any of the following circumstances:
   a. The buyer does not pay the seller at the time of sale, and the buyer is not obligated to pay the seller at a specified date or dates.
   b. The buyer does not pay the seller at the time of sale but rather is obligated to pay at a specified date or dates, and the buyer's obligation to pay is contractually or implicitly excused until the buyer resells the product or subsequently consumes or uses the product.
   c. The buyer's obligation to the seller would be changed (e.g., the seller would forgive the obligation or grant a refund) in the event of theft or physical destruction or damage of the product.
   d. The buyer acquiring the product for resale does not have economic substance apart from that provided by the seller.
   e. The seller has significant obligations for future performance to directly bring about resale of the product by the buyer.
2. The seller is required to repurchase the product (or a substantially identical product or processed goods of which the product is a component) at specified prices that are not subject to change except for fluctuations due to finance and holding costs, and the amounts to be paid by the seller will be adjusted, as necessary, to cover substantially all fluctuations in costs incurred by the buyer in purchasing and holding the product (including interest).

The staff believes that indicators of the latter condition include any of the following:

a. The seller provides interest-free or significantly below-market financing to the buyer beyond the seller's customary sales terms and until the products are resold.
b. The seller pays interest costs on behalf of the buyer under a third-party financing arrangement.
c. The seller has a practice of refunding (or intends to refund) a portion of the original sales price representative of interest expense for the period from when the buyer paid the seller until the buyer resells the product.

3. The transaction possesses the characteristics set forth in Emerging Issues Task Force (EITF) Issue 95-1 and does not qualify for sales-type lease accounting.
4. The product is delivered for demonstration purposes

From a revenue recognition perspective, the primary fraud risk here involves recognition of revenue by the manufacturer or wholesaler upon delivery to the retail customer, when the transaction qualifies as a consignment transaction. This results in early revenue recognition.

One example of improper revenue recognition in connection with a consignment inventory transaction involved Nortel Networks Corporation. In a complaint filed by the SEC, Nortel was charged with a variety of financial reporting misstatements. One of these charges involved Nortel's transactions with Telamon Corporation, a company that served as a pass-through entity for certain business deals that required the involvement of a minority- or women-owned business. In these cases, Telamon, a minority-owned business, would be the seller of Nortel products to the final end users.

Nortel's practice was to recognize revenue when it delivered products to Telamon. However, the usual risks of ownership were not transferred from Nortel to Telamon, who was not required to pay Nortel until the products were resold and Telamon collected payment from the end customer. In addition, Telamon routinely returned unsold products to Nortel. The complaint noted that during 2000, Telamon returned hundreds of millions of dollars' worth of unsold products to Nortel due to softening orders. Revenues for the fourth quarter of 2000 were overstated by approximately $150 million in connection with these consignment deliveries to Telamon.

Terms, like those in the Nortel case, allowing a customer to delay paying for merchandise until that customer has, in turn, sold the products to some other customer, usually an end user, are the telltale sign of a consignment arrangement.

Characteristics of sales transactions that may indicate that a recorded sale is, in fact, a consignment transaction include the following:

- The seller requires payment only after the goods have been resold.
- The buyer is financed by the seller directly or through guarantees.
- The buyer has a relatively unlimited right of return.
- The buyer lacks economic substance apart from the seller.
- The buyer is charged prices higher than those charged to other customers.
- The buyer is forced to make purchases beyond its normal needs.
- The seller imposes constraints on the buyer's sales, credit, and advertising policies.

CHAPTER FOUR

Misclassification Schemes

RECORDING FINANCING ARRANGEMENTS AS REVENUE

One way to quickly improve a company's financial statements is to find a party willing to temporarily take some inventory off its hands, purportedly as a sale, with an understanding that the inventory will be returned after year-end.

U.S. GAAP addresses this issue at ASC 470-40-25 under the topic of product financing arrangements by distinguishing such arrangements from ones generating sales revenue. Generally, transactions that purport to be a sale of inventory should be treated as financing arrangements when the risks and rewards of ownership have not been transferred to the purchaser. Under ASC 470-40-25, if a company sells a product to another entity and, in a related transaction, agrees to repurchase the product (or a substantially identical product) or processed goods of which the product is a component, the company must record a liability at the time the proceeds are received from the other entity to the extent that the product is covered by the financing arrangement. The company may not record the transaction as a sale nor may it remove the covered product from its balance sheet.

The Delphi Corporation case is an excellent example of improperly recorded income in connection with a financing transaction. Delphi, an auto parts supplier, had planned to sell an inventory of precious metals, earmarked for use in coating catalytic converters, to another company (its former parent company and largest customer) by the end of December 2000. However, in November 2000, Delphi learned that this transaction would not come to fruition in 2000, but would instead be postponed to early 2001. In a desperate attempt to record a gain from the precious metals in its 2000 financial statements while remaining able to honor its commitment to transfer the precious metals to its former parent, Delphi concocted an alternative transaction. This transaction involved the sale of the precious metals to a bank in December 2000 for approximately $200 million. However, Delphi simultaneously entered into a forward purchase agreement to acquire precious metals of the same specifications and in the same quantities in January 2001, to coincide with the postponed transfer of metals to Delphi's former parent. As a result of this arrangement, Delphi recorded a gain on the sale of the precious metals in December 2000, followed by a purchase in January 2001.

So, how is Delphi falsely stating its 2000 income for this transaction? The answer lies in the terms of the agreement to purchase the precious metals back from the bank. The agreement called for Delphi to purchase the metals at a price that was fixed at the time of the agreement, the same date as when Delphi sold the metals to the bank. The price at which Delphi was required to repurchase the metals from the bank was about $3.25 million higher than the price at which Delphi sold the metals to the bank.

Hmmm, sounds like interest, doesn't it? In fact, that's exactly what it is. The establishment of a fixed, and slightly higher, price at which virtually the same quantity and specifications of assets were to be transferred back to Delphi was the accounting equivalent of Delphi borrowing funds from the bank in December 2000 and repaying the funds, with interest, in January 2001. Looking at it from the bank's perspective, the bank had no market risk (since the price at which it would be able to resell the metals back to Delphi was fixed to ensure a profit). The bank simply stored the metals for Delphi.

Adding to the dubious nature of the transaction was the fact that there was no fixed date for the delivery of the metals by Delphi to the bank. Delphi had the right to not actually deliver the metals. Instead, it was permitted to simply pay the bank a fixed rate per ounce for any undelivered metals. Indeed, some of the metals purportedly sold by Delphi to the bank were actually still in the possession of Delphi suppliers. Just as Delphi was not required to deliver the metals to the bank in December 2000, the bank was not required to deliver them to Delphi in

January 2001. All the bank had to do was present a bill of sale in January 2001 for the metals remaining in the possession of Delphi. Since Delphi utilized the last-in, first-out (LIFO) method of accounting for its inventory, this arrangement with the bank resulted in the improper recognition of $54 million in LIFO gains for 2000.

But Delphi wasn't finished with its abuse of the accounting rules governing financing agreements. On December 27, 2000, it sold $70 million of bulk inventories to a company primarily involved in providing consulting services. Sound odd? There was even a written sales agreement documenting the transaction. However, there was also an unwritten side deal under which the consulting company sold an identical inventory of items to Delphi on January 5, 2001, all at the original price, plus a transaction fee. This enabled Delphi to improperly recognize another $27 million of LIFO gains at December 31, 2000.

ONE-TIME CREDITS REPORTED AS REVENUE

When financial statements are analyzed, special one-time income transactions (as well as one-time, nonrecurring costs) are often eliminated in order to get a better picture of a business. Elimination of these transactions allows an analyst to normalize a company's profits or losses over a period of time in order to better evaluate a company.

As a result, a company may be tempted to misclassify one-time income or gain transactions and erroneously include these items with revenue from the company's core lines of business (especially in cases where one or more lines of business are underperforming). While the net profit or loss of the company is not misstated when this is done, an incorrect picture of its operations is presented.

This is one of the charges aimed at Cardinal Health by the SEC in 2007 (see AAER 2654). Cardinal is a provider of health care services and products, including its pharmaceutical distribution operation, which accounted for more than 80 percent of its revenues. Through one of its subsidiaries, Cardinal was involved in litigation against certain vitamin manufacturers who had pled guilty to charges of price-fixing. The lawsuit was filed in May 2000. For the quarter ended December 31, 2000 (the second quarter of FY 2001), in an effort to close an earnings gap for the quarter, Cardinal recognized a $10 million contingent gain on the vitamin litigation. Never mind the fact that recognition of such a gain contingency could not be supported under U.S. GAAP. Not only did Cardinal inappropriately record a gain contingency, they recorded it as a reduction to cost of goods sold in order to improperly pump up operating income for the quarter. For the quarter ended September 30, 2001, Cardinal recorded another $12 million gain in anticipation of success in its litigation. Once again, this amount was recorded as a reduction in cost of sales.

Cardinal's optimism in this case was well founded. It was rewarded in 2002 with a $35 million settlement, at which time the additional $13 million was recorded. In 2007, Cardinal agreed to pay a $35 million penalty to settle these and other charges stemming from the SEC's complaint.

SALES INCENTIVE SCHEMES

Vendors can provide a wide variety of incentives to their customers in an effort to maintain customer loyalty and to encourage additional purchases, as well as to receive certain benefits from customers. Earlier, the accounting for customer loyalty programs was addressed. In this section, the topic of special incentives is covered. Other incentives, also known as promotional allowances, involve cash payments, rebates, or reductions in amounts due in exchange for a variety of benefits. Examples of these benefits include:

- Special displays
- Exclusivity
- Advertising

In a simple example, Vendor A, a wholesaler, sells goods to Customer 1, a retailer, for a specified amount. Vendor A also offers to Customer 1 a reduced price if Customer 1 displays Vendor A's products in a prominent, well-trafficked area of Customer 1's store.

Accounting schemes associated with sales incentives fall into two of the revenue categories explained in connection with other schemes:

1. Misclassification schemes
2. Timing schemes

These schemes can potentially impact the revenues or sales of either the vendor or the customer.

From the Customer's Perspective—Incentives Received from a Vendor

Under ASC 605-45, when cash is received by a customer from a vendor, it should be accounted for as a reduction of the cost of sales when recognized in the income statement of the customer. However, there are two possible exceptions from this treatment:

1. If the payment received represents a payment for an identifiable benefit (goods or services) delivered to the vendor, the payment should be classified as revenue when recognized.
2. If the payment received represents a reimbursement of costs incurred by the customer in selling the vendor's products, the payment should be recorded as a reduction of that cost when recognized.

From the Vendor's Perspective—Incentives Provided by the Vendor

In many respects, the accounting from the vendor's perspective mirrors that described above for the customer. Cash incentives provided to a customer by a vendor should generally be accounted for as a reduction in the vendor's revenue, unless *both* of the following conditions are met, in which case the transaction should be classified as a cost:

1. The vendor receives an identifiable benefit (goods or services) that is "sufficiently separable" from the customer's purchase of the vendor's products such that the vendor could have entered into a separate transaction with another party to receive the benefit.
2. The vendor can reasonably estimate the fair value of the benefit.

The logic behind the second condition is that if the consideration paid by the vendor exceeds the fair value of the benefit received from the customer, the excess should be classified as a reduction in revenue earned from the customer.

Either the customer or the vendor could engage in misclassification schemes. There is no impact on net income in a misclassification scheme. However, other key performance measures could be manipulated using a misclassification scheme. The most common performance measures that can be manipulated are:

- Total sales or revenue
- Gross profit margin

Each of these measures, when manipulated, may provide a significant boost to the company's value in the eyes of analysts, investors, lenders, or, in the case of a privately held business, potential buyers.

Take the simple example of a customer with sales of $100 million and cost of sales of $40 million. This company shows a gross profit of 60 percent. Now let's assume a $1 million incentive is earned from a vendor. If that $1 million is classified as revenue, total revenues are increased to $101 million. Depending on whether the $1 million is classified with other sales, gross profit may stay at 60 percent (if the revenue is reported separately from the $100 million in sales), or it may increase to 60.4 percent (if classified with sales). However, if the $1 million incentive is recorded as a reduction on cost of sales, gross profit jumps to 61 percent, since cost of sales is reduced to $39 million, while sales remain at $100 million.

Which statistic is more important to the customer—the increase in sales and revenue to $101 million, or the bigger jump in gross profit to 61 percent? The answer might depend on a lot of factors, including trends from recent years, analysts' expectations, the model used to determine a company's fair value for purposes of an acquisition, and many others.

A similar impact could be derived by a vendor wishing to improperly account for incentives provided to customers.

Timing schemes, however, can impact the net profits (or losses) of a company, usually by inflating the current year's profits at the expense of future years. This is what happened in the case of Wickes Building Supplies, Ltd, a UK-based group of companies that was the subject of an investigation by the Serious Fraud Office beginning in 1996, culminating in charges filed in 1999. The essence of the Wickes case revolves around the early recognition in 1994 and 1995 of rebates from suppliers, resulting in overstatement of profits by more than £20 million. The rebates should have been recognized only when agreed purchasing thresholds were met. However, the documentation for the real purchasing thresholds was substituted with phony documents supporting the early recognition. The documents containing the false terms were provided to Wickes's auditors in connection with their audits of the company's financial statements.

To understand how these schemes can work, let's look at two real-life examples in greater detail, one from a customer's perspective (the recipient and beneficiary of discounts provided by a supplier), and one from a vendor's (supplier's) perspective (a provider of discounts).

Example of Scheme Perpetrated by a Customer—The Royal Ahold Case

Koninklijke Ahold N.V. is a company organized in the Netherlands that operates under the name Royal Ahold in the United States. In 2004, Royal Ahold was charged with two accounting frauds. One of these involved the recognition of promotional allowances received from vendors by U.S. Foodservice (USF), a wholly owned subsidiary of Royal Ahold. During the years in question, 2001 and 2002, the majority of USF's operating income came from promotional allowance payments received from vendors. Very little profit resulted from USF's end-sales to customers.

The typical promotional allowance agreement involved USF committing to purchase a certain minimum volume from a vendor at established prices, in exchange for which the vendor would pay a per unit rebate of a portion of the original purchase price charged to USF, based on a payment schedule. Some promotional allowances were paid as they were earned. However, on multi-year contracts it was common practice for vendors to prepay some portion of the projected rebate based on targets in the contract.

In order to meet its earnings targets, USF recorded completely fictitious promotional allowances in amounts sufficient to cover any budget shortfalls in earnings. According to the complaint filed by the SEC, USF did not even maintain any form of comprehensive, automated system for tracking amounts owed by vendors under these agreements, instead utilizing an estimated "promotional allowance rate" to be applied to sales. USF executives attempted to cover up their scheme using a variety of techniques, including lying to the auditors, who were incorrectly informed that none of these promotional allowance arrangements were documented in the form of agreements.

As a result of this scheme, Royal Ahold's financial statements (which included the statements of its wholly owned subsidiary, USF) were materially misstated.

What clearly places this case in the category of fraud, as opposed to an unintentional error or misapplication of an accounting rule, are the great lengths that USF executives went to in order to hide their scheme. In addition to lying to the auditors, USF executives rigged the confirmation process used by the auditors. Confirmation requests were sent to various vendors. These requests reported greatly exaggerated amounts of promotional allowances and receivables due from vendors, since they were based on USF's fraudulent financial statements. USF contacted vendors informing them to sign the confirmations without question. When vendors objected, they were told that the confirmation was just "an internal number" and that USF did not consider the receivable stated in the confirmation to be an actual obligation. In some cases, side letters were sent to vendors assuring them that they did not owe the amounts stated in the confirmation requests.

Example of Scheme Perpetrated by a Vendor—The Carter's Case

The second example illustrates another variation on this type of scheme. It involves the timing of the recognition of revenue reductions associated with incentives provided to customers by a supplier.

Carter's, Inc. is an example of a timing difference scheme perpetrated by a vendor (supplier). In a 2010 complaint filed by the SEC, Carter's was charged with manipulating discounts granted by Carter's to its largest retail customer, Kohl's Corporation, from at least 2004 through 2009. The Carter's case is also a good illustration showing that not all financial statement frauds originate in or even involve the accounting department. In fact, some involve the deception of the accounting department by other personnel.

Carter's is a maker of apparel designed for babies and children, selling under the brand names of *Carter's* and *OshKosh*. Consistent with standard business practices in the industry, Carter's provided some of its customers with discounts (known as "accommodations") that could be applied against outstanding invoices. These accommodations, based on the rules described earlier, are normally accounted for as reductions in sales revenue.

The Carter's scheme involved mismatching, resulting in a timing difference. Under the matching principle inherent in U.S. GAAP and IFRS, expenses or revenue reductions associated with revenue transactions should be recognized in the same accounting period as the revenue. However, in the case of Carter's, accommodations provided to Kohl's were often not finalized until either the very end of, or even after, the end of each quarter. Internal controls at Carter's provided for the creation and approval of internal documentation for accommodations prepared by the sales department that would be forwarded to the accounting department for recording and matching with subsequent use of the discount by a customer.

However, from 2004 through 2009, a senior sales executive of Carter's began granting excessive accommodations to Kohl's and concealing these excess accommodations from the accounting department. This sales executive arranged with Kohl's for Kohl's to "delay taking those accommodations for a sufficient amount of time such that each accommodation could be mischaracterized to Carter's accounting department as an expense of the later period in which it was taken, rather than an expense of the earlier period in which the sale was made."

Internally, supporting documentation was rigged to coincide with the fraudulent accounting treatment. For each of the falsely deferred accommodations, the sales executive instructed his assistant to wait to generate the documentation for the accommodation until about one week before Kohl's was "scheduled" to utilize the discount (which could be several quarters after the accommodation was actually granted). The assistant was also instructed to include inaccurate data on the supporting documentation, particularly information about the original sales date to which the accommodation applied. This tricked the accounting department into matching the accommodations with the wrong (later) sales.

Similar to many other timing difference fraud schemes, the fraudulent deferral of accommodations provided to Kohl's by Carter's grew from year to year before it all unraveled. When the scheme began in 2004, total unrecognized accommodations amounted to a little more than $3 million at year-end. By 2009, the unrecorded accommodations had grown to more than $18 million.

Of course, as the amounts involved escalated, the lies extended beyond merely creating false supporting documentation. Even in 2012, additional charges continue to be made in connection with this scheme.

CHAPTER FIVE

Gross-Up Schemes

IN SOME CASES, a company's reporting objective is not necessarily to improve the appearance of profitability. The goal can also be to appear larger, processing a greater volume of transactions and activities. This objective can lead the company to engage in gross-up schemes.

Under both U.S. GAAP and IFRS, certain amounts collected from customers should not be reported as revenue. For example:

- Sales taxes, service taxes, and value added taxes
- Amounts collected on behalf of a principal with whom the reporting entity has an agency relationship

However, reimbursements for out-of-pocket expenses are generally to be recognized as revenue (rather than as an offset to expenses).

In addition, IAS 18 notes when goods or services are exchanged for other goods or services that are similar in nature, revenue should not be recognized.

AGENT VERSUS PRINCIPAL

If a company receives a payment but is acting in the capacity as an agent for another entity (the principal), the company should not record the entire amount as revenue, and the amount remitted to the principal separately as costs. Instead, the agent company should merely record any net amount from the transaction as revenue. The amount to be remitted to the principal should be accounted for as a liability when it is received. The liability is then eliminated when payment is remitted to the principal.

Examples of transactions in which this issue emerges are plentiful. One of the most common examples involves a company that sells products and services to customers. The products that it provides to its customers, however, are provided by an unrelated supplier. A series of characteristics of this transaction will determine whether the company is acting as a principal or as an agent for the supplier, though the determination is not always easy to make.

Under ASC 605, eight questions should be addressed in making this determination:

1. Who is the primary obligor in the transaction? If the company is responsible for fulfilling the obligations to a customer in an arrangement, this is consistent with the company recording amounts it receives as revenue. However, if a supplier to the company has the primary responsibility for fulfilling an order for products or services to be provided to a customer, this is an indicator that the company should not recognize revenue for the portion of the transaction for which the supplier has primary responsibility. Simply having responsibility for arranging for transportation of products is not an indicator of being the primary obligor in a transaction.
2. Who has inventory risk in the transaction? Inventory risk exists when a company assumes ownership of inventory before the inventory has been ordered by a customer. Thus, if a company does not own the inventory until after it has been ordered by a customer (e.g., the company does not even order items from a supplier until it receives an order from or makes a sale to a customer), it does not have inventory risk. Having inventory risk is consistent with being a principal in a transaction. No inventory risk is an indicator of being an agent.
3. Does the reporting entity have latitude in pricing? If a company has latitude in establishing the price it charges its customer, this indicates it is acting as principal by the fact that it possesses the risks and rewards consistent with such relationships. However, if the price it charges a customer is fixed by the supplier, this is consistent with acting as an agent.

4. Does the entity change the product or provide part of the service?
5. Does the entity have supplier discretion?
6. Does the entity have a role in determining product or service specifications?
7. Does the entity have physical loss inventory risk?
8. Does the entity have credit risk? Credit risk exists when a sales price has not been fully collected at the time a product or service is delivered. While requiring prepayment, by itself, does not preclude recognition of revenue as principal, the existence of credit risk is a common characteristic of being a principal in a transaction. Whereas, if the supplier does not receive payment (from the agent) until after the agent receives payment from the customer, the intermediary company may be serving in the capacity of an agent.

With one exception, agent transactions improperly recorded as principal transactions affect gross operations, but do not generally have an impact on profits or loss, unless the transactions overlap accounting periods. However, consignment sales transactions, described in Chapter 3, are a form of agent transaction in which profits can be affected, since improperly recorded sales are offset by cost of goods sold, resulting in profits being recorded in the wrong period, or where none should be recognized (e.g., consignment inventory that remains unsold by a retailer).

BARTER AND ROUND-TRIP TRANSACTIONS

In a barter transaction, two entities swap products or services. Often the products or services are of a similar nature (e.g., advertising), but in some cases, they are not. Generally, barter transactions result in revenue and expenses (or assets) for both companies involved in the transaction.

Candie's, Inc., a designer, marketer, and distributor of women's shoes, handbags, and accessories, was the target of the SEC in AAER 1770 in April 2003. The SEC charged Candie's with improperly recognizing revenue from barter transactions. In August 1997, Candie's entered into an agreement with another company under which Candie's would provide 160,000 pairs of shoes at $10 per pair, to be paid using a combination of cash and advertising credits. On October 31, 1997, the last day of its fiscal quarter, Candie's recorded $1.3 million in revenue from the purported shipment of 133,000 pairs of shoes. One minor problem—the shoes weren't shipped until July 1999. In October 1998, another agreement was signed with the same barter company that increased the value of the shoes that had already supposedly been shipped (and were previously recorded as being shipped) by $600,000. The October 1998 agreement also described another sale of 62,000 pairs of shoes. Between these two agreements, Candie's recorded another $1.8 million in revenue. Once again, the shoes in the second agreement were not shipped. Obviously, a major element of this fraud deals with the failure to ship any shoes associated with the recording of revenue. However, the valuation of the barter arrangement is also questionable, based on the second agreement's adjustment in value of a transaction that supposedly already took place in the previous period. As a result, revenue for the one transaction was recorded in two different accounting periods.

Round-trip transactions have certain similarities to barter transactions. However, while cash is not necessary to a barter agreement, cash always exchanges hands in round-trip transactions. For example, Company A sells a product to Company B for cash, while at the same time, Company B sells a product to Company A for cash, often for an equivalent or similar amount as the first transaction.

To attempt to disguise the transaction, round-tripping is sometimes carried out through subsidiaries or other affiliates used as intermediaries. In other cases, unrelated third parties may be utilized to perpetrate the fraud.

This is exactly the nature of the charges brought by the SEC in 2002 against former executives of Homestore, Inc. (formerly Homestore.com, Inc.) According to the SEC (release 2002-141):

> Throughout 2000 and 2001, Homestore's sale of online advertisements was one of its primary revenue sources. Homestore engaged in a series of complex round-trip barter transactions to inflate revenues and meet Wall Street estimates. The essence of these transactions was a circular flow of money by which Homestore recognized its own cash as revenue. Specifically, Homestore paid inflated sums to various vendors for services or products; in turn, the vendors used these funds to buy advertising from two media companies. The media companies then bought advertising from Homestore either on their own behalf or as agents for other advertisers. Homestore recorded the funds it received from the media companies as revenue in its financial statements, in violation of applicable accounting principles.
>
> Using this structure, Homestore paid a total of $49.8 million to various vendors in the first two quarters of 2001. These vendors then paid $45.1 million to a major media company to purchase online advertisements. Homestore, in turn, recorded $36.7 million in revenue from the major media company's related purchase of Homestore online advertisements. In short, Homestore recycled its own money

to generate revenues. Homestore used this same general plan with another media company in the second and third quarters of 2001 to fraudulently recognize an additional $9.7 million in revenue.

Another round-trip transaction case involved Duane Reade, the operator of a chain of drug stores in the New York metropolitan area. In 2008 (see AAER 2894), the SEC charged Duane Reade's CEO with engaging in round-trip transactions that falsely inflated the company's revenue. The transactions purportedly involved payments to Duane Reade for the company's agreement to relinquish supposedly valuable leases or other real estate rights. According to the SEC, these transactions were shams in which Duane Reade's CEO "persuaded counterparties to make payments to Duane Reade in exchange for his promise to repay them through other fictitious transactions." These transactions were supported with phony documentation prepared by Duane Reade's CFO.

A second category of round-trip transactions was also perpetrated by Duane Reade. Under this scheme, vendors, at the direction of Duane Reade's CEO, issued bogus credits to the company. These credits were recorded as current income. However, the CEO then directed the vendors to rebill Duane Reade for the credited amounts in later periods using fictitious invoices. This timing scheme resulted in the fraudulent recording of income in one period, offset by the recording of expenses in a subsequent period.

PHONY REVENUE AND EXPENSES

Another incentive in certain financial reporting fraud cases is to simply appear to be a larger company. In these cases, the fraud may be so simple as to only involve the recording of artificial revenue and expenses in equal amounts. There is no effect on net profit with this scheme. However, by appearing larger, it can help a company meet market expectations for overall growth in sales.

One example was the case of The BISYS Group, Inc., which engaged in a variety of improper accounting in connection with its Insurance Services division from 2000 to 2003. One of the schemes perpetrated by BISYS was the simultaneous accrual of $1 million of commission income and $1 million of expense for the quarter ended December 31, 2000. These accruals were immediately reversed in January 2001. But, by making the accruals, BISYS only narrowly missed the revenue expectations stated by analysts. The exact same technique was used again for the quarter ended December 31, 2001, only this time for $2.05 million, enabling BISYS to exceed revenue expectations.

PART TWO

Asset-Based Schemes

THE REVENUE-BASED SCHEMES described in Part I involve situations in which the primary motive was to inflate revenue. Since accounting involves two sides to every transaction, schemes involving revenue inflation can impact financial statements in several other manners:

1. Overstating assets (e.g., accounts receivable)
2. Understating liabilities (e.g., deferred revenue)
3. Overstating expenses (e.g., gross-up schemes)
4. Understating gains or other nonoperating revenue (e.g., misclassification schemes)

In Part II, schemes involving the overstatement of assets, excluding those impacted through the inflation of revenue, will be the focus. The primary categories of asset-based schemes explained here include:

- Improper capitalization of costs that should be expensed
- Inventory schemes
- Overvaluing assets in connection with fair value accounting
- Failure to properly recognize asset impairments

CHAPTER SIX

Improper Capitalization of Costs

ONE OF THE MOST common methods of fraudulently making a company appear financially stronger is through the capitalization or deferral of expenses. This method instantly takes expenses, which reduce net income, and converts them into assets.

There are several categories of expenses that are the most likely candidates for improper capitalization, including the following:

1. Start-up costs
2. Research and development costs
3. Repairs and maintenance (capitalized as property and equipment)
4. Software development and acquisition
5. Websites
6. Development of intangible assets
7. Advertising
8. Other deferrals and prepaid expenses

While WorldCom may be the most well-publicized and most material case of improper capitalization of expenses (to the tune of more than $3 billion), the American Italian Pasta Company (AIPC) case may be even more useful for illustrating the many methods with which this category of fraud can be perpetrated.

AIPC engaged in no fewer than four different methods of expense capitalization, resulting in overstatement of earnings from 2002 through 2004. Three of the methods involved improper capitalization of costs associated with the installation of new pasta production lines in the company's manufacturing plants. Normally, the costs capitalized in adding new production lines included internal plant labor and other internal costs, in addition to amounts paid to third parties. Capitalizing internal labor costs is consistent with accounting principles. However, one of AIPC's many downfalls in this case was the company's lack of adequate procedures for measuring internal plant labor utilized on capital projects. This led to the first method of improperly capitalizing expenses—AIPC capitalized internal costs based on its budget rather than on any actual measurement of those costs (note that the lack of internal controls in this case raised doubts about all capitalized internal costs, even though some portion of the internal costs likely were legitimately capitalized).

The second method AIPC used involved the capitalization of normal manufacturing expenses that exceeded the original manufacturing budget. In other words, any excess manufacturing costs simply got dumped into fixed assets. AIPC simply recorded plant-wide cost variances without any analysis of whether these costs had any relation to a capital project.

The third approach utilized by AIPC was to capitalize the impact on profit of sales shortfalls. For example, if sales fell short of expectations in one period, the profit shortfall would be restored by increasing a capital asset. In assigning the increased basis to specific assets, in some cases AIPC even charged the amounts to assets that had already been installed and were in operation.

The fourth method of improper expense capitalization involved internal and external information technology costs and really involved multiple methods. As explained later, certain internal and external costs of developing software for internal use may be capitalized. However, much like with its plant labor, AIPC capitalized internal information technology labor costs based solely on a budget, without any supporting documentation or correlation to specific capitalizable tasks. In addition, AIPC improperly capitalized numerous other types of internal and external information technology costs, such as hardware leasing, software maintenance, communications, and noncapitalizable outside labor.

START-UP COSTS

Under ASC 720-15, all start-up costs and organization costs should be expensed as incurred. Start-up activities are defined as "those one-time activities related to opening a new facility, introducing a new product or service, conducting business in a new territory, conducting business with a new class of customer or beneficiary, initiating a new process in an existing facility, or commencing some new operation. Start-up activities include activities related to organizing a new entity (commonly referred to as organization costs)."

Activities related to routine, ongoing efforts to refine, enrich, or otherwise improve upon the qualities of an existing product, service, process, or facility are not "start-up activities" and are not within the scope of ASC 720-15. In addition, activities related to a merger or acquisition and to ongoing customer acquisition are not "start-up activities."

In addition, certain costs are specifically excluded from the scope of ASC 720-15 on the basis that other authoritative literature already exists that addresses these costs:

- Costs of acquiring or constructing long-lived assets and getting them ready for their intended uses (however, the costs of using long-lived assets that are allocated to start-up activities are within the scope of ASC 720-15).
- Costs of acquiring or producing inventory.
- Costs of acquiring intangible assets (however, the costs of using such assets that are allocated to start-up activities are within the scope of ASC 720-15).
- Costs related to internally developed assets, such as internal-use software costs (however, the costs of using those assets that are allocated to start-up activities are within the scope of ASC 720-15).
- Costs that are within the scope of guidance on accounting for research and development costs.
- Costs of fund-raising incurred by nonprofit organizations.
- Costs of raising capital.
- Costs of advertising.
- Costs incurred in connection with existing construction-type and certain production-type contracts.

Auditors and investigators should always carefully scrutinize assets that have been capitalized in connection with a company that is going through a start-up phase, including starting up new locations, divisions, product lines, and so on, as these are areas that are ripe for improper capitalization.

RESEARCH AND DEVELOPMENT COSTS

One of the categories identified that is a likely candidate for improper capitalization is research and development, addressed in U.S. GAAP at ASC 730.

Research is defined as a planned search or critical investigation aimed at discovery of new knowledge with the hope that such knowledge will be useful in developing a new product or service (referred to as product), or a new process or technique (referred to as process), or in bringing about a significant improvement to an existing product or process.

Development is described as the translation of research findings or other knowledge into a plan or design for a new product or process, or for a significant improvement to an existing product or process, whether intended for sale or use. It includes the conceptual formulation, design, and testing of product alternatives, construction of prototypes, and operation of pilot plants.

Research and development costs are to be expensed as incurred.

There are several examples of cases in which research and development costs were improperly capitalized as a way of inflating profits. The SmartForce PLC case, introduced in Chapter 2 in connection with a revenue recognition scheme, is one such example. One of the allegations against SmartForce was that it improperly capitalized research and development costs associated with some of its courseware content. In its Restatement 8-K/A filed with the SEC, in which it corrected this error, SmartForce noted that the capitalization was "inconsistent with SmartForce's general policy of expensing content development as it is incurred."

PROPERTY AND EQUIPMENT

Included among the reported assets of an entity is property and equipment. Most reported property and equipment is owned by the reporting entity. However there are certain exceptions to this ownership requirement, most notably for property utilized under leases that qualify as capital leases.

U.S. GAAP for property and equipment is found at ASC 360. IFRS is found primarily in IAS 16. With one important exception that will be explained later in this section, U.S. GAAP and IFRS are mostly consistent in the accounting for property and equipment.

Accounting for the Acquisition

Property and equipment should be initially recorded at cost. Cost is generally based on the cash paid for an asset, or the amount borrowed to acquire an asset. However, when consideration other than cash is provided in exchange for property and equipment, fair value of the consideration is generally utilized to measure the acquired asset.

Cost basis of property and equipment includes all costs directly related to the acquisition. This includes the purchase price, related taxes associated with the purchase (e.g., sales tax), import duties, direct costs associated with bringing the asset to the location, and costs of establishing working conditions necessary for it to be operated as intended. If the property is real estate and construction, acquisition costs may also include architect fees, remodeling costs, excavation costs, payments to construction contractors, materials, building permits, and labor.

Costs must be specifically identified in order to be eligible for capitalization. In the case of Qwest Communications International, Inc. (see AAER 2127), the SEC claimed that the company improperly capitalized costs associated with the construction of design service centers because the amounts capitalized were simply based on estimates rather than any specific asset construction or acquisition. The result was an overstatement of $103 million of 2000 pre-tax income and $97 million of 2001 pre-tax income.

If an asset retirement obligation exists, the estimated cost of dismantling and removing the asset should also be capitalized, with a corresponding credit to a liability account. See Chapter 10 for further explanation of this liability.

Costs Incurred during Ownership

Once an entity has capitalized an asset, additional costs are usually incurred on an ongoing basis to maintain the asset. This introduces another financial reporting fraud risk.

Generally, costs that result in appreciably extending an asset's useful life, or that increase the asset's capacity, or that improve the efficiency or safety of the asset, should be capitalized when incurred. Those costs that do not meet one of these criteria should be expensed. Thus, repair and maintenance costs associated with merely maintaining an asset in proper working condition, ensuring it lasts for its expected useful life, should be expensed rather than capitalized.

If a component part of an asset is replaced, the cost of the component replacement part may be capitalized and the component part that was replaced would be derecognized (its cost and accumulated depreciation removed from the books).

One excellent example of the improper capitalization of expenses involves Buca, Inc. In a complaint filed by the SEC, Buca, a Minneapolis-based holding company for two restaurant chains, was charged with using several schemes involving the improper capitalization of $12 million of expenses from 2000 to 2004. Starting with repairs, Buca capitalized $4.67 million of everyday repair and maintenance expenses, along with general and administrative expenses.

Buca also utilized a worker misclassification scheme to disguise another capitalization fraud. Under this scheme, Buca misclassified certain workers as independent contractors who should have been classified as employees. This helped in improperly capitalizing amounts paid to these workers. For example, during 2002, amounts paid to Buca's assistant controller (which should have been expensed as salaries) were capitalized as though these amounts were part of the acquisition of another restaurant chain that Buca was involved in at the time. Similarly, Buca laid off its vice president of real estate, then hired her as an independent contractor shortly thereafter. She was then paid a $100,000 "finder's fee" for two leases she had previously negotiated and Buca capitalized this amount. In effect, the severance payment made to the laid off employee was recorded as an asset.

Buca also improperly capitalized payments made to legitimate independent contractors. In one instance, $572,000 in payments made to one contractor for permitting services provided for Buca restaurants was capitalized without any basis for doing so.

Buca is discussed again later in connection with an asset inflation scheme (see Chapter 7).

One final consideration involves the subsequent revaluation of property and equipment. As will be explained in the section on impairment losses in Chapter 7, property and equipment should be assessed for impairment. But what about those situations in which the fair value of property and equipment has increased to an amount greater than recorded net book value?

Under IFRS, revaluing property and equipment to reflect these unrealized gains is permissible. Under U.S. GAAP, recording such increases is prohibited.

When recording these increases in accordance with IFRS, consideration must be given to the type of property and equipment involved. In this section, internal-use assets are covered. Investment property is also addressed in Chapter 7.

If an entity elects to carry internal-use property at fair value, the election should be made with respect to an entire class of property (e.g., land and buildings, machinery, etc.) rather than on an asset-by-asset basis. Increases in an asset's carrying amount in excess of its net book value are not credited to income in the income statement. Rather, these increases are credited directly to equity as a revaluation surplus (unless a previous revaluation resulted in an expense, in which case the revaluation would first restore the previously recognized expense). Accordingly, the surplus is reflected in other comprehensive income rather than in the income statement.

SOFTWARE DEVELOPMENT AND ACQUISITION COSTS

Under U.S. GAAP, the accounting for costs incurred in the development or acquisition of software is covered in two areas, depending on whether the software is for internal use only (e.g., a company's accounting software) or for the generation of revenue through licensing, sale, and so on.

ASC 350-40 prescribes accounting treatment for "internal-use software," which is described as software that is acquired or internally developed solely to meet a company's internal needs (i.e., it is not to be sold) and in the absence of any substantive plan (during its development or modification phase) for external marketing. Examples of internal-use software include a company's accounting system, business intelligence and analytical software, customer management systems and databases, content management systems, and many others.

The following costs associated with internal-use software should be capitalized and amortized on a straight-line basis, unless another method is more representative of the software's use:

- External direct costs of materials and services for developing or obtaining internal-use software (i.e., design, coding, installation, and testing)
- Internal payroll and related costs for employees who are directly associated with and who devote time to the internal-use software project
- Interest costs incurred in developing computer software
- Costs related to upgrades and enhancements, when it is probable that those expenditures will result in additional functionality

Costs that should be expensed as incurred include the following:

- Costs incurred in the preliminary project phase (making decisions to allocate resources to the project, determining performance requirements, and reviewing and selecting vendors and consultants)
- Research and development
- General and administrative costs and overhead
- Data conversion
- Training costs
- Internal maintenance costs

Amortization should begin when the computer software is ready for its intended use, regardless of whether the software will be placed in service in planned stages that may extend beyond the reporting period. In determining and periodically reassessing the estimated useful life over which capitalized costs should be amortized, organizations should consider the effects of obsolescence, changes in technology, competition, and other economic factors. Changes in software and management's plans for replacing technologically inferior software or hardware should also be considered.

Software designed to generate revenue is covered under ASC 985-20. Internal costs incurred to create computer software are expensed as incurred until technological feasibility for the product has been reached. Technological feasibility is established upon completion of a detailed program design or, in its absence, completion of a working model. After technological feasibility is established, the costs of coding and testing and other costs of producing product masters are capitalized. Capitalization stops when the product is available for general release to customers. Subsequent costs are expensed as incurred.

Capitalized software costs are amortized on a product-by-product basis, starting when the product is available for general release to customers. Annual amortization is the greater of:

1. Straight-line over the product's estimated useful life
2. The percentage of the product's current-year revenues as compared to the product's expected future revenues

Capitalized software costs are evaluated for impairment on a product-by-product basis through a comparison of the unamortized capitalized costs to the product's net realizable value. The amount by which the unamortized capitalized costs exceed the net realizable value is recognized as an impairment charge.

IFRS does not provide specific guidance on the capitalization or expensing of costs associated with software development. Rather, such costs are generally treated as intangible assets and are accounted for in accordance with IAS 38, explained later in this chapter.

An example of improper capitalization of software development costs is found in the case of Winners Internet Network, Inc. The SEC charged Winners with inflating its reported assets as of December 31, 1999, by $421,000 in connection with its propriety-processing software. The SEC alleged that Winners improperly capitalized wages, payroll taxes, rent, travel, marketing, and consulting expenses that were purportedly associated with the development of this software. The SEC found that the costs were unrelated in any way to the development of the software. Further, the costs were incurred after January 1999, which is the date the software was available for general release to customers.

All capitalizable development work should have taken place by that date. As a result, even if the costs in question had some relation to the software, they were incurred in the post-development phase and therefore would not be eligible for capitalization.

WEBSITE COSTS

Many companies expense all costs associated with the development and maintenance of their websites. However, accounting principles allow for the capitalization of some of these costs. As a result, one of the risks of fraudulent financial reporting is the improper capitalization of website costs.

Accounting for the costs of developing a website is covered in ASC 350-50, which uses much of the same logic as ASC 350-40 does for internal-use software. The costs of developing a website can be classified in four phases:

1. Planning stage
2. Application and infrastructure development stage
3. Graphics and content development stage
4. Operating stage

Consistent with ASC 350-40, all planning-stage costs should be expensed as incurred. Examples of planning-stage costs include the following:

- Development of a project or business plan
- Determining functionalities of the site
- Determining the hardware and technologies necessary
- Conceptual formulation of the graphics and content
- Evaluation of vendors
- Addressing legal considerations, such as copyright and trademark issues

Most of the costs associated with the next phase, the application and infrastructure development, should be capitalized and amortized over an estimated useful life. Examples of the costs incurred during this phase include the following:

- Acquisition or development of any software necessary to develop or operate the website (such as HTML editor, graphics software, server operating systems, web browser software, etc.)

- Development or acquisition and customization of code for web applications (such as search engines, order processing systems, payment systems, catalog software, e-mail, security features, etc.)
- Development or acquisition and customization of database software needed to integrate applications
- Development of HTML web pages or development of templates and writing of code to automatically create HTML pages
- Obtaining and registering an Internet domain name
- Installation of developed applications on the server(s)
- Creation of initial hypertext links to other websites or to destinations within the site
- Testing the site applications

In the third stage, graphics and content development, again, many costs should be capitalized. Most importantly, the initial creation of graphics to be used on the site should be capitalized. This includes the design or layout of each page, color, images, and the overall "look and feel" and "usability" of the site (including buttons, borders, etc.).

Initial entering of content into the website, however, should be expensed as incurred. These costs are analogous to "data conversion" costs associated with internal-use software (which are to be expensed as incurred).

Most operating-stage costs are to be expensed as incurred (ASC 350-50). Examples of operating costs that should be expensed include the following:

- Training employees involved in support of the site
- Registering the site with search engines
- User administration activities
- Updating site graphics
- Performing backups
- Creating new links
- Verifying that links are operating properly
- Adding new functionalities or features
- Performing routine security reviews
- Performing usage analysis

One important exception to the preceding rule regarding expensing of operating stage costs (especially with respect to updating site graphics and adding new functionalities or features) concerns "upgrades and enhancements." Upgrades and enhancements should be capitalized if it is likely that they will result in added functionality (again, just like the rules for internal-use software). Determination of whether an upgrade or enhancement adds functionality is a matter of judgment. Organizations that cannot separate internal costs on a reasonably cost-effective basis between maintenance and relatively minor upgrades and enhancements should expense such costs as they are incurred.

One of the difficulties in applying the principles of ASC 350-50 to some websites is the availability (or lack thereof) of documentation associated with developing the sites. This can be particularly true when outside contractors are utilized. These contractors often quote and bill one lump-sum amount for a variety of services, some of which should be expensed and others which should be established as assets. Allocating such lump-sum fees can be extremely difficult without significant cooperation from the contractor. The same problem is encountered with respect to internal payroll costs when contemporaneous time reports are not maintained by employees involved with the website.

IFRS for website development costs was addressed in SIC 32, issued in 2002, which concluded that websites represent a form of internally developed intangible asset covered under IAS 38, covered in the next section.

INTANGIBLE ASSETS

Intangible assets are assets lacking a physical substance, but which provide future economic benefits, generally in the form of the ability to produce income. Examples include copyrights, trademarks and service marks, patents, customer lists, contracts or sales backlogs, and various contractually based assets. Generally, intangible assets may result from any of the following activities or transactions:

- An intangible asset purchased as a stand-alone transaction
- An intangible asset (or multiple intangible assets) included as part of a larger purchase of multiple assets
- An intangible asset that is transferred to a company by its owner (e.g., in exchange for equity in the company or as part of a start-up operation)
- An intangible asset that is developed internally by a company
- Intangible assets acquired in connection with a merger or acquisition, as explained in Chapter 11

Intangible assets acquired individually or with a group of other assets (but not those acquired as part of a merger or acquisition) should be initially measured and recognized at fair value. From a practical perspective, this means that if an organization *purchases* an intangible asset, the purchase price will usually be considered to be the fair value. An intangible asset included in a purchase of multiple assets may be more difficult to measure if there is a single purchase price for the sum of the assets. However, an allocation of the purchase price based on the fair value of each individual asset should be identified.

Under ASC 350, costs of internally developing an intangible asset may be capitalized only if all three of the following characteristics are present:

1. The intangible asset is specifically identifiable.
2. The asset has a determinate life (it has a limited and determinable life).
3. The asset is not inherent in a continuing business and related to an entity as a whole.

Failing to meet any of these criteria results in the requirement to expense rather than capitalize the costs associated with internally developing an intangible asset. Fraud in the form of inappropriately capitalizing costs that should be reported as expenses could result if management misrepresents any of the preceding factors. The effect of this type of fraud is to overstate assets, understate expenses, and overstate profits.

IFRS rules for intangible assets are found in IAS 38. Under IAS 38, costs of developing an intangible asset may be capitalized only if certain criteria are met. But these criteria deal primarily with the feasibility of the entity completing the development of the asset and the probability of the entity generating future economic benefits from the asset.

In addition, IAS 38 states that an intangible asset must be identifiable, similar to the first and third criteria under ASC 350. In order to be identifiable, the asset must meet one of the following criteria:

1. It must either be separate or capable of being separated from the entity and sold, transferred, licensed, or rented.
2. It must arise from contractual or other legal rights, regardless of whether those rights are transferable or separable from the entity or from other rights and obligations.

Where the IFRS criteria are less stringent than U.S. GAAP is with respect to the second criterion described under ASC 350. IFRS has no such requirement for an internally developed intangible asset to have a limited and determinable life. As explained in Chapter 7, intangible assets with finite useful lives must be amortized over these lives, whereas those assets that do not have a determinable useful life are subject to annual impairment testing.

Under both IAS 38 and ASC 350, separately acquired intangible assets (outside of those acquired in a business combination, explained in Chapter 11), such as those purchased from another entity or from an individual, would ordinarily be capitalized, assuming they meet the criteria of being identifiable and having future economic benefit.

ADVERTISING COSTS

Guidance on accounting for advertising is found in ASC 720-35 as well as in ASC 340-20. ASC 340-20 provides the criteria for capitalization of advertising costs.

Advertising is defined as "the promotion of an industry, an entity, a brand, a product name, or specific products or services so as to create or stimulate a positive entity image or to create or stimulate a desire to buy the entity's products or services." Examples of advertising include the following:

- Direct-mail advertising (paper and e-mail)
- Product catalogs
- Television and radio advertising
- Printed advertisements in newspapers, publications, and directories
- Billboards
- Sponsorship of public events

Advertising costs should be expensed either as incurred or the first time the advertising takes place. A company should select one of these two methods for recognizing advertising expense and disclose this method in the financial statements. An exception from the general requirement to expense advertising costs exists for direct-response advertising, which may be reported as an asset.

Direct-response advertising whose primary purpose is to elicit sales to customers who could be shown to have responded specifically to the advertising should be capitalized if it is expected to result in future benefits, as in sales resulting from direct-response advertising of merchandise in excess of future costs to be incurred in realizing those revenues. If no future revenues are anticipated, however, because the products or services advertised are being provided by the organization without charge, there is no basis for capitalizing the costs of direct-response advertising after the first time the advertising takes place.

Under ASC 340-20, demonstrating that direct-response advertising will result in future benefits requires persuasive evidence that its effects will be similar to the effects or responses to past direct-response advertising of the organization that resulted in future benefits. Such evidence should include verifiable historical patterns of results for the organization. Attributes to consider in determining whether the responses will be similar include the following:

- The demographics of the audience
- The method of advertising
- The product
- Economic conditions

Industry statistics would *not* be considered objective evidence that direct-response advertising will result in future benefits in the absence of the specific organization's operating history. If an organization does not have a past history for a particular product or service but does have operating histories for other new products or services, statistics for these other new products or services may be used if it can be demonstrated that these statistics are likely to be highly correlated to the statistics of the particular new product or service. Test marketing is identified as one method of demonstrating such a correlation.

Direct-response advertising costs that are not capitalized, due to the inability to demonstrate the probability of future benefits, may not be retroactively capitalized in subsequent periods based on historical evidence in the subsequent periods indicating that the advertising did in fact result in future benefits.

If direct-response advertising costs are reported as assets, the costs so treated may only include the following:

1. Incremental direct costs of direct-response advertising incurred in transactions with independent third parties (e.g., concept development, writing advertising copy, artwork, printing, magazine space, mailing, etc.)
2. Payroll and payroll-related costs (employee benefits) for the direct-response advertising activities of employees who are directly associated with and devote time to the advertising reported as assets

For purposes of this rule, administrative costs, rent, depreciation other than depreciation of assets used directly for advertising activities, and other occupancy costs are not costs of direct-response advertising activities.

Amounts that are reported as assets should be amortized on a cost-pool-by-cost-pool basis over the period during which the future benefits are expected to be received. The method of amortization involves the ratio that current period revenues for the direct-response advertising cost pool bear to the total of current and estimated future revenue for that cost pool. These amounts should not be discounted to their net present values. Estimated amounts of future revenues may change over time. Accordingly, this ratio should be recalculated at the end of each reporting period in those rare instances in which the asset may be amortized over multiple reporting periods.

OTHER DEFERRALS AND PREPAID EXPENSES

Financial statement fraud in the form of overstatement of assets can be accomplished in many different manners. One additional category to consider is prepaid expenses.

Generally, an asset should be established when a company has paid for some service that has not been fully delivered by the end of an accounting period. For example, when a full 12-month premium for business insurance is paid and the coverage overlaps fiscal years, it is common that a prepaid expense will be established as of the end of the period for the remaining months of coverage.

But, in some cases, a company may attempt to represent as an asset a payment for services that have already been rendered, falsely claiming that the benefit from the service will last into the future. Such a claim can be supported only in very specific instances, such as with the creation of an intangible asset.

In the case of Huntington Bancshares, Inc., a financial holding company, the SEC asserted in a 2005 complaint (see AAER 2251) that the company established an asset when no such future service or benefit supported such treatment. From 1997 to 2002, Huntington improperly deferred, rather than expensed, sales commissions paid to employees in connection with the opening of new customer deposit accounts.

In another case (AAER 2202), the SEC charged TALX Corporation, a provider of automated employment verification services and automated employee self-service applications, with capitalizing a payment that was associated with past service. Among the many charges against TALX was one concerning the payment associated with settling a patent infringement claim. In March 2001, TALX entered into a license agreement with the patent holder relating to the claim. The payment made to the patent holder included a portion as compensation for claimed past use of the patented technology. This portion of the payment should have been expensed at that time. However, TALX included the entire amount of the payment in a capitalized asset account. This resulted in an overstatement of TALX's income of $1.6 million, or 49 percent, for fiscal year 2001.

Prepaid expenses that have been paid to related parties should be scrutinized with great care. As noted in Chapter 3, transactions with related parties are often subject to special terms and are prime candidates for fraudulent reporting.

In one case, payments to related parties were utilized as part of a scheme to improperly capitalize costs. The case involved Friedman's Inc., a large jewelry retailer. In a 2005 complaint filed by the SEC, Friedman's was charged with engaging in a variety of methods of financial reporting fraud from 2001 to 2003. One of those assertions pertained to a $700,000 cash "gross-up" bonus paid during the second quarter of 2003 to three Friedman's executives. The bonuses allowed them to pay their personal income tax liabilities on restricted stock that had been granted by the company. This, of course, should have been expensed as compensation. However, Friedman's instead offset the payment against a liability for accrued professional fees payable to an affiliated investment bank, Morgan Schiff. That liability had been $800,000. Further, during the fiscal year ended September 28, 2002, Friedman's improperly capitalized fees paid to the Morgan Schiff affiliate for work purportedly done on a financing and a securities offering. In fact, according to the SEC complaint, at least $720,000 of those fees had nothing to do with the financing or offering and should have been expensed as incurred.

INVENTORY CAPITALIZATION SCHEMES

Inventory is an important income-producing asset for many companies, including manufacturers, wholesalers, distributors, and retailers. Generally, under both U.S. GAAP (ASC 330) and IFRS (IAS 2), inventory is to be carried at cost.

Accounting for inventory held by wholesalers or distributors and retailers is relatively straightforward, as the initial unit cost is easily identified and is usually associated with a single specific purchase transaction. Accounting for inventory of a manufacturer is much more complex, as it generally consists of three categories:

1. Raw materials—items that will serve as inputs in a production process
2. Work in process—partially manufactured items that are at some stage of completion
3. Finished goods—completed products that are available for sale

The first risk of financial reporting fraud involving inventory of a manufacturer pertains to improper capitalization of the costs associated with manufacturing or acquiring inventory.

The Aerosonic Corporation case is an excellent example of the numerous methods which can be employed to overstate inventory. Aerosonic is an airplane instruments manufacturer. Inventory was an important asset to Aerosonic, representing almost 50 percent of the company's total assets for the years in question, 1999 through 2002. As explained in a complaint filed by the SEC, a variety of techniques were utilized to overstate Aerosonic's inventory. One of those methods involved the use of outdated and unsupported labor and overhead rates in the calculation of the cost of manufacturing inventory. As a result, approximately $900,000 of internal labor and overhead was improperly capitalized into inventory.

A similar approach of improperly capitalizing overhead costs to inventory was carried out by OM Group, Inc., based on the SEC's AAER 2643 from 2007. This scheme went on from 1999 to 2002 and was executed through the use of top-side adjustments to OM Group's consolidated financial statements. These entries were in some cases completely unsupported and in others were duplicative of entries previously made at the lower, operating unit level.

As explained in Chapter 3, another type of inventory is consignment inventory. This category of inventory represents products that have been delivered by a manufacturer or distributor to a retailer, but without the risks of ownership being transferred to the retailer. While the retailer holds and displays the inventory for sale to customers, it still belongs to the manufacturer or distributor. Consignment inventory that has not yet been sold to final customers should be reported as an asset of the manufacturer or distributor, not as an asset of the retailer.

INVENTORY FLOW ASSUMPTIONS

Inventory is often an asset that turns over many times during a year. Sometimes, inventory turns over at a steady rate, sometimes on seasonal or cyclical patterns, and other times in unpredictable patterns. And the inventory acquired (or manufactured) during the year may have different costs depending on when it was acquired. Take the following simple example:

> On January 1, Company A had 1,000 units of a particular inventory item on hand. These units each had a cost of $25, for a total inventory

on hand of $25,000. During the year, Company A purchased 7,000 additional units on three separate occasions, as follows:

February 1—3,000 units at $26 each
April 15—2,000 units at $27 each
October 1—2,000 units at $28 each

During the year, 6,000 units were sold, leaving 2,000 units in inventory on December 31.

The accounting question is, which 2,000 units were on hand at year-end? The answer to this question will affect the book value of inventory.

There are several inventory flow models that may be acceptable. However, there is a difference between U.S. GAAP and IFRS in this area. Inventory flow models include the following:

1. **Specific identification.** This method, acceptable under U.S. GAAP and IFRS, means exactly what it sounds like. Each time a unit is sold, the determination of which batch it came from is specifically identified and the cost of that specific item becomes the cost of goods sold. Likewise, inventory on hand at year-end is valued based on a specific identification of the items with the production batch or purchase. In the example, the 2,000 units on hand at year-end may be comprised of units from each of the four batches (i.e., some costing $25, $26, $27, and $28).
2. **FIFO (first-in, first-out).** Under this assumption, each sale is assumed to come from the oldest inventory on hand. Thus, inventory on hand at year-end is costed based on the most recent additions to inventory. In the example, FIFO would result in year-end inventory of $56,000 (2,000 units at $28) and cost of goods sold would be $157,000. FIFO is acceptable under both U.S. GAAP and IFRS.
3. **LIFO (last-in, first-out).** This model assumes that sales always come from the most recently acquired inventory. As a result, the oldest items stay in inventory. In the example, LIFO would result in year-end inventory of $51,000 (1,000 units at $25 and 1,000 units at $26). Cost of goods sold would be $162,000. LIFO is allowed under U.S. GAAP, but is not permitted under IFRS.
4. **Weighted-average.** This method assumes that inventory available for sale, consisting of beginning inventory plus all purchases during the year, have identical unit costs, based on a weighted average. In the example, there are 8,000 total units available for sale. Those 8,000 units have a

total cost of $213,000, resulting in a weighted-average unit cost of $26, 625. Accordingly, the year-end inventory of 2,000 units would be reported at $53,250 and cost of goods sold would be $159,750. Weighted-average costing is permissible under both U.S. GAAP and IFRS.

There are other inventory flow models as well, such as the retail method (in which ending inventory is priced at retail, then multiplied by a cost-to-retail ratio to arrive at estimated cost), but these four are the most frequently encountered and illustrate an important point—that the inventory flow assumption can have a material effect on financial statements.

CHAPTER SEVEN

Asset Valuation Schemes

FICTITIOUS ASSETS

Let's start with the simplest method of inflating the value of assets—by reporting assets that a company does not even own. Verifying that assets reported by a company are actually owned by that company and not by some other party is an essential part of any audit. But, it is also one that has slipped through the cracks during some audits. A company must own and control an asset in order to report it on its balance sheet. If the asset is owned by another entity, a related party for example, the asset should not be included in the balance sheet.

Supporting documentation for assets should verify the ownership of an asset. One of the more remarkable overstatements of assets involved Parmalat Finanziaria S.p.A., an Italian seller of dairy products. Parmalat was charged with overstating its 2002 reported assets by at least €3.95 billion. The company claimed to hold this amount in cash and marketable securities in an account at Bank of America in New York City in the name of Bonlat Financing Corporation, a wholly owned (and, therefore, consolidated) subsidiary incorporated in the Cayman Islands. Bonlat's auditors confirmed the account with Bank of America—or so they thought. The assets did not exist and the confirmation had been forged. Yet the purported balance in this account was included in the audited financial statements.

INVENTORY VALUATION SCHEMES

In Chapter 6, schemes involving improper capitalization of costs incurred in manufacturing or acquiring inventory were introduced. In this chapter, schemes associated with the subsequent counting and valuation of inventory is the subject.

Opportunities for financial reporting fraud involving inventory normally involve overstating inventory (and, as a result, understating cost of goods sold and inflating profit). The most common financial reporting fraud risks involving inventory include:

1. Manipulating the year-end inventory count to inflate the quantity reported in inventory, using any of a variety of methods:
   a. Altering count sheets or records
   b. Inserting phony additional count sheets or records
   c. Counting the same items multiple times by moving them from one location to another
   d. Including items in inventory that do not exist, such as by counting empty boxes
   e. Utilizing a computer program that systematically assigns improper counts or creates phony records of inventory supposedly on hand
   f. Utilization of a fictitious vendor that supposedly provides inventory to the company (i.e., the inventory count sheets appear to be supported by invoices from a provider of the items)
   g. Improperly including in inventory items owned by an affiliate
   h. Including consignment inventory on hand of a retailer when it is rightfully owned by the supplier

   Recall from Chapter 2 the case of Del Global Technologies Corp., charged with a variety of financial reporting fraud schemes by the SEC. One of those schemes involved the overstatement of inventory through the creation of phony inventory tags prepared in connection with the 1999 physical inventory. This resulted in a $1.8 million overstatement of inventory. This scheme was carried out from 1997 to 2000, resulting in more than $13 million of overstated inventory. More than 30 percent of the company's reported inventory didn't exist!
2. Improper sales cut-off techniques at year-end (e.g., manipulation of bill-and-hold transactions, etc. See Chapter 3 for details on several sales cut-off manipulation techniques)

3. Overvaluing items in inventory by misclassifying them (e.g., characterizing a low-cost inventory item as a higher-cost item), through use of techniques such as mislabeling, resulting in an inflated unit cost
4. Improper application of the adopted inventory flow model
5. Use of improper top-side adjustments to inventory (i.e., adjustments made at only the general ledger level that are not reflected in the detailed inventory system), as was the case with the OM Group (see Chapter 6)
6. Improper application of labor and overhead rates to manufactured items, such as with the Aerosonic case (discussed in Chapter 6)
7. Altering vendor invoices or other supporting documents to inflate per-unit costs
8. Failing to recognize an impairment loss on inventory resulting from any of the following:
   a. Intentionally failing to identify obsolete or very slow-moving inventory items
   b. Offering a sales incentive to customers (i.e., certain incentives offered to customers, sometimes done just to sell slow-moving inventory, may result in unit sales prices that are less than unit cost)

   The team at Del Global Technologies Corp. engaged in this practice as well, with senior management directing employees to list obsolete inventory at full values as part of the company's inventory inflation scheme.

Another example of overvaluing inventory on hand comes from a case involving Fischer Imaging Corporation (Fischer), a manufacturer and servicer of medical imaging system used for the diagnosis and screening of disease. In AAER 2134 of 2004, the SEC charged Fischer with overstating its reported inventory by overvaluing its excess and obsolete inventory associated with discontinued product lines. Fischer also was alleged to have inflated reported inventory by valuing malfunctioning parts that had been returned by customers as if the parts were fully operational. Finally, Fischer was charged with double-counting certain raw materials among their inventory items.

Inventory is also the first of what will be several categories of assets discussed in this book as potential subjects of impairment, which results when an asset must be written down from its current book value.

Under U.S. GAAP, at ASC 330-10-35, inventory must be carried at the lower of cost or market. Market is defined as current replacement cost, which is further defined as net realizable value. IFRS is the same, directly stating that inventory is to be carried at the lower of cost or net realizable value.

Net realizable value is the estimated selling price in the ordinary course of business, reduced by any anticipated costs of completion and sale.

Reserves for impairment losses, or direct reductions in basis, are usually recorded in connection with damaged, slow-moving, or obsolete inventory items.

U.S. GAAP and IFRS differ regarding the treatment of subsequent recoveries of impairment write-downs. Under IFRS, if inventory that has been written down for an impairment loss subsequently recovers in value prior to sale, the recovery can be recognized (up to, but not exceeding, the original cost). Under U.S. GAAP, however, impairment losses result in a permanent write-down in the basis of inventory. Recognition of subsequent recoveries is limited to any gain made when the inventory is sold.

Unlike certain other nonfinancial assets (see IAS 16 for property and equipment and IAS 40 for investment property), there is no option under IFRS to increase the book value of inventory from cost to fair value when fair value exceeds cost. In this respect, IFRS mirrors U.S. GAAP.

The folks at Aerosonic (see Chapter 6) also improperly applied the impairment loss rules in addition to the improper capitalization scheme described earlier. According to the SEC complaint, senior management at Aerosonic "took the position that Aerosonic's inventory never became obsolete, and that additional reserves were unnecessary because all slow-moving inventory would eventually be sold." The SEC found that the reported levels of inventory were enough to support several thousand years' worth of future sales of certain parts, based on recent sales levels. Senior management was aware that a reserve of $3 to $4 million would be appropriate in 2001, but, nonetheless authorized just $500,000 in reserves between 2000 and 2003. When Aerosonic eventually restated its financial statements, almost $2.62 million of losses were recorded in connection with this scheme.

INFLATING THE BASIS OF PROPERTY AND EQUIPMENT

In Chapter 6, improper capitalization of costs that should be recorded as expenses was explained. However, in some cases, there is a legitimate asset to be recorded, but the fraud involves inflating the carrying amount of the asset.

Recall the case of Buca, Inc., the restaurant chain that improperly capitalized $12 million of expenses from 2000 to 2004. Buca was involved in one other scheme that involved the inflation in basis of legitimate capital assets. This scheme required the cooperation of a willing vendor.

This scheme could best be called a bill-back arrangement. The scheme involved the cooperation of certain Buca vendors that typically provided capital assets to Buca (e.g., construction and information technology vendors). The scheme also involved an annual conference, the "Paisano Partners Conference," held by Buca for its store managers. The Buca vendors were solicited to make "contributions" to fund the costs of the conference, but with the clear understanding that they could invoice these contributions back to Buca. As a result, what would ordinarily be reported as an operating expense of Buca for the conference was recorded as part of the cost (albeit an inflated cost) of various capital assets that were provided by these vendors. The total amount improperly capitalized under this scheme was $713,000. Construction vendors that participated in this bill-back scheme typically billed Buca for their contributions in vaguely worded change orders, invoices, or inflated project bids.

Extending this scheme one step further, one of Buca's information technology vendors was used to bill back certain ordinary operating expenses of Buca, such as the company's monthly telephone bill. Once again, after paying an operating expense on behalf of Buca, the vendor would add the amount to an otherwise legitimate invoice for a capital item. This scheme resulted in another $130,000 of inflated asset amounts.

INFLATING THE BASIS OF ASSETS ACQUIRED IN NONCASH TRANSACTIONS

There are many methods of inflating the basis of an asset. One category of transaction especially prone to this treatment involves assets acquired in noncash transactions.

U.S. GAAP for these transactions is found in ASC 845, *Nonmonetary Transactions.*

In general, the accounting for nonmonetary transactions is based on the fair values of the assets (or services) involved, similar to monetary transactions. Accordingly, the initial basis of a nonmonetary asset acquired in exchange for another nonmonetary asset is the fair value of the asset surrendered to obtain it. A gain or loss may be recognized in connection with the exchange. The fair value of the asset *received* should be used to measure the cost only if it is more clearly evident than the fair value of the asset surrendered.

In some cases, such as the one involving JBI, Inc. described next, the asset received is in the form of barter credits. These barter credits can be used to purchase goods or services, such as advertising time, from either the barter entity or members of its barter exchange network.

In reporting the exchange of a nonmonetary asset for barter credits, it is presumed that the fair value of the nonmonetary asset exchanged is more clearly evident than the fair value of the barter credits received and that the barter credits should be reported at the fair value of the nonmonetary asset exchanged.

This presumption can only be overcome if an entity can convert the barter credits into cash in the near term. There should be evidence of this right, such as a historical practice of converting barter credits into cash shortly after receipt. Alternatively, if independent quoted market prices exist for items to be received upon exchange of the barter credits, this could also overcome the presumption that the credits should be valued based on the value of asset surrendered. It also is to be presumed that the fair value of the nonmonetary asset does not exceed its carrying amount unless there is persuasive evidence supporting a higher value.

Similar to the impairment criteria described in other chapters, an impairment loss on the barter credits must be recognized if it subsequently becomes apparent that either of the following conditions exists:

1. The fair value of any remaining barter credits is less than the carrying amount.
2. It is probable that the entity will not use all of the remaining barter credits.

In 2012, JBI, Inc. was charged with an accounting fraud stemming from its purchase of "media credits" comprised of prepaid print and radio advertisements to be used for future marketing activities. The media credits purportedly had a value of $9,997,134. However, the agreed upon price for the credits was $1 million, payable in the form of 1,000,000 shares of common stock valued at $1 million (a $1.00 per share market price) on August 24, 2009, by JBI (then known as 310 Holdings).

Instead of reporting the purchased media credits at the purchase price of $1 million, JBI recorded an asset of $9,997,134 (with the credit side of the entry going to additional paid-in capital). This inflated the assets and net worth of JBI substantially. The company reported assets of $24.1 million and stockholders' equity of $22.9 million as of December 31, 2009.

The $9,997,134 valuation was not entirely without basis. It could be traced to a transaction between the original acquirer (who sold them to JBI) and a company called Media4Equity LLC in August 2008. However, according to the SEC's complaint, this original valuation was "severely flawed." And under no circumstances, even if the valuation was proper, was there any basis for recording the credits on JBI's books at $9,997,134 when the consideration paid reflected "the perceived value of the media credits at the time of the transaction."

In addition, the SEC alleged that the media credits were actually worthless and should, after being initially recorded at $1 million, have been subsequently remeasured to zero on September 30 and December 31, 2009. The SEC based this conclusion on "the unreliability of the probable future economic benefits attributable to the media credits."

The motive behind this scheme was to "use JBI and its valuation as a vehicle for acquisitions," according to the SEC. In fact, when JBI restated its 2009 financial statements, the removal of the media credits was just one (albeit the largest) of several adjustments that were made. Among the other adjustments were two related to reallocating the purchase prices of two subsidiaries—discussed further in Chapter 11.

JBI was primarily a technology company, focusing on data restoration and recovery, and it had several large clients, like NASA. However, its founder, John Bordynuik, became involved in the research and development of a process designed to convert plastic waste into oil. This process was called "Plastic2Oil" or "P2O." It is this process, and the need for capital to pursue the process, that really motivated Bordynuik to engage in financial reporting fraud.

As a result of JBI's inflated financial statements, more than $8.4 million was raised from investors. Soon after raising these funds, JBI announced it would be restating its 2009 financial statements.

But the story leading up to the restatement is even more interesting. JBI hired an accountant who was not a certified public accountant, and in fact only had six credit hours of accounting classes, to prepare its financial statements using the $10 million inflated figure for the media credits. According to the SEC complaint, at one point Bordynuik sent an instant message to the accountant stating, "please get the pro formas as juicy as you can so I can acquire a chemical company for less," a reference to JBI's plans to use the inflated financial statements as a means of acquiring other companies needed to pursue the Plastic2Oil venture. In this case, "pro formas" is a reference to unaudited financial statements that would be presented to (and designed to deceive) investors.

IFRS for nonmonetary transactions is found in two standards. In IAS 18, *Revenue*, it is stated that revenue should be measured at the fair value of the consideration received or receivable. However, there is an important caveat. When goods or services are exchanged or swapped for other goods or services of a similar nature and value, the exchange is not regarded as a transaction that generates revenue.

When goods are sold or services are rendered in exchange for dissimilar goods or services, the exchange is considered to be a transaction that generates revenue. The revenue is measured at the fair value of the goods or services received, adjusted by the amount of any cash or cash equivalents transferred. When the fair value of the goods or services received cannot be measured reliably, the revenue is measured at the fair value of the goods or services given up, adjusted by the amount of any cash or cash equivalents transferred.

IFRS also includes SIC-31, *Revenue—Barter Transactions Involving Advertising Services*. And this document takes the opposite approach from IAS 18.

In some cases, an entity may enter into a barter transaction to provide advertising services in exchange for receiving advertising services from a customer. This may involve printed advertising, radio or television advertising, Internet advertising, or any other form. SIC-31 states that revenue from a barter transaction involving advertising cannot be measured reliably at the fair value of advertising services received. However, a seller can reliably measure revenue at the fair value of the advertising services it provides in a barter transaction, by reference only to nonbarter transactions that:

- Involve advertising similar to the advertising in the barter transaction
- Occur frequently
- Represent a predominant number of transactions and amount when compared to all transactions to provide advertising that is similar to the advertising in the barter transaction
- Involve cash and/or another form of consideration that has a reliably measurable fair value (such as marketable securities)
- Do not involve the same counterparty as in the barter transaction

While IAS 18 and SIC-31 frame their explanations in the context of revenue recognition, the logic would be similar for measuring the value of an asset conferred (such as advertising benefits not yet received) to an entity in a barter transaction.

ASSETS ACQUIRED FROM RELATED PARTIES

Some of the most egregious cases of overvaluing assets either purchased or obtained in barter transactions involve acquisitions from related parties.

Just as revenue from related parties should be closely scrutinized (see Chapter 3), the acquisition of assets from related parties, whether by cash or by nonmonetary means, should be examined carefully for signs of overvaluation.

One such case involved Great American Financial, Inc., which acquired two assets from officers of the company. One of those assets, reported at $225,000, was for patents that did not exist. According to the SEC, the other asset, a $1.1 million racehorse, had "lifetime race earnings of $1,000, earned stud fees of less than $1,000, and been recently purchased by the persons who contracted to sell it to Great American for only $5,000." Keep in mind that this case dates all the way back to 1984. For a horse, $1 million is a lot by any standard, but this was a huge sum in 1984.

No discussion of improperly accounted-for related party transactions would be complete without a mention of Tyco and Enron. Tyco International (see SEC AAERs 1627 and 1839) was charged in 2002 and 2003 with improper accounting and reporting of a wide variety of asset purchase and asset sale transactions with related parties. One of these transactions involved the purchase by Tyco of real estate from the company's chief financial officer at an amount "far more than its fair market value."

In the case of Enron, assets were sold to nonconsolidated special purpose entities, only to later be repurchased. In each case, the amounts recorded were manipulated to achieve a particular purpose, sometimes to report a gain or avoid having to report a loss, in other cases to warehouse an asset off Enron's balance sheet for later use (via a repurchase). Some estimates have the inflation in Enron's reported profits from 1997 to 2001 as a result of related party transactions to be as high as $1.5 billion.

UNDERSTATING DEPRECIATION AND AMORTIZATION EXPENSE

Long-lived tangible assets and intangible assets may be subject to a depreciation or amortization requirement over an estimated useful life. Several techniques can be used to overstate the net book value of these assets through the manipulation of depreciation or amortization entries:

1. Establishing useful lives in excess of the realistic lives of the assets, resulting in the postponement of the recording of expenses
2. Delaying the start of depreciation or amortization by using an improper in-service date

3. Establishing an inappropriately high salvage value for an asset (this is the remaining book value beneath which no further depreciation will be recorded)

The American Italian Pasta Company (AIPC), the company which first appeared in Chapter 6, engaged in the second technique to reduce its operating expenses and improperly increase net profits. AIPC's policy was to begin depreciating property and equipment starting on the first day of the quarter following the day an asset was placed in service. This is a reasonable policy that would be acceptable under U.S. GAAP and IFRS. However, during 2002 and 2003, depreciation expense was fraudulently reduced by delaying for multiple quarters the start dates of certain manufacturing assets and information technology assets.

There are a variety of factors that should be considered when initially establishing, as well as subsequently evaluating, useful lives of property and equipment:

- How long the asset will have an economic benefit to the entity
- Historical experience with similar assets
- Estimates provided by manufacturers of the assets
- Third-party appraisals
- Signs of physical deterioration of an asset
- Technical obsolescence
- Plans of the entity, such as plans to relocate
- Environmental factors (e.g., the extent to which weather impacts the lives of assets)
- Legal restrictions on an asset's use (length of use, nature of use, etc.)
- An asset's relationship to other assets (e.g., improvements to a building where the building may not last as long as the improvement otherwise would have)
- An entity's policies and practices regarding maintenance of its assets.
- Anticipated level of use of an asset (e.g., rigorous and continuous versus sporadic or infrequent)

Useful lives should be periodically reviewed and adjustments (lengthening or shortening) made as necessary.

Methods of depreciation generally fall into two categories:

1. Straight-line
2. Accelerated

Under straight-line depreciation, the same amount of depreciation expense is recorded in each period. With accelerated methods (e.g., declining balance, sum-of-the-years digits, etc.), greater expense is recorded in the first period, followed by gradually decreasing amounts of expense in subsequent periods.

If evidence available when an asset is acquired indicates that an asset's decline in value is greater in the earliest years of its life, or its maintenance costs rise significantly in later years, an accelerated method may be preferable. Absent factors indicating that accelerated depreciation is preferable, straight-line depreciation should be applied.

If units of production associated with an asset are estimable, this may be utilized as a method of calculating depreciation expense. Accordingly, if there is a period of nonuse, no depreciation expense would be recorded for such a period.

INVESTMENT PROPERTY

IAS 40 permits the use of a fair value model of accounting for properties that are designated as investment property. Investment property is land and/or buildings held by an owner (or lessee under a finance lease) to earn rentals or for capital appreciation purposes, or both, as opposed to being held as owner-occupied property or as property held for sale in the ordinary course of business.

Unlike the IAS 16 fair value model, the IAS 40 model results in the appreciation or depreciation in fair value being reported as part of profit or loss (much like the IAS 39 designation of certain investments as being carried at fair value through profit or loss).

Generally, if the fair value model is used, it must be used for all investment property. However an entity may choose either the fair value model or the cost model for all investment property backing liabilities that pay a return linked directly to the fair value of, or returns from, specified assets including that investment property and choose either the fair value or cost model for all other investment property.

Changing from one model to the other (e.g., fair value to cost) is permitted only if the change results in a more appropriate presentation. IAS 40 states that this is highly unlikely to be the case for a change from the fair value model to the cost model.

IAS 40 provides a significant amount of guidance on fair value determinations for investment properties. Some of this guidance is similar to the fair value input hierarchy found in U.S. GAAP and, recently, in IFRS 13, such as the greater reliability of using prices obtained from an active market over the use of internal estimates, and the need for making appropriate adjustments to market prices for assets that are similar but not identical to the asset in question. IAS 40 also suggests, but does not require, the use of independent appraisers.

Fair value determinations also should not consider the effects of internal synergies between the property and other assets, tax benefits, or other factors unique to the owner. Nor should it factor in any elements of the owner's financing arrangement or other factors that would not have a bearing on what knowledgeable and willing buyers and sellers would consider in negotiating a value.

Fair value determinations of investment property that generates rent income should be customized to the terms of the lease. For example, if the property is furnished, fair value should factor in not only the building, but the furnishings as well. When this is done, the furnishings should not also be recognized as a separate asset in the financial statements. This concept of not double-counting assets is an important element of the accounting for investment property and the subsequent fair value determination.

There is no U.S. GAAP counterpart to IAS 40. Therefore, no literature exists in U.S. GAAP that specifically addresses investment property. Accordingly, most investment property, including that held by most real estate companies, is accounted for using the cost model, as with other property and equipment, for U.S. GAAP purposes. There are, however, certain types of specialized entities, such as certain investment companies, employee benefit plans that invest in real estate, and bank-sponsored real estate trusts, that carry all investments at fair value.

Financial reporting fraud risks associated with investment property accounted for under IFRS are as follows:

1. Use of improper fair values to inflate the carrying amount of investment property
2. Failing to recognize impairment losses
3. Changing from one method to another (e.g., fair value to cost, or vice versa) without justification

IMPROPER VALUATION OF INVESTMENTS—FINANCIAL ASSETS

Financial assets include cash, equity instruments (ownership interests), contracts to receive cash or a financial asset from another entity, and contracts to exchange financial instruments with another entity on potentially favorable terms. The IFRS definition of financial assets includes a fourth category—certain contracts that will or may be settled in the entity's own equity instruments.

Most commonly held forms of investments are covered under this definition—including debt securities, stocks, mutual funds, and so on. However, with respect to equity interests, the accounting can differ depending on the type of interest, as follows:

- Majority ownership interests that result in a company controlling another entity, normally requiring consolidation—explained in Chapter 11
- Ownership interests accounted for using the equity method of accounting, applied when there is less than a majority ownership interest, but enough so that substantial influence can be exerted—explained further later in this chapter
- Interests in publicly traded equities
- Interests in nonpublic (unlisted) companies

Under U.S. GAAP, accounting for debt and equity securities with readily determinable fair values, and where neither consolidation nor the equity method of accounting is applied, is found at ASC 320. IFRS is found at IAS 39, *Financial Instruments: Recognition and Measurement,* and IFRS 9, which takes effect for annual reporting periods beginning on or after January 1, 2015 (however, earlier adoption of FRS 9 is permitted).

Under ASC 320, debt and marketable equity securities are to be accounted for based on their classification, as follows:

1. **Held-to-maturity securities**—Debt securities that the holder has the intent and ability to hold to maturity. These securities are to be carried at amortized cost, unless it is a hedged item. Although generally carried at amortized cost, held-to-maturity securities are subject to recognition of unrealized loss if there is an other-than-temporary impairment.
2. **Trading securities**—Debt and equity securities that are bought and held primarily for the purpose of selling them in the near term. These securities are to be reported at fair value on a recurring basis, with unrealized gains and losses included in earnings (i.e., included in profit or loss of the entity).
3. **Available-for-sale securities**—Debt and equity securities not classified as either held-to-maturity securities or trading securities. These securities are carried at fair value, with unrealized gains and losses excluded from earnings and reported in other comprehensive income rather than in profit or loss.

IAS 39 requires that financial instruments, with certain exceptions, be measured at fair value on a recurring basis. Two types of investments are exempt from the requirement to record financial instruments at fair value:

1. Any held-to-maturity investment, which should be measured at amortized cost (including deductions for impairment), similar to U.S. GAAP explained earlier
2. An equity security that does not have a quoted market price in an active market and whose fair value cannot be reliably measured, which should be measured at cost, subject to possible impairment if fair value is less than cost

As with U.S. GAAP, IFRS states that changes in fair value of available-for-sale debt securities be reported in other comprehensive income, rather than in profit or loss (with the exception of foreign exchange gains or losses on the amortized cost basis, which are to be included in profit or loss).

When IFRS 9 is implemented for years beginning after January 1, 2015, the held-to-maturity classification will no longer impact the accounting for investments. In its place will be a business model exception from the fair value measurement requirement. If the business model is to hold assets primarily to collect contractual cash flows (as with a loan or bond), and the contract terms provide for cash flows that are solely payments of principal and interest on specified dates, then amortized cost should be used as the carrying amount.

The primary financial reporting fraud risks with investments in financial instruments are as follows:

- Failure to recognize unrealized losses on investments with fair values that have declined below their book values
- Improper classification of investments—especially with respect to improper classification of an investment as available-for-sale, which enables any recorded unrealized losses to be excluded from profit or loss and reported instead as a component of comprehensive income

Amortized cost may be calculated differently depending on whether U.S. GAAP or IFRS is applied. Under U.S. GAAP, amortized cost is calculated based on contractual cash flows over the contractual life of the asset. Under IFRS, however, the calculation is based on estimated cash flows over the expected life of the asset. This is called the effective interest method. Only in cases in which cash flows or expected lives cannot be reliably estimated should contract terms be used. Only under certain specific and very limited situations would expected life be used under U.S. GAAP.

Management's estimates of cash flows and the period over which cash flows will be received may differ from the terms stated in a contract. When such differences exist, the amortized cost calculation will also differ, resulting in one additional risk of manipulation.

Unlisted Equity Instruments

Unlisted (not publicly traded) equity instruments may be accounted for differently under U.S. GAAP and IFRS. Under U.S. GAAP, unlisted equities are scoped out of ASC 320 and are generally carried at cost, unless they are impaired. However, a fair value option can be elected under ASC 825, resulting in carrying these instruments at fair value on a recurring basis. It should be noted, however, that certain industry-specific standards require that unlisted equity instruments be carried at fair value on a recurring basis (e.g., investment companies, defined benefit plans, broker/dealers, and insurance companies).

Under IFRS, as noted above, IAS 39 requires all financial instruments to be carried at fair value unless a fair value cannot be reliably measured. There are no industry-specific exceptions or guidance under IFRS.

How an Impaired Investment Becomes Goodwill

A major recent case involving a company's attempts to hide impairment losses is the Olympus Corporation case, which came to light in October 2011. What makes the Olympus case so fascinating is the duration of the scheme (more than 20 years), as well as the methodology.

In response to the increased value of the Japanese yen after 1985, Olympus embarked on a "speculative investment strategy" involving the purchase of higher risk securities. However, by the late 1990s, unrealized losses on these investments accumulated to nearly JPY 100 billion ($1.3 billion USD). But what really triggered the scheme was the looming introduction of new fair value accounting rules that would require the recognition of these unrealized losses. Olympus designed a "loss separation scheme" to hide these losses.

Under this plan, impaired assets were sold to off-balance-sheet "receiver funds" that were established and controlled by Olympus. Since these funds were controlled by Olympus, the sales of assets were done at the assets' book values, not at the lower, impaired values.

The receiver funds were able to pay Olympus for the acquired assets because the funds were financed by third-party financial institutions. These loans were secured with collateral pledged by Olympus. The receiver funds then acquired certain growth companies (three Japanese companies between 2003 and 2005 and one British company, Gyrus Group PLC, in 2008).

Later, Olympus purchased these growth companies from the receiver funds. These purchases were at inflated prices and included the payment of exorbitant advisory fees, enabling the receiver funds to repay the financial institutions, get the Olympus collateral released, and cover their operating expenses. Basically, the inflated purchase prices and advisory fees covered the hidden unrealized losses on the assets initially sold by Olympus to the receiver funds.

The excess purchase price paid by Olympus for the growth companies was then recorded as goodwill, which could then be written down over time. The end result of this scheme is that unrealized losses of Olympus were converted into goodwill, enabling the deferral of any loss to future periods, when the goodwill could then be impaired. In some cases, Olympus recorded a write-down in value very soon after the acquisition. Some of the companies that were acquired had no revenue or business history, raising doubts about whether these companies were even legitimate businesses.

One of the factors that aided in this accounting trick, referred to as "tobashi," was the fact that the transactions were supported by cash changing hands. This was not merely an accounting journal entry made to hide losses.

Shares of Olympus fell by more than 80 percent from October 13, 2011, just prior to the fraud becoming public, to November 11, 2011, three days after the company admitted to the wrongdoing.

Impairment Losses

The general concept of an impairment is that the carrying amount of an investment exceeds the amount that the investment could be sold for—its fair value. This concept runs through the myriad of rules found under both U.S. GAAP and IFRS. However, there are some important differences in the approach taken under each of the two sets of accounting standards.

First, U.S. GAAP, under ASC 320, makes an important distinction between a temporary impairment and an "other than temporary" impairment in available-for-sale investments. Recall that this category of investment is the one in which unrealized gains or losses are reported as a component of other comprehensive income rather than in profit or loss. That classification changes if the impairment is other-than-temporary, in which case an unrealized loss must be reported in profit or loss in the income statement.

Making the determination of whether a decline is temporary or not requires much judgment and the careful consideration of many factors. This, of course, means that it can be susceptible to fraud. Some factors to be considered in making the determination of whether an impairment loss is other-than-temporary include the following:

- The length of time (duration) and extent to which the security's fair value has been less than its cost (i.e., the severity and magnitude of the impairment)
- The financial condition and near-term prospects of the issuer, including any known events that have occurred, such as changes in technology that could impair earnings potential, the discontinuance of a line of business, and so on
- The intent and ability of the holder to retain its investment for a period of time that is long enough to allow for an expected recovery in fair value (i.e., even if a security can be expected to subsequently increase in value, can the entity afford to hold on to it for that long?)
- Whether the decline in fair value was affected by macroeconomic conditions or by specific information pertaining to an individual security (declines attributable to adverse conditions that are related to a specific issuer, industry, or geographic area are considered to be stronger indicators that an impairment is other-than-temporary than conditions such as uncertainty regarding a category of investment or other market-wide factors)
- Downgrades by rating agencies or negative reports by analysts
- Reductions or elimination of expected dividend payments
- Missing interest payments or scheduled repayments of principal

For equity instruments, an other-than-temporary impairment must be recognized even if a decision to sell has not been made. For debt securities, an impairment loss should be recognized if the decision to sell the security has been made. If a company does not intend to sell the debt security, it should consider all available evidence to assess whether it more likely than not will be required to sell the security before the recovery of its amortized cost basis, in which case an other-than-temporary impairment loss should be recognized. In other words, if management asserts that it will be able to hold on to the debt security long enough to enable the company to recover its amortized cost, then an impairment loss will not need to be recorded.

A 2008 SEC order illustrates some of the complexities involved in assessing impairment losses. AAER 2838 concerns Citigroup, Inc., the global financial services company and, in particular, its activities in Argentina, where it was the largest foreign bank in 2001. While the order does not imply any form of fraud, it clearly states that Citigroup improperly valued a financial asset.

During late 2001 and continuing into 2002, Argentina was in a severe economic and political crisis. This crisis triggered a number of accounting decisions at Citigroup, decisions with which the SEC strongly disagreed. Citigroup held $681 million of Argentine bonds that were eligible for swaps for guaranteed promissory notes (GPNs), which were for longer terms and lower interest rates. The bond swap transaction took place in December 2001.

The swap was to be accounted for at fair value. But instead of using the market value of the bonds that were surrendered, as suggested by the SEC and Citigroup's auditor, the company elected to utilize an alternative approach that involved valuing the GPNs received in exchange. Citigroup used a discounted cash flow analysis to determine the fair value of the GPNs. In its order, the SEC claimed that Citigroup utilized unreasonable assumptions in calculating the discount rate used in the valuation, resulting in an overstatement of the fair value of the GPNs. The SEC noted that Citigroup "used a precrisis rate that assumed that the collapsing Argentine economy would recover in the short term" and that the company assumed that "in the event the Argentine government defaulted on the GPNs, there was a high likelihood that the government would honor the collateral features of the GPNs, enabling Citigroup to recover all principal and interest."

The SEC's conclusion was that "While Citigroup's approach may have been appropriate under the then existing circumstances, the assumptions that Citigroup applied were not reasonable and resulted in Citigroup understating its losses on the bond swap." In other words, switching from a market approach (the market approach to measuring fair value is described more fully in Chapter 8) to a different approach, based on present values of expected cash flows, was acceptable. But Citigroup's assumptions in calculating present value were not. Instead of the $416 million in losses that should have been recognized, Citigroup recorded losses of just $82 million by improperly calculating impairment loss.

Adding to Citigroup's problems was the SEC's conclusion regarding Argentine bonds that were not eligible for the bond swap. Not all bonds were eligible for the swap. Thus, for the nonswapped bonds, Citigroup was required to determine whether the decline in fair values of the bonds was temporary or other-than-temporary. Citigroup's conclusion was that the unrealized losses were temporary. The SEC argued that it should have been clear that these losses were other-than-temporary based on the fact that the Argentine government had announced that it intended to default on its sovereign debt and that credit rating agencies had significantly downgraded Argentina's sovereign debt rating. At the time, the majority of Argentine government bonds were trading at less than $0.50 on the dollar. The SEC's conclusion was that Citigroup's determination that these bonds were not impaired was "not reasonable."

IFRS for impairments also follows a model that is dependent on the type of financial asset. For assets carried at amortized cost (e.g., held to maturity investments, loans, and receivables), an impairment is measured as the difference between the carrying amount and the present value of expected future cash flows, discounted using the instrument's original discount rate.

For assets carried at cost, due to the inability to reliably measure fair value, impairment is measured as the difference between the carrying amount of the asset and the present value of estimated future cash flows discounted at the current market rate of return for similar financial assets.

For assets that are carried at fair value on a recurring basis (available for sale instruments), impairment is measured as the difference between the acquisition cost (net of any principal repayment and amortization) and current fair value, less any impairment loss previously recognized in profit or loss.

As suggested by the preceding point, declines in the fair value of an available-for-sale financial instrument do not necessarily indicate that an impairment has occurred. This is similar to the temporary or other-than-temporary distinction made under U.S. GAAP. Declines in fair value are reported within other comprehensive income. If objective evidence of an impairment exists, these losses are then moved from other comprehensive income to profit or loss for the period. Under IFRS, objective evidence of an impairment includes any of the following:

- Significant financial difficulties of an issuer of securities held by an entity
- High probability of bankruptcy
- Disappearance of a market caused by financial difficulties
- Defaults or other breaches of contract
- Observable information that brings into doubt the reliability of expected future cash flows
- Significant or prolonged declines in fair value below cost
- Significant adverse changes in technological, market, economic, or legal environments

There are certain differences between U.S. GAAP and IFRS regarding subsequent treatment of financial assets after an impairment loss has been recognized, such as the conditions under which impairments can be reversed. These differences are beyond the scope of this book, but could possibly lead to slightly different financial reporting fraud risks under IFRS and U.S. GAAP.

LOANS

A particularly important financial asset of many businesses is loans receivable. Accounting for loans is addressed in U.S. GAAP at ASC 310 and in IFRS at IAS 39 (which covers all financial instruments) and IAS 18.

Under U.S. GAAP, loans (as well as trade receivables) that are not measured at fair value and that a company has the intent and ability to hold for the foreseeable future or until maturity or payoff should be reported on the balance sheet at outstanding principal adjusted for the following:

- Any charge-offs
- Any allowance for loan losses (or the allowance for doubtful accounts)
- Any deferred fees or costs on originated loans
- Any unamortized premiums or discounts (other than sales discounts) on purchased loans

U.S. GAAP, in ASC 825, provides an option for loans and most other financial instruments to be carried at fair value on a recurring basis. If such option is selected, it should be indicated in the notes to the financial statements.

Under IAS 39, when any financial asset or financial liability is recognized initially, it should be measured at its fair value (which for loans and most other receivables will generally be equal to cost or principal at inception). In the case of a loan or receivable that is not carried at fair value through profit or loss, transaction costs that are directly attributable to the acquisition or issue of the asset should also be included in this fair value measurement.

Subsequent to initial recognition, however, loans and receivables are to be measured at amortized cost using the effective interest method. The effective interest method is a method of calculating the amortized cost of a loan (or other financial asset or liability) and of allocating the interest income over the loan term. The effective interest rate is the rate that discounts estimated future cash receipts through the expected life of the loan or, if appropriate, a shorter period to the net carrying amount of the loan. When calculating the effective interest rate, an entity should estimate cash flows considering all contractual terms of the loan (e.g., prepayment options) but should not consider future credit losses. The calculation includes all fees and points received between parties to the contract that are an integral part of the effective interest rate, transaction costs, and all other premiums or discounts. There is a presumption that the cash flows can be estimated reliably. However, in situations in which it is not possible to estimate reliably the cash flows or the expected life of a loan, the entity should utilize the contractual cash flows over the full contractual term.

Loans inherently have some element of uncertainty regarding collectibility. If anything less than the book value of a loan is to be collected, an impairment has been incurred and should be recognized. Entities with loan portfolios generally record an allowance (reserve) for the estimated amount of uncollectible loans. In some cases, the allowance is based on identification and estimation of collectibility of specific loans. In other cases, the allowance is a broad calculation based on characteristics of an entire loan portfolio, as well as on historical results.

Under U.S. GAAP, guidance on impairments of receivables generally falls under the rules of ASC 450, which covers contingencies (in particular, ASC 450-20 on loss contingencies). ASC 450 requires recognition of a loss when both of the following conditions are met:

1. Information available before the financial statements are issued indicates that it is probable that an asset has been impaired at the date of the financial statements
2. The amount of the loss can be reasonably estimated

Losses for uncollectible loans and other receivables should be accrued when both of the preceding conditions are met.

ASC 310-10-35, however, provides additional guidance on impairments of loans. Under this guidance, loans are considered to be impaired when it becomes probable that the creditor will be unable to collect all the contractual interest and principal payments as scheduled in the loan agreement. When a loan is impaired, ASC 310-10-35 requires that the impairment be measured based on either of the following:

- The present value of expected future cash flows discounted at the loan's effective interest rate
- The loan's observable market price or the fair value of collateral if the loan is expected to be repaid by the underlying collateral

For purposes of the present value calculation, a loan's effective interest rate is the rate implicit in the loan, meaning its contractual interest rate adjusted for any deferred loan fees or discount existing at the loan's origination (or acquisition).

IFRS guidance is similar, stating that a loan or other receivable is considered impaired if its carrying amount is greater than its estimated recoverable amount. The amount of the loss is the difference between the carrying amount and the fair value of expected future cash flows discounted at the *original effective interest rate*. Estimated future cash flows should be reduced based on current estimates of collectibility. Impairment losses should be recognized as a reduction to the carrying amount of the asset, either directly or through use of an allowance account.

If the collection of interest becomes questionable, this is a sign of impairment under either U.S. GAAP or IFRS. In addition to recognizing an impairment, suspension of the accrual of additional interest income as it becomes due under the original terms of a loan should be considered.

In addition, many loans include provisions for additional fees being charged in the event of default or delinquency. Since delinquency is inherently a sign of impairment and uncollectibility, delinquency fees should only be accrued if they are considered collectible.

Two cases provide illustrations of some of the most common fraud schemes involving loan portfolios.

In January 2011, the SEC charged one company and certain of its executives with an elaborate scheme designed to improve the appearance of a loan portfolio. This case involved Sterling Financial Corp. and, in particular, a wholly owned subsidiary of Sterling, Equipment Finance, LLC (EF). EF was a commercial lender, holding financing contracts with forestry and land equipment dealers through which EF provided loans. The SEC complaint charged two of EF's executives with subverting "virtually every aspect of EF's loan process and internal controls" to engage in a variety of schemes designed to inflate the size and quality of EF's loan portfolio. Among the fraudulent tactics employed were the following:

- Creating fictitious loans for the purpose of making payments on delinquent loans (these loans were made in the names of legitimate customers but without the customers' knowledge)
- Altering of documents in loan files to hide delinquent and fictitious loans, including falsifying loan documents to reflect a 20 percent down payment, as required by EF policy, when there was no such down payment, creating

fictitious uniform commercial code (UCC) filing documents, and altering of credit reports
- Granting of excessive deferrals (moving delinquent loan payments to the end of the loan term) without the customers' consent and resets (which result in a refinancing) of delinquent loans in order to make them appear current
- Reassignment of loan payments to unrelated accounts to fund payments on delinquent loans
- Use of aliases for borrowers to circumvent EF's maximum lending limitations

As a result of the fraud, Sterling ultimately charged off $281 million of EF finance receivables, which represented a large majority of EF's loan portfolio, and approximately 13 percent of Sterling's total loan portfolio during the period of the fraud. Sterling reported the fraud in 2007, and the company was acquired by another financial institution in 2008.

Another case with fraudulent presentation of a loan portfolio involves Franklin Bank Corp., a Texas-based savings and loan holding company. In April 2012 the SEC charged Franklin's CEO and CFO with a series of violations motivated by attempts to conceal the deteriorating condition of a loan portfolio during the financial crisis beginning in 2007.

Franklin's mortgage loan portfolio, like those of many other financial institutions, started showing signs of delinquencies soon after the financial crisis began. One of the schemes that was perpetrated involved a loan modification program known as "Fresh Start," in which Franklin unilaterally sent letters to borrowers who were four or more payments past due on their loans. The letters advised these delinquent borrowers that Franklin would consider their loans to be current if the borrowers:

- Contacted the bank by October 1, 2007
- Agreed to make one payment
- Agreed to move all past due amounts to the end of the loan due at maturity
- Made a payment on or before October 13, 2007

As a result of this program, Franklin modified more than $10 million of loans, including $4 million in loans that Franklin had previously classified as non-performing.

The nature of the loan modifications made by Franklin constituted a troubled debt restructuring, defined as occurring when a creditor for economic or legal reasons related to a debtor's financial difficulties grants concessions to the debt that it would not otherwise consider. ASC 310-40 provides guidance on troubled debt restructurings. As noted earlier, loans are considered to be impaired when it becomes probable that a creditor will be unable to collect all amounts due according to the contractual terms of the loan agreement. If a loan has been restructured, as is the case with Franklin, the reference here is to the terms of the original loan, not the restructured loan. Accordingly, Franklin's loans should have been considered impaired.

The result of this treatment was the under-reporting of non-performing loans by 24 percent and a 17 percent overstatement of earnings. In addition to the "Fresh Start" program, Franklin also misstated its financial statements in connection with two other loan modification programs.

In summary, some of the most common financial reporting fraud risks associated with loans include the following:

- Improper amortization of loan principal
- Bogus/sham loans
- Misrepresented loans (e.g., loans to related parties that are disguised as though they are other loans, multiple loans to the same individual or entity, etc.)
- Failure to recognize impairment or bad debt losses on loans
- Misrepresented or forged/altered supporting documents (e.g., appraisals, applications, insurance, guarantees, etc.)
- Improper assessment of the fair value of loans
- Misrepresentations regarding collateral supporting a loan

EQUITY METHOD INVESTMENTS

The equity method of accounting is to be applied when a company can exercise significant influence over another entity, without holding a controlling interest (which would require consolidation). Generally, this means that when a company holds between a 20 and 50 percent voting interest in another entity, the equity method is the likely method of accounting.

The minimum of 20 percent is generally considered to be a rebuttable presumption of significant influence. Other factors that may be considered include the following:

- Representation on the board of directors
- Participation in the policymaking processes

- Significance of intercompany transactions
- Technology dependency
- Investee dependence on the investor
- Interchange of managerial personnel
- Extent of ownership by an investor in relation to the concentration of other shareholders

ASC 323, as well as IAS 28 and IFRS 11, makes equity accounting mandatory for participants in joint ventures.

Under the equity method of accounting, the holder maintains an asset account to reflect its investment in the other entity. Generally, this asset is measured based on the percentage of the equity the company holds in the other entity, plus or minus certain adjustments. An income statement account is reported that generally reflects the holder's percentage interest in the profits or losses of the other entity. The entity in which the holder has an interest may be a corporation, partnership, or other form of entity.

Take the following simple example. Assume that Company A has $100 million of assets and $60 million of liabilities. One of Company A's owners is Company B. Company B owns 30 percent of the outstanding stock of Company A and utilizes the equity method of accounting for its investment in Company A.

As a result, Company B would report a $12 million asset for its investment in A (net assets of $40 million multiplied by 30 percent). If during the next year Company A made a $10 million profit, and ended the year with total assets of $105 million and total liabilities of $55 million, Company B would report a $3 million income item in its income statement ($10 million times 30 percent) and a $15 million investment balance at year-end (net assets of $50 million times 30 percent).

A financial reporting fraud risk exists regarding the accounting at the investee level. If the assets, revenues, or gains of the 30-percent-owned business are overstated, or its liabilities, expenses, or losses are understated, as a result of a fair value accounting fraud, then the owner's financial statements will, in turn, reflect an inflated asset account and an inflated income statement effect. Intentional manipulation of the fair value accounting rules or any other financial reporting fraud at Company A will result in misstatements in the financial statements of Company B.

PROPORTIONATE CONSOLIDATION

Somewhere between consolidation and the equity method of accounting is one additional method of accounting—proportionate consolidation. The application of this method is limited to situations involving jointly controlled entities as described in IAS 31. There is no specific standard addressing the use of proportionate consolidation under U.S. GAAP. However, if an investor owns an undivided interest in each asset and is proportionately liable for its share of each liability of another entity, the equity method of accounting may not be appropriate, and proportionate consolidation is sometimes applied. A proportionate consolidation presentation is not appropriate, however, for an investment in an unincorporated legal entity accounted for by the equity method of accounting unless the investee is in either the construction industry or an extractive industry. In these two industry groups, the proportionate consolidation method has sometimes been applied.

Under IAS 31, a jointly controlled entity exists when each partner in a joint venture has a form of control (but not majority control), rather than simply significant influence (which would result in the equity method). A common example would be a 50-50 equal partnership (regardless of the form of entity as partnership, corporation, etc.). With a 50-50 venture, neither party owns a majority, and it is common that the two partners must effectively agree on all key decisions (as opposed to a situation in which one is an active partner and one is a silent partner). Likewise, a venture with three equal partners may be a jointly controlled entity, particularly if unanimity is required among the partners for key decisions.

Under the proportionate consolidation method, the holder of an interest in another business reports its proportionate share of the assets, liabilities, revenues, expenses, gains, and losses of the other entity. In the example used in the preceding section on the equity method of accounting, Company B, the 30-percent owner of Company A, would not reflect a single asset equal to 30 percent of the net assets or net equity of Company A as it did under the equity method. Under the proportionate consolidation method, Company B would report separate assets each equal to 30 percent of the assets of Company A, and liabilities equal to 30 percent of each of Company B's liabilities, and so on. Likewise with revenues and expenses.

The financial reporting fraud risks with proportionate consolidation, therefore, include the same risks as under the equity method (improper reporting of the underlying assets, liabilities, revenues, or expenses of the venture), as well as a risk of improper application of the guidance regarding whether or not the proportionate consolidation method should be used in the first place. For example, a company wanting to simply appear to be larger or to report higher gross revenues may apply the proportionate consolidation method in a situation that does not warrant such treatment.

It is important to note that with the introduction of IFRS 11, *Joint Arrangements*, the use of proportionate consolidation will be eliminated. Therefore, readers of this book may encounter proportionate consolidation accounting for periods up to the adoption of IFRS 11, which is to be applied to periods beginning on or after January 1, 2013.

IMPROPER CLASSIFICATION OR AMORTIZATION OF INTANGIBLE ASSETS

Intangible assets that are recognized as assets generally fall into one of three categories, each of which impacts subsequent accounting treatment:

1. Assets with finite and precise useful lives
2. Assets with finite, but imprecise, useful lives
3. Assets with indefinite useful lives

Each of the first two categories of intangible assets should be amortized over their useful lives. The method of amortization should reflect the pattern in which the economic benefits of the intangible asset are consumed or otherwise used up (i.e., either straight-line or accelerated methods may be utilized). If such a pattern cannot be readily determined, then straight-line amortization should be used.

In addition, in connection with the second category of intangible assets, an estimate of the asset's useful life should be established by the organization. Some considerations in determining useful lives for intangible assets include:

- Product life cycles of similar assets
- Pace of technological change
- Historical experience in estimating useful lives of other intangible assets
- The expected use of the asset by the entity
- Whether the expected use is dependent on other assets or other entities
- The level and cost of maintenance that would be necessary to prolong or maintain a useful life
- Expected or known actions of industry competitors
- Management's plans for the asset (e.g., is a replacement technology already in the research phase, and management hopes to have it on the market soon?)
- The level of obsolescence that is evident

The third category of intangible assets, those with indefinite lives, is not subject to amortization. Instead, at the end of each reporting period (i.e., at the end of each fiscal year), two determinations must be made with respect to each such asset:

1. Whether the asset continues to have an indefinite life (i.e., if it is determined that the asset now has a finite life, amortization over the remaining life should begin)
2. Whether an impairment loss has occurred

Impairment losses on intangible assets are covered in the next section.

IMPAIRMENT LOSSES—NONFINANCIAL ASSETS

An impairment loss occurs when the fair value of an asset declines below the carrying value of the asset on the company's books. Depending on which type of asset is involved (e.g., an investment, a tangible asset, or an intangible asset), different rules may apply to the assessment and measurement of an impairment loss.

A significant financial reporting fraud risk, therefore, is the risk that a company fails to recognize an impairment loss.

Impairment losses of long-lived assets are covered in two areas, depending on the nature of the asset:

1. ASC 360-10, which covers impairments of property and equipment and intangible assets with finite useful lives (i.e., intangible assets that are being amortized over a useful life)
2. ASC 350-30-08, which requires annual impairment testing of goodwill and other intangible assets with indefinite lives (i.e., those intangible assets that are not being amortized over a useful life)

ASC 360

ASC 360-10 carries forward the guidance introduced in SFAS No. 144, *Accounting for the Impairment or Disposal of Long-Lived Assets* and SFAS No. 121. Under this guidance, an impairment loss must be recognized if the carrying amount of a long-lived asset (or asset group) meets both of two requirements:

1. It is not recoverable.
2. It exceeds fair value.

To determine whether the carrying value of long-lived assets is recoverable, an organization should estimate future cash flows expected to result from use of a long-lived asset and its eventual disposition. If the resulting anticipated undiscounted cash flows are less than an asset's carrying value, an impairment loss should be recorded based on the fair market value of the asset. However, many long-lived assets do not directly result in future cash inflows, so the determination of fair value becomes important as the determining factor in assessing whether an impairment loss has occurred.

A long-lived asset (or asset group) should be tested for recoverability whenever events or changes in circumstances indicate that its carrying amount may not be recoverable. Examples of such events or changes in circumstances include the following:

- A significant decrease in the market price of a long-lived asset
- A significant adverse change in the physical condition of a long-lived asset or in the extent or manner in which it is being used
- A significant adverse change in legal factors or in the business climate that could affect the value of a long-lived asset, including an adverse action or assessment by a regulator
- An accumulation of costs significantly in excess of the amount originally expected for the acquisition or construction of a long-lived asset
- A current-period operating or cash flow loss combined with a history of operating or cash flow losses, or a projection or forecast that demonstrates continuing losses associated with the use of a long-lived asset
- A current expectation that a long-lived asset will be sold or otherwise disposed of significantly before the end of its previously estimated useful life

If an impairment loss is recognized, the adjusted carrying amount of a long-lived asset is its new cost basis. Thus, for depreciable assets, the new cost basis becomes the basis for depreciation/amortization over the remaining useful life of that asset (note that changes in estimates of useful lives are not among the examples of events warranting a testing for impairment, as such changes affect accounting estimates and should be taken into consideration accordingly). Recoveries of impairment losses resulting from increases in fair value may not be recorded.

ASC 350

ASC 350-30-08 requires *annual* impairment testing of goodwill and other intangible assets with indefinite lives. If the carrying amount of an intangible asset exceeds its fair value, an impairment loss is to be recognized in an amount equal to that excess. Once an impairment loss is recognized, the reduced basis becomes the new basis of the asset—subsequent reversals of the impairment loss are prohibited.

Separately recorded indefinite-lived intangible assets should be combined into a single unit of accounting for purposes of testing impairment if they are operated as a single asset and, as such, are essentially inseparable from one another. Determining whether several indefinite-lived intangible assets are essentially inseparable is a matter of judgment.

IFRS guidance on impairments in long-lived assets is found in two sources. IAS 36, *Impairment of Assets*, covers assets that are in use by an entity. However, if a non-current asset is classified as held for sale, it is covered under IFRS 5, *Non-current Assets held for Sale and Discontinued Operations*, rather than IAS 36. An asset is held for sale when its carrying amount will be recovered primarily through its sale, rather than through ongoing use of the asset. Accordingly, most long-lived non-current assets are covered under IAS 36 when they are first acquired, but later may be held for sale, at which point they are covered under IFRS 5. IFRS 5 requires that non-current assets held for sale be carried at the lower of cost or fair value, less selling costs.

IAS 36 utilizes slightly different language to arrive at a similar concept to the one explained under U.S. GAAP, but one that can potentially lead to a different conclusion for some assets. IAS 36 states that an impairment loss occurs when the carrying amount of an asset exceeds its recoverable amount. The recoverable amount is defined as the higher of an asset's fair value, less costs to sell, or its value in use. Value in use is defined as the present value of future cash flows expected to be derived.

In other words, an impairment loss exists under IAS 36 if the carrying amount of an asset exceeds its recoverable amount, which is the greater of:

1. Fair value, less costs to sell
2. Present value of future cash flows

Recall that IAS 36 applies only to assets in use by an entity—not to assets held for sale. Therefore, fair value is measured based on the greater of fair value or that asset's "value in use." Value in use should be assessed based on the following factors:

- The estimated future cash flows the entity expects to derive from use of the asset (i.e., the net of cash inflows and outflows considered necessary to generate the cash inflows)

- Expectations about possible variations in the amount or timing of those future cash flows
- The time value of money, represented by the current market risk-free rate of interest
- The price for bearing the uncertainty inherent in the asset
- Other factors, such as illiquidity, that market participants would reflect in pricing the future cash flows the entity expects to derive from the asset

INVESTMENTS IN INSURANCE CONTRACTS

Increasingly, financial statements of certain companies include investments in insurance contracts. Guidance on the accounting for these investments is contained in ASC 325-30, *Investments in Insurance Contracts.* ASC 325-30 states that a purchaser may elect to account for its investments in life settlement contracts using either the investment method or the fair value method. The choice is made on an instrument-by-instrument basis and is irrevocable. Under the investment method, a purchaser recognizes the initial investment at the purchase price plus all initial direct costs. Continuing costs (e.g., policy premiums and direct external costs, if any) to keep the policy in force are capitalized. Under the fair value method, a purchaser recognizes the initial investment at the purchase price. In subsequent periods, the purchaser remeasures the investment at fair value in its entirety at each reporting period and recognizes changes in fair value earnings (or other performance indicators for entities that do not report earnings) in the period in which the changes occur.

While adjustments up or down to fair value are implicit in the fair value method, even under the investment method, recognition of an impairment loss must be considered when conditions indicate that a company may not be able to recover the book value of its investment. In cases where undiscounted expected proceeds from future maturities are less than the carrying value, plus undiscounted future premiums, a company should recognize an impairment loss equal to the amount by which the carrying value (including expected future costs to maintain the policies) exceeds the expected proceeds.

The preceding explanation of the investment method mirrors the explanation found in the notes to the financial statements of Life Partners Holdings, Inc. (LPHI), a company that generates almost all of its revenue from brokering life settlements, primarily with high-income or terminally ill life insurance policy holders. Unfortunately, the company apparently did not do a very good job of following its own policies for recognizing impairment losses, according to a complaint filed in January 2012 by the SEC.

Life settlements involve purchasing life insurance policies from the original policy holder. The purchase price is less than the face amount of the policy (i.e., the proceeds upon death of the insured). The purchase amount is determined using a variety of factors, such as the insured's life expectancy, based on the person's age, health, lifestyle (e.g., whether the insured is a smoker), geographic location, and other factors. Like others in this industry, LPHI initially focused on "viatical" settlements—those involving terminally ill persons. However, over the past 10 years, more settlements have involved insured persons who are not terminally ill, many of whom are high-income individuals who sell their interests in life insurance policies as part of their financial planning. After the settlement, the purchaser is responsible for paying subsequent premiums on the policy.

In its year-end financial statements from February 28, 2010, LPHI reported an asset called "Investment in Policies" at $16.46 million, representing interests in life insurance policies purchased by the company. However, it subsequently restated this amount to $12.15 million, after recognizing it had used improper life expectancy estimates in assessing the existence of impairment losses in connection with life insurance policies. By initially using estimated life expectancies that were too short, expected future cash flows exceeded the carrying amount of the investment plus future premiums. LPHI used one outside doctor for all of its life expectancy determinations, something that the company has been criticized for. In its litigation announcement, the SEC noted that this doctor had "no actuarial training or prior experience rendering life expectancy estimates." Once longer, more realistic, life expectancies were utilized, the original policy costs plus projected future premiums exceeded estimated maturity value, resulting in an impairment loss. The footnotes to LPHI's financial statements of February 28, 2011, in explaining the restatement of the February 2010 statements, noted that "In general, life expectancies increased with the addition of more data." Really? We can actually live longer if we get more data? What a great way to explain what the SEC characterized as a financial statement fraud.

In AAER 3351, the SEC announced it had filed charges against LPHI and three of its officials for their involvement in a fraudulent disclosure and accounting scheme. The SEC charged LPHI with misstating its net income from 2007 through 2011 in connection with the failure to recognize impairment losses, as well as with a premature revenue recognition scheme. LPHI also materially understated a liability associated with its life settlements—called "Long-Term Deferred Policy Monitoring Costs."

CHAPTER EIGHT

Fair Value Accounting

FAIR VALUE CONSIDERATIONS

Throughout this section on asset-based financial reporting fraud schemes, the term *fair value* has been used extensively. The measurement of fair value is critical to the application of numerous accounting standards associated with assets, as well as with certain liabilities, covered later. A significant amount of professional judgment is required with many fair value measurements. As a result, this is an area that is very susceptible to manipulation and fraud.

Under U.S. GAAP, fair value is defined as the price that would be received to sell an asset or paid to transfer a liability in an orderly transaction between market participants at the measurement date (an exit price). The term *market participant* excludes related parties.

Until the issuance of IFRS 13 in 2011, the IFRS definition of fair value was "the amount for which an asset could be exchanged between knowledgeable, willing parties in an arm's-length transaction." This IFRS definition and the explanation of fair value concepts were spread out among several standards.

But with the release of IFRS 13, a comprehensive standard on fair value now exists. IFRS 13 will be effective for annual periods beginning on or after January 1, 2013. The IFRS 13 definition of fair value is identical to the U.S. GAAP definition just provided. Most other concepts in IFRS are consistent with those found in U.S. GAAP. Accordingly, a detailed comparison will not be provided here.

METHODS OF MEASURING FAIR VALUE

Most fair value measurements utilize one of the following approaches to determining fair value:

1. Market approach
2. Income approach
3. Cost approach

Market Approach

The market approach uses prices and other information generated by market transactions involving identical or comparable assets or liabilities. The use of the market approach sometimes involves estimating the point within a range of multiples or other inputs where an appropriate multiple or input should be. This requires the use of judgment and therefore all factors that are specific to the asset or liability being measured should be considered. Some of these factors may be quantitative, but they are often qualitative.

One of the most significant benefits of using the market approach is that it is often based primarily on readily available data. This data is often in the form of well-documented, publicly available prices recorded in active markets, such as with stock trades. Other data used in the market approach, such as the prices at which specific entities, lines of business, operating divisions or locations have been sold, may not be as readily available as prices from stock markets, but is nonetheless objective and useful.

Of course, important potential downsides to the market approach are that either active markets do not exist for a particular item or the comparison of the item in question with the known transactions in the market is complicated.

Often, there are known transactions in a market, but none are for assets or liabilities that are identical to the one for which a value is needed. The process of drawing this comparison can be an extremely complex task.

Income Approach

The income approach uses valuation techniques to convert future amounts to a single present amount (discounted). The most commonly used future amounts used in the formula are cash flows, earnings, or some component of earnings (e.g., earnings before taxes and interest). Consideration of future amounts can extend for many periods into the future or only a few. This requires much judgment. In certain industries or for certain assets, certain time periods have become standard. But in most cases, the number of future periods to consider is a matter of judgment.

Fair value determined using the income approach varies based on three primary factors:

1. The amount of cash flow—the higher the cash flow, the higher the value
2. The timing of the cash flows—the sooner the cash flow, the higher the value
3. The risks associated with the cash flows—the lower the risk, the higher the value

Each of these three factors can be a target for misrepresentation in a fraudulent determination of fair value under the income approach.

Within the income approach, valuation experts frequently utilize three distinct methods to value businesses:

1. Discounted cash flow
2. Capitalized cash flow
3. Excess cash flow

Discounted Cash Flow Method

The discounted cash flow method is the most commonly used. Using this approach, a value is derived by calculating the present value of estimated future cash flows. This method can be applied to a single asset, a group of assets, a division, a region, or an entire company. Cash flows may be estimated for a very short period of time or very long periods, up to infinity if an income stream is expected to continue forever.

When cash flows are anticipated over multiple periods, discounted cash flow is normally expressed as the following equation:

$$DCF = \frac{CF_1}{(1+r)^1} + \frac{CF_2}{(1+r)^2} + \ldots + \frac{CF_n}{(1+r)^n}$$

Where:

DCF = Discounted cash flow

CF = Cash flow for a period (1, 2, and so on, up to period n)

r = Discount rate

When a calculation involves multiple periods, it is also commonly referred to as present value and is represented by the following formula:

$$DPV = \sum_{t=0}^{N} \frac{FV_t}{(1+i)^t}$$

Where:

DPV = Discounted present value

Σ = Sum of

N = The last period for which cash flow (income) is expected

FV = The expected future value (cash flow) for each period

i = The discount rate

t = The period over which cash flows are anticipated

The discount rate used in the income approach represents the rate of return that an investor would require. This rate considers three elements:

1. A basic rate of return without any consideration of risk, or how much of a return an investor desires in exchange for the use of the investor's money
2. Anticipated rates of inflation, which correspond to the expected depreciation in purchasing power while funds are invested
3. Risk associated with the amount or timing of the estimated future cash flows

Each of these three elements requires the use of judgment, making them prone to potential manipulation in a fair value accounting fraud.

Capitalized Cash Flow Method

The capitalized cash flow method is a shortcut version of the discounted cash flow method. Unlike the discounted cash flow method, however, both the discount rate and the rate of growth in cash flow are assumed to remain constant in perpetuity.

The capitalized cash flow method is also known as the dividend discount model. It is expressed as follows:

$$\text{PV} = \text{NCF}/(k-g)$$

Where:

PV = Present value

NCF = Cash flow for the next full period

k = Present value discount rate

g = Expected long-term rate of growth

Unlike the discounted cash flow model, in which separate cash flow projections can be developed for each future period, and different discount rates can be applied to each future period's cash flow, the capitalized cash flow method is more simplistic.

Hitchner identifies several common mistakes that are made when applying the capitalized cash flow model. Several of these common mistakes can, when done intentionally, become a basis for committing financial statement fraud, such as:

1. Using an inaccurate long-term growth rate
2. Using an inappropriate discount rate
3. Failing to normalize earnings when estimating future cash flow

Excess Cash Flow Method

The excess cash flow method, also known as the excess earnings method, is sometimes used to value the intangible assets of a business rather than an entire business. It is referred to in the Internal Revenue Service's Revenue Ruling 68-609 as having application to intangible asset valuation. The basic steps involved in the excess cash flow approach are as follows:

1. Determine the fair value of net tangible assets of an entity
2. Determine normalized future cash flows in total (the concept of normalization is explained below), and break those cash flows down as follows:
   a. Cash flows attributable to net tangible assets
   b. Cash flows attributable to intangible assets, which are simply the difference between total cash flows and cash flows attributable to net tangible assets (i.e., separate determination of cash flows from intangible assets is not done)
3. Determine what an appropriate rate of return on net tangible assets would be (also referred to as the weighted average cost of capital)
4. Determine an appropriate rate of return on the intangible assets
5. Determine the fair value of intangible assets based on the capitalization rate determined in step 4
6. Determine a total fair value by adding the fair value of the net tangible assets to the fair value of the intangible assets
7. Determine the fair value of the entity's equity by subtracting any interest-bearing debt obligations from the amount determined in step 6

To properly apply the income approach, future cash flows must be normalized. Normalization represents the process of making projections of future cash flows most representative of what can be expected of the future. In other words, certain items that have historically impacted cash flows and that may be considered in estimates of future cash flows may need to be eliminated in order to get a true picture of what future cash flows will be like. For example, one of the more common adjustments necessary to normalize cash flows is for nonrecurring items, such as one-time expenditures.

Generally, there are many more considerations in normalizing the cash flows when valuing an entire business than there would be for valuing a single asset. In valuing an entire business, adjustments may be necessary for a variety of ownership, capitalization, debt, income tax, and other factors that may not be necessary when valuing a single asset.

Expected Cash Flow

A fourth possible approach to determining present values of future cash flows takes a different approach to measuring risk. It is referred to as the expected cash flow approach.

In the three methods of applying the income approach explained so far, the various risks associated with future cash flows are considered in developing a single discount rate that is applied to those future cash flows. Under the expected cash flow approach, risk is handled in a different manner. Instead of incorporating it into the discount rate, it is handled by determining multiple expectations of future cash flows and assigning probabilities to each. The element of risk is removed from the discount rate, leaving a much more reliable discount rate based primarily on an expected rate of return.

Under the expected cash flow approach, a weighted average of the various present values is calculated, based on the probabilities assigned to each calculation.

A Case of Improper Application of the Income Approach

An excellent example of fraudulent application of a valuation model is a case involving Bank of Montreal, which restated its financial statements by $237 million Canadian (CAD) in 2007 as a result of a valuation fraud. The valuations involved natural gas options that were traded by one of the bank's senior commodity traders.

At Bank of Montreal, similar to other financial institutions, each commodity trader was responsible for assigning fair values to their books each day. If the derivatives involved were actively traded on a recognized market, the mark-to-market basis was utilized in valuing the derivatives (i.e., the market method, as explained earlier). However, when no such market existed, a computerized mark-to-model approach was used (generally, a variation on one of the many income approaches described in the preceding section). The mark-to-model method involved having the traders provide the data inputs, which included fixed inputs, such as an option's expiration date, as well as variable inputs that required some calculation on the part of the trader.

When a mark-to-model method was used, Bank of Montreal's internal controls required that an independent price verification be obtained from a third party. If the independent price was lower than the value calculated by the trader, a valuation reserve for the difference would be established. The selection of the outside party was made by personnel from a department separate from that of the trader, providing for a segregation of duties.

This is where things begin to unravel for Bank of Montreal. The trading unit had successfully resisted efforts by other departments of the bank to utilize a multicontributor independent valuation service. As a result, the same outside company, Optionable, had been used exclusively as the broker for the trades and to verify the trader's valuations since 2003. A relationship developed between the Bank of Montreal trader and three individuals at Optionable. By its own account, Optionable earned 24 percent of its 2006 brokerage revenues from the trades carried out by the one Bank of Montreal trader. In effect, earning so much of its revenue from a single source impaired Optionable's independence, creating the incentive to cooperate with the trader at Bank of Montreal.

This relationship led to the practice of "U-turning," in which the three individuals at Optionable simply returned values to Bank of Montreal's back office mirroring those provided by the trader. How this worked was simple. Optionable provided Bank of Montreal's back office with fair value quotes twice a month. The trader engaging in the fraudulent valuations would e-mail his list of inflated values to his contacts at Optionable, easily circumventing the internal control that Bank of Montreal thought was in place. Later that same day, Optionable would e-mail its list of supposedly independent values to Bank of Montreal's back office. These e-mails contained values exactly matching those of the trader, thus covering up the inflated values. Over the six quarters from November 1, 2005, through April 30, 2007, the Bank of Montreal trader overvalued his book by a total of $680 million (CAD), of which $432 million (CAD) was attributable to the trader's fraud.

The Bank of Montreal trader's compensation grew enormously as a result of his fraud. In 2003 and 2004, he received annual bonuses of approximately $650,000 (CAD). However, the bonus jumped to more than $3 million in 2005, the year the fraud began in earnest. His 2006 bonus rose to $5.35 million.

The three individuals at Optionable also profited. Two senior executives who owned stock in the company made $10 million when they sold shares in Optionable stock in 2007. And a third person, who assisted the two executives, received large bonuses for cooperating.

The unraveling of the fraud scheme began in the summer of 2006 when the Bank of Montreal finally subscribed to a multi-contributor valuation service called Totem. Totem's valuations came in below those of the trader and Optionable. After repeated efforts by the fraudulent trader to manipulate these values, by early 2007 the scheme came to an end.

In addition to the impact on Bank of Montreal, the shareholders of Optionable also felt the effects of the fraud once it came to light. Shares of Optionable stock fell by 82 percent in just two days after the Bank of Montreal reported it would suspend its relationship with Optionable. Additional subsequent declines brought the total hit to more than 90 percent.

See Chapter 7 for a discussion of the Citigroup case, which involved a change in valuation models from the market approach to the income approach.

Cost Approach

The cost approach to determining fair value is based on assessing what the cost would be to replace an asset, or the service capacity of an asset, and then making adjustments to that cost figure. The primary adjustment to the cost figure is for obsolescence.

The obvious risks associated with the cost approach concern the replacement cost estimate and adjustments for obsolescence and any other relevant factors. Replacement cost estimates may in some cases be fairly easy, such as when an asset was purchased fairly recently and the same model of that asset is still being sold. Estimating the replacement cost of unusual or custom-designed, custom-built assets becomes much more complicated and may require external assistance.

Adjustments for obsolescence can also be very easy or very difficult. But these adjustments, as well as other adjustments to the initial replacement cost, are an easy target for manipulation.

INTERNAL VERSUS EXTERNALLY DEVELOPED VALUATIONS

Fair values can be determined internally or externally. When they are determined internally, management should make sure that the personnel involved in the process have the proper expertise for the specific valuation issues involved.

Externally developed valuations should be prepared by independent valuation experts with experience in valuing the specific types of assets, liabilities, or businesses in question. Management should determine that external valuation specialists are properly credentialed and experienced in the specific types of valuations needed. References should be checked and licenses and certifications verified.

But in other cases, including some involving fair value accounting fraud, management doesn't want the best valuation specialist. Instead, management wants to find a valuation specialist willing to provide a report that supports what management wants to use as a fair value in the financial statements.

Unscrupulous members of management may go to great lengths to obtain a report in support of a preferred fair value, all to dupe auditors and others who may question a particular value in the financial statements. Improper valuations used in support of a fair value accounting fraud can be generated internally or may come from third-party experts. When third-party valuation experts are involved, there are five situations in which a fraudulent valuation can result:

1. **Bribed appraiser.** In a worst-case scenario, an outside party may be bribed in order to issue a valuation report that supports a fair value accounting position of management. This is the most egregious offense in this area and also one of the most difficult to detect.
2. **Conflict of interest.** If there is a concealed financial or other relationship between either the entity or a member of management and the outside valuation specialist, the specialist is not independent and the report may support a fraudulent valuation preferred by management.
3. **Unwitting accomplice.** In the first two cases, the appraiser is an accomplice to the fraud and he or she knows it. In other cases, a third-party valuation specialist may unwittingly prepare a valuation report in support of a fraud, as a result of pressures applied by management, suppression of information by management, reliance on phony data provided by management, or other tactics. This is most likely to occur when the outside party is either inexperienced or careless in their work.
4. **Sham valuation specialist.** One other method that could be used to perpetrate fraud is the preparation of a completely fictitious valuation report from a nonexistent valuation specialist. This approach is similar to any other phony vendor scheme in that the perpetrator prepares false documentation that makes it appear that an actual vendor exists.

5. **Altered report.** A company may have arranged for and received a valuation report from a respected professional valuation expert. But the report does not support the position preferred by management. Could it be possible for management to make alterations to the report prepared by the valuation expert to make it appear that the expert supported the fraudulent valuation reflected in the financial statements? Reports should be reviewed carefully for signs of alteration, missing pages, additions inserted into the report, or other signs of alteration.

Other than the obvious signs of alteration described in the last situation, there can be a number of other signs that a valuation report may be flawed. Those flaws may be a sign of fraud, not merely carelessness by an appraiser. Some other signs to watch out for in valuation reports include the following:

- Mathematical and clerical errors, including cross-references that don't agree, grammatical mistakes, and similar careless errors
- Apparent exaggeration and excessive reliance on positive factors, or downplaying negative factors
- A report that lacks a sufficient level of detail, especially details involving the data used in support of the valuation (interest rates, cash flow assumptions, etc.) and descriptions of valuation methodologies utilized
- Misrepresentation of the specialist's licenses, education and training, or credentials (don't be fooled by a specialist with a lot of certifications after his or her name—verify those licenses and other credentials)
- The use of unusual valuation methods or methods that are not commonly accepted for a particular type of valuation (or making unexplained modifications to a commonly accepted method)
- A report that does not contain a statement certifying the valuation specialist's independence from the entity
- Use of data that would not be known to prospective buyers of an asset—remember that the definition of fair value is based on what market participants would pay for the asset
- Evidence that there was an extremely short turnaround time on the report—this could be a sign that not much effort was put into the valuation, or that the report was prepared quickly to satisfy an urgent need of management
- Evidence that the report was cut and pasted from other reports—we've seen reports that had the name of the wrong client, clearly a sign that the report was prepared using a "cookie cutter" mentality

- Excessive reliance on mathematics and formulas, without adequate narrative explanation

Valuation reports should be reviewed carefully for these warning signs. Just because a fair value is supported by a professional-looking report doesn't mean it should be blindly accepted as accurate.

INPUTS USED IN MEASURING FAIR VALUE

A final consideration in the use of fair value in financial reporting is the nature of the data used in measuring fair value. Both U.S. GAAP and the new IFRS 13 classify data used in measuring fair value into three levels of inputs.

Level 1 inputs are quoted (unadjusted) prices in active markets for identical assets or liabilities that the reporting entity has the ability to access at the measurement date. In theory, there should be minimal doubt associated with Level 1 inputs.

Level 2 inputs are inputs other than quoted prices included within Level 1 that are either directly (i.e., as prices) or indirectly (i.e., derived from prices) observable for the asset or liability. Examples of Level 2 inputs include the following:

- Quoted prices for similar assets or liabilities in active markets
- Quoted prices for identical or similar assets or liabilities in markets that are not active (i.e., markets in which there are few transactions, the prices are not current, or price quotations vary substantially over time or among market makers, or those in which little information is released publicly)
- Inputs other than quoted prices that are observable (e.g., interest rates and yield curves observable at commonly quoted intervals, volatilities, prepayment speeds, loss severities, credit risks, and default rates)
- Inputs that are derived principally from or corroborated by observable market data by correlation or other means

Since Level 2 inputs do not involve identical assets or liabilities, it may be necessary to make adjustments to Level 2 price information, as well as other Level 2 inputs. Adjustments to Level 2 quoted prices and other inputs should be tailored to the specific asset or liability. These adjustments should customize any Level 2 quoted prices or other inputs to arrive an appropriate fair value for the asset or liability. Examples of adjustments to Level 2 prices or other inputs that may be necessary include the following:

- The condition of the asset or liability
- The degree to which the inputs are comparable to the asset or liability
- The volume and level of activity in the market(s) within which the inputs were observed
- The amount of time that has lapsed since the observed transaction or other input
- The terms of the instruments subject to the transaction
- The existence and nature of any transactions that are related to transaction(s) being evaluated or used as inputs (i.e., is the transaction one of several related transactions that could impact the input?)

Level 3 inputs are those inputs that are "unobservable," meaning verifiable data from outside the reporting does not exist. Therefore, internally developed data (e.g., projections of future cash flows) used in developing an estimate of fair value is classified as Level 3.

Financial statements are required to disclose in the notes section information about whether Level 1, 2, or 3 inputs were utilized in measuring fair value.

As one progresses from Level 1 to Level 2 and on to Level 3, an increasing level of judgment is required. As a result, the risk of fraud is normally higher in connection with the use of Level 2 inputs over Level 1 inputs, and even more so with Level 3 inputs over Level 2 inputs. The very idea of an "unobservable" input used to measure the fair value of an asset or liability reported in the financial statements should be a clear indicator to any auditor that significant audit work should be performed. Level 3 inputs often consist of a series of management estimates, some with more support than others. These should be scrutinized carefully.

PART THREE

Expense and Liability Schemes

THE PURPOSEFUL OMISSION of liabilities for expenses incurred is another common technique used to fraudulently make it appear that a company is financially strong. What makes this type of fraud difficult to detect is the fact that the fraud lies in something that is *not* on the books, rather than a misstatement of something that has actually been recorded on the balance sheet. Omissions therefore require a different approach by auditors and investigators.

In most cases, failing to accrue expenses represents a timing difference, as the expense eventually becomes due and is paid, at which time the expense is usually recorded. However, pushing expenses off until a future period makes the current period appear more profitable, and that may be exactly what a company is attempting to do.

For a simple example, take the case of Symbol Technologies, Inc. Symbol paid quarterly bonuses to employees in the first quarter of 2000. Payment of compensation would normally trigger an automatic accrual for payroll taxes owed by an employer. In a complaint filed by the SEC, Symbol was charged with failing to accrue $3.5 million of FICA taxes owed by the company in connection with bonuses paid that quarter. Instead, the company recorded the expense in a later period in which the taxes were paid. This resulted in an increase in net income of 7.5 percent for the first quarter.

CHAPTER NINE

Shifting Expenses to Future Periods

TIMING SCHEMES INVOLVING LIABILITIES

One of the simplest methods of improving profits is to fail to record a liability for an expense that has been incurred by an entity. One of the basic concepts behind accrual accounting is the recognition of an expense when the expense has been incurred and the benefits received. When a company postpones recognition of an expense until it pays a vendor, the company is practicing a cash basis of accounting, which does not conform to U.S. GAAP or IFRS.

Thus, auditors and investigators should always be on the lookout for a company attempting to postpone recognition of expenses until a future period rather than accruing a liability for those costs in the current period.

ACCOUNTS PAYABLE

The most common liability that is underreported in an attempt to improve a company's balance sheet is accounts payable. Auditors perform a search for unrecorded accounts payable by analyzing disbursements made subsequent to year-end. The supporting documentation for these disbursements is examined for signs that the underlying goods or services were delivered prior to the end of the year and, therefore, subject to a requirement to accrue them as liabilities on the balance sheet at year-end.

Techniques that may be utilized to omit accounts payable from the balance sheet include the following:

- Hiding invoices for goods and services received prior to year-end from the auditor and waiting until after the audit is completed to pay the vendors
- Making arrangements with vendors to delay payment until after the auditors have completed the audit
- Making arrangements with vendors to delay invoicing the company until well after the end of the year
- Arranging for undisclosed financing of vendor payables, so that vendors receive payment from a third-party finance company, and omitting the liability to the finance company from the balance sheet
- Altering vendor invoices so that the dates of goods or services delivered appear to be after the end of the company's fiscal year
- Entering into non-cash arrangements with vendors for the settlement of accounts payable after year-end and making it appear that the non-cash "payment" is not connected to the settlement of the accounts payable

COMPENSATED ABSENCES

Recall from Chapters 2 and 6 the case of Qwest Communications, charged by the SEC in 2004 with a variety of schemes resulting in material inflation of the company's profits. One of those schemes involved unsupported reductions in a liability previously recorded for compensated absences of employees (i.e., vacation or holiday leave).

Under ASC 710-10-25 of U.S. GAAP, a liability should be accrued for compensated absences (e.g., vacation or sick pay) if all of the following conditions are met:

1. The employer's obligation is attributable to employees' services already rendered
2. The obligation relates to rights that either:
   a. Vest—those rights for which the employer has an obligation to make payment even if an employee terminates; thus, they are not contingent on an employee's future service

   b. Accumulate—those rights that are earned and when unused may be carried forward to one or more periods subsequent to that in which they are earned (although the amount an employee can carry forward may be limited)
3. Payment of the compensation is probable
4. The amount of the liability can be reasonably estimated

The basis for this accrual is that accumulating or vesting benefits are earned by employees as services are rendered. The distinction between vested and accumulated (nonvested) benefits is that vested benefits would be paid out in cash if an employee were to leave the employer. Accumulated benefits carry forward from one year to the next, but are not paid out in cash if an employee leaves. When measuring the liability at the end of a period, an employer should consider an estimate of the forfeitures of accumulated benefits.

IFRS for compensated absences is found in IAS 19, *Employee Benefits*. The guidance here is similar to U.S. GAAP, noting that the accrual should occur as the services are rendered that entitle the employee to the benefit. The accrual should reflect vested and nonvested benefits. However, the possibility that employees may leave before they use an accumulated entitlement affects the measurement of that obligation (i.e., an estimate should be made regarding the portion of accumulated benefits that will likely be used).

Prior to June 2001, Qwest had recorded a liability for compensated absences utilizing a policy under which the liability was measured at 100 percent of the vacation time owed to employees for the year. This liability had stood at approximately $118 million. However, over a seven-month period, the liability was inexplicably reduced by 81 percent, to $23 million, without any basis. This was done, according to the SEC, in order to meet "various financial targets." The actual amount of vacation time owed to its employees was not reduced. Only the amount recorded as a liability in the financial statements was.

CONTINGENT LIABILITIES

Contingencies represent gains or losses that may occur, but for which there is some degree of uncertainty. It is this uncertainty that distinguishes contingent assets and liabilities from other recognized assets and liabilities.

One common example of a contingency that could result in a gain or a loss is the outcome of a court case. When lawsuits are filed on behalf of, or against, an entity, the outcome of the case is often a cash settlement—either paid by the entity or to be received by the entity. Depending on the stage of the case at the time the financial statements are prepared, there could be a low or high degree of certainty that management of an entity feels regarding the eventual outcome of the case.

Fraud risks regarding reporting of contingent liabilities can involve either omission or postponement (timing differences). However, since the contingencies that require recognition are those that are likely to result in a liability, these schemes are better qualified as timing schemes, as the fraudulent company is attempting to postpone the recognition of a liability until the inevitable future period in which it is paid.

U.S. GAAP for contingencies is found at ASC 450. IFRS is provided in IAS 37, *Provisions, Contingent Liabilities and Contingent Assets*.

Contingencies can be classified as gain or loss contingencies. Under U.S. GAAP, loss contingencies can result in either of the following:

1. The incurrence of a liability
2. An impairment of an asset

A liability is to be recorded in the financial statements for a contingent loss only if all three of the following conditions are present:

1. The underlying causal event occurred prior to the balance sheet date.
2. It is probable (i.e., likely) that a loss has been incurred.
3. There is a reasonable basis for estimating the loss.

When all three of the criteria are met, the balance sheet should reflect a liability. All three criteria can be subject to manipulation, especially the second and third criteria. Claiming that a loss is not likely or that there is not a reasonable basis for estimating the amount of the loss are both potential methods to avoid recognizing a liability in the financial statements.

Of course, if a liability is inevitable, it will eventually have to be recorded. But management may wish to defer recognition of the liability until a future period. Many financial statement frauds are based on attempts to put off negative transactions and accelerate the positive ones—all timing differences to make the current period appear stronger.

The critical element in determining whether a liability should be recognized is the likelihood that a loss has been incurred. If the likelihood of a loss is remote (defined as slight) or only possible (somewhere between remote and probable), a liability should not be recognized. Only if it is probable that a loss has been incurred should a liability be recognized.

Likelihood that a loss has been incurred also impacts whether disclosure of a loss contingency is required in a footnote disclosure. Recognized liabilities for probable loss contingencies should always be explained in the footnotes. In addition, loss contingencies that are possible should be disclosed, even though they are not recognized as liabilities on the balance sheet. It is only with respect to loss contingencies with a remote likelihood of incurrence that neither recognition nor disclosure is required.

Careful reading of footnote disclosures regarding loss contingencies is another important step in determining whether financial statements are misstated. If a loss contingency is disclosed but not recognized, it means that the entity considers the likelihood of the incurrence of a loss to be more than remote but less than probable.

Gain contingencies can result in either the acquisition of an asset (e.g., cash in the settlement of a lawsuit) or a reduction of a liability (e.g., reduction in the amount recorded as payable to a vendor as a result of suing the vendor for nonperformance or substandard performance). A recovery associated with a contingent loss is included in the scope of the definition of a gain contingency. For example, if an entity has incurred a contingent liability that may be recoverable in the form of insurance, the amount that may be recovered via insurance is considered to be a gain contingency.

Generally, gain contingencies are not to be recorded in the financial statements until all contingencies have been resolved. However, if the gain contingency involves a recovery related to a contingent loss, it should be recorded if it is both probable and reasonably estimable.

If such a gain contingency is recorded, its amount is generally limited to the amount of the contingent loss. Only when all contingencies related to the recovery have been resolved can a gain contingency in excess of the loss contingency be recorded.

If the recognition criteria for contingent liabilities explained earlier have been met, a liability should be recorded in an amount equal to the best estimate of the future amount to be paid (or the amount of the asset impairment). If there is a range of losses that could be incurred, the amount representing the best estimate should be accrued. If none of the amounts within the range of possible losses is better than the others, the liability should be recognized at the lowest amount in the range.

Clearly, a significant degree of judgment is necessary to estimate many contingent liabilities. In some cases, an entity may have a history with similar losses that can form a reliable basis for an estimate. Outside experts, including legal counsel, can also provide reliable information in formulating an estimate, as can the experience of other entities with similar losses. Estimates that are based solely on internal information in situations in which an entity has no prior experience should be viewed as the most susceptible to manipulation. These are also the most difficult to audit.

As it relates to liabilities, what U.S. GAAP refers to as loss contingencies are classified into two categories under IAS 37, based on the likelihood of loss—provisions and contingent liabilities. Whereas U.S. GAAP requires the recognition of some contingent losses but not others, based on their likelihood, IFRS uses different terms for the different degrees of likelihood.

A provision is recognized as a liability in the financial statements only when all three of the following conditions are present:

1. An enterprise has a present obligation as a result of a past event. Such an obligation can be either a legal obligation (i.e., based on a contract or law) or a constructive obligation (one that is based on the entity's actions, established patterns of prior practices, policies, etc.).
2. It is probable (meaning, it is more likely than not) that an outflow of resources embodying economic benefits will be required to settle the obligation.
3. A reliable estimate can be made of the amount of the obligation.

If all three of these conditions are present, an entity should recognize a liability. These three conditions are substantially similar to the three conditions requiring the recognition of a loss contingency under U.S. GAAP. Measurement of the liability is explained later.

A contingent liability, however, is not to be recognized. These are liabilities that are possible (rather than probable) based on past events, but whose existence will be confirmed through the occurrence or nonoccurrence of future events that are uncertain and not within the control of the entity. Also included within the scope of contingent liabilities are present obligations that result from past events but which either cannot be reliably estimated or will not likely require an outflow of economic resources to settle.

Contingent liabilities are not to be recognized as liabilities. However, they should be disclosed in the footnotes to the financial statements unless the possibility of an outflow of resources to settle the obligation is remote. Again, this treatment mirrors U.S. GAAP, only with a slight difference in terminology.

Provisions should be recognized as liabilities based on the expected expenditures necessary to settle the obligation. Expected expenditures should be the best estimate of the expenditure required to settle the obligation.

When a variety of different levels of expenditure are possible, IFRS suggests use of the expected value method. Similar to the expected value method as described in U.S. GAAP, this method involves assigning probabilities to various possible outcomes and developing a weighted average of those outcomes based on the probabilities assigned to each. For example:

Estimated Loss		Probability		Expected Value
$ 30,000,000	X	10%	=	$ 3,000,000
$ 20,000,000	X	40%	=	$ 8,000,000
$ 15,000,000	X	30 %	=	$ 4,500,000
$ 10,000,000	X	20%	=	$ 2,000,000
Expected Value				$17,500,000

When the effect of the time value of money is material, a provision should be recognized at the present value of the best estimate of expenditures expected to settle the obligation. This may be the case when the expected timing of settling an obligation extends beyond the near future. The discount rate(s) used in the calculation should be pre-tax rates that reflect current market assessments of the time value of money, as well as any risks that are specific to the liability.

The financial statement fraud risk here is clear-cut. A company may attempt to avoid recording a contingent liability (under U.S. GAAP) or provision (under IFRS) even though the recognition criteria have been met. Detecting this type of omission, however, can be difficult. These types of liabilities tend to be known only among the most senior members of management and few others within a company. The existence of these liabilities may be documented in the form of correspondence between the company and the third party to which the liability accrues. This correspondence may be extensive, as in the case of litigation. But it may be limited to e-mail messages and not much more in other cases.

ACCRUED COMPENSATION

Another liability subject to timing scheme manipulation involves the liability for compensation owed to employees. Particularly prone to abuse is the accrual of liabilities for bonuses and other incentives earned in one period but paid in the next.

One example of this occurred in the case of SCB Computer Technology, Inc., a provider of information technology–related consulting, outsourcing, and staffing services. In AAER 1622, the SEC charged SCB with underreporting its liabilities at the end of the company's fiscal year 1999, at which time the company owed certain employee bonuses totaling $380,000. SCB paid the bonuses in the first quarter of fiscal year 2000, but did not accrue the expense at the end of 1999. Consistent with U.S. GAAP, SCB should have expensed the bonuses in the period in which they were earned, which was fiscal year 1999. Instead, SCB improperly capitalized these bonuses when they were paid in 2000 as prepaid commissions associated with a 44-month contract awarded to SCB and The Partners Group (a partnership acquired by SCB in 1997) in the first quarter of fiscal year 2000.

SCB intentionally failed to properly record these bonuses as expenses in 1999 in order to avoid the negative impact the employee bonuses had on SCB's earnings for fiscal year 1999. By amortizing the bonuses over the term of this 44-month contract, SCB improperly spread out the earnings impact of the bonus payment over future periods. As a result, SCB overstated its pre-tax income by an additional 5% for fiscal year 1999.

IMPROPER USE OF LIABILITY "RESERVES"

As explained in Part I concerning revenue-based schemes, not all financial reporting frauds involve an overstatement of earnings. Some initially involve an understatement of earnings in a period that can accommodate such treatment due to already-met expectations, in order to have a cushion for future periods.

Just like the use of contra-asset reserves as a form of cookie jar, into which a company can dip in order to smooth out earnings, reserves can also take the form of liability accounts.

Among the many charges faced by Symbol Technologies, Inc. was the assertion that company executives inappropriately recorded decreases in an overstated liability account in order to bridge earnings gaps in five quarters from 1999 to 2001. The liability account had been established for legitimate reasons—to create a reserve for contributions that Symbol would make to a special retirement plan for senior executives. However, in 1999 and 2000, some senior executives elected to swap these retirement benefits for "split" life insurance policies. This swap should have triggered a removal of the liability at the time of the swap. But Symbol instead kept the liabilities on the books, recognizing an opportunity that could be utilized in future periods. In order to meet earnings expectations in future quarters, Symbol decreased these reserves in the periods needed, rather than in the periods in which the swaps took place. Going one step further, as these schemes often do, Symbol eventually reduced the reserve for swaps that did not even take place in order to meet earnings goals, effectively removing a liability that still existed.

CHAPTER TEN

Omissions and Underreporting of Liabilities

DEBT

Debt obligations are liabilities associated with money that has been borrowed by an entity. Examples of debt obligations include:

- Loans from financial institutions (mortgages, lines of credit, commercial loans, and other loans provided by banks and other financial institutions)
- Unsecured promissory notes
- Bonds issued by the company
- Mortgage-backed securities
- Asset-backed securities

In addition to a stated rate of interest (often referred to as the coupon rate) debt instruments can have several other important features that can impact their accounting treatment:

- **Call provisions.** These provisions permit the issuer of the debt to repay the obligation prior to the stated maturity date, usually at some premium (to compensate the holder of the debt instrument for the reduction in interest income that the holder will receive).

- **Put provisions.** These provisions enable the lender (the holder of the debt instrument) to require the borrower to repay the debt obligation prior to the scheduled maturity date, usually on specified dates and also often at par (face) value (thus enabling the lender to reinvest in other, more attractive investment options).

Under both U.S. GAAP and IFRS, debt is generally initially recognized at an amount equal to the proceeds received or, if proceeds are not provided in cash, the fair value of the consideration received. After the initial issuance of debt, the subsequent measurement of debt is to be at amortized cost using the effective interest method (unless a fair value option is elected, as explained below). However, U.S. GAAP and IFRS differ in how the effective interest method is applied.

Under U.S. GAAP, amortization is based on contractual cash flows over the contractual life of the instrument, with only two possible exceptions:

1. Puttable debt is to be amortized over the period from the date of issuance to the first put date.
2. Callable debt is to be amortized over *either* the contractual life or the estimated life of the instrument (once either of these options is selected, it must be applied consistently).

IFRS, on the other hand, bases effective interest rate calculations on *estimated* cash flows over the *expected* life of the instrument. Under IAS 39, contractual terms of debt are used only if it is not possible to otherwise estimate cash flows or the life of the instrument. This difference, using estimated rather than contractual cash flows and lives, can potentially lead to significant differences in calculations between IFRS and U.S. GAAP.

The primary financial reporting fraud risk associated with debt obligations is the exclusion of such liabilities from the financial statements. The Parmalat case is good example of this risk.

Parmalat Finanziaria S.p.A. (Parmalat), a seller of dairy products based in Italy, admitted to overstating assets in its 2002 audited financial statements by at least €3.95 billion (see Chapter 7) and excluding certain debt obligations from its reported liabilities. The debt obligations that were excluded amounted to approximately €2.9 billion. They were excluded on the basis that the company had repurchased Parmalat bonds. In fact, no such repurchase ever took place.

Both U.S. GAAP and IFRS provide for a fair value option for debt. The fair value option for debt and other financial instruments under U.S. GAAP is found at ASC 825. Under IAS 39, debt may be designated as "at fair value through profit or loss" similar to the classification of investments explained in Chapter 7.

The option to measure debt obligations at fair value creates an additional fraud risk in the form of underreporting a debt obligation, as explained below. Contrary to the assumption held by some, the fair value of a debt obligation its par (stated) value. While it may seem counterintuitive to report a debt obligation at an amount other than face amount to be repaid, this is exactly what can, and often does, result when fair value accounting is applied.

One of the most important factors in determining the fair value of debt is whether or not the debt is collateralized. Uncollateralized debt will usually carry a greater risk than collateralized debt. With collateralized debt, its fair value is usually at least equal to the liquidation value of the underlying assets that have been pledged as collateral. Of course, determining the liquidation value of the underlying assets may not always be a simple task.

The primary factor that can lead to the fair value of a debt obligation being different from par value is the debt instrument's yield to maturity. If the calculated yield to maturity differs from the interest rate stated in the debt instrument (e.g., the coupon rate of a bond), the fair value will differ from the face value of the debt, as follows:

If coupon rate > yield to maturity, then fair value > face value
If yield to maturity > coupon rate, then face value > fair value

So, what are the primary factors that impact yield to maturity? Here is where it gets interesting. Calculating yield to maturity requires judgment regarding various risk factors. And when judgment is involved, the risk of fraud is greater.

There are three primary risk factors to consider in developing a yield to maturity:

1. **Default risk.** This represents the risk that the issuer/borrower will fail to pay some or all of a debt obligation. The primary factor impacting default risk is the financial condition of the issuer/borrower. Default risk falls under the broader category of nonperformance risk, a risk factor that is required to be considered in measuring fair value. Default risk may be mitigated based on the existence, nature, and liquidation value of collateral.
2. **Interest rate risk.** This is the risk associated with changes in interest rates available in the market over time. If market rates of interest increase to levels in excess of a bond's rate of interest, the trading price of the bond decreases, and vice versa. When determining market rates of interest, rates should be located for debt instruments that are as similar as possible to the debt being evaluated in terms of amounts and maturity dates, as well as other relevant factors, such as the bond's rating.

3. **Call risk.** As explained earlier, a call feature enables the issuer to repay an obligation before its stated due date. Call risk represents the likelihood of such a call feature being exercised, which would impact the value of the debt to other participants in the market, since one of the considerations in calculating fair value is the duration of the expected cash flows.

The fair value of a debt obligation, after assessing these and other relevant risks, is then equal to the present value of future cash flows. However, in performing the calculation, the yield to maturity rate should be used as the discount rate rather than the stated rate in the debt instrument. As a result, fair value may differ from the instrument's face value.

As with other fair value measurements, the information used to determine fair value of debt obligations may be internally generated or come from external sources (i.e., observable versus unobservable inputs). In some cases, a similar debt that is publicly traded can serve as a reliable benchmark. In other cases, the discounted cash flow methodology summarized in the preceding paragraphs would be a more appropriate and reliable estimate of fair value.

But even under the discounted cash flow approach, the inputs used may be a combination of internal data and external market data. For instance, the determination of a yield to maturity may best be determined by locating a similar company and utilizing information gathered from that company. This is particularly useful when assessing fair value of debt obligations of companies that are not publicly traded. Benchmarking a privately held business to a similar but publicly traded company may be a useful technique for determining fair value of that company's debt instrument.

A financial reporting fraud risk with respect to debt obligation (or other financial liability) exists when these liabilities are designated as being carried at fair value on a recurring basis. Manipulation of fair value techniques and/or inputs may result in a liability being reported at a lower amount than what it should be—resulting in an overall understatement of liabilities.

Of course, if a company wishes to understate its liabilities, completely omitting debt obligations from the financial statements may be even more effective than merely undervaluing them. Let's look at an example to understand how this might work.

Adelphia Communications Corporation, a cable television operator, and six of its senior officers, were charged by the SEC with fraudulently excluding more than $2.3 billion in bank debt from its reported liabilities from 1999 to 2001. It did so by transferring the debt to unconsolidated affiliated entities that were under the control of Adelphia's founder and the founder's various family members. There were 63 identified affiliates, referred to as "Rigas Entities" after the family name of the company's founder. Only 14 of the Rigas Entities were involved in the cable television industry. The remaining 49 were engaged in activities that were unrelated to the cable television business, including ventures such as interior design, furniture retailing, landscaping, honey cultivation, and film production.

Beginning in 1996, Adelphia, certain Adelphia subsidiaries, and various Rigas Entities entered into co-borrowing arrangements with financial institutions. Each co-borrower would pledge collateral and each would be able to borrow up to the entire amount available under the agreement. Under the first co-borrowing in 1996, Rigas co-borrowers contributed 66 percent of total collateral. However, under subsequent borrowings, Adelphia and its subsidiaries contributed substantially more of the collateral, to the point that one 2001 borrowing involved only 4 percent of the collateral from Rigas co-borrowers.

By December 31, 2000, total available borrowing capacity was $3.75 billion and the entire amount was borrowed and outstanding. Of this amount, $1.6 billion was improperly excluded from Adelphia's financial statements, purportedly because Adelphia was merely a guarantor of the Rigas co-borrowers (this argument might not work under the current rules covering guarantees, which were adopted subsequent to this case and which are covered in the next section). However, this assertion was fraudulent, as the underlying agreements clearly specified that Adelphia was jointly and severally liable for the full amount of the debt. This discrepancy in 2005 also became a key element of an administrative proceeding (see AAER 2237) filed against Adelphia's auditors, who were aware of the terms of the agreements.

The SEC asserted that almost all of the excluded debt had at one point been on Adelphia's books, but was subsequently transferred off the financial statements. This was done in several manners:

- Sham reclassification journal entries that moved debt to the books of Rigas co-borrowers
- Improper transfers in connection with direct placements of Adelphia securities to Rigas family members
- Recording debt directly on the books of Rigas co-borrowers even though Adelphia was liable for the debt (and ignoring the fact that loan proceeds were deposited directly into Adelphia bank accounts)

The effect of this practice was interesting. First, what should have been reported as a debt obligation was instead recorded as a payable to affiliates.

However, another trend that was going on for some time was the draining of Adelphia cash by transferring it to Rigas Entities. These transfers had been recorded as receivables from Rigas Entities, an asset. Once the debt was improperly reclassified to payables to Rigas Entities, these liabilities were offset against the receivables from the Rigas Entities. And the whole thing disappears!

In essence, what happened was that funds borrowed from banks by Adelphia were used to fund unrelated business ventures carried out by various members of the Rigas family.

GUARANTEES

In a guarantee, one party provides assurance that a performance requirement of another party is met. Examples of guarantees include the following:

- One company has a loan payable to a financial institution, and payment of the note is guaranteed by another company.
- A manufacturer has a contract with a customer to provide a certain quantity of products, and the commitment to meet the quantity expectation is guaranteed by another manufacturer.
- One entity leases its office space from a landlord that requires the guarantee of another entity.

Guarantees result in two types of liabilities (in the terminology used in U.S. GAAP, as explained in Chapter 9 on contingencies):

1. A noncontingent liability
2. A contingent liability

The noncontingent liability represents the guarantor's ongoing obligation to perform under the terms and for the duration of the guarantee – the equivalent of being on "standby" and available for performance during the guarantee period. The contingent liability represents the guarantor's potential obligation to make payments in the future in case events trigger such an obligation.

Guarantees create special recognition, reporting, and disclosure requirements in connection with the financial statements of the guarantor. U.S. GAAP for the contingent liability inherent in a guarantee is addressed at ASC 450, covered in Chapter 9. The topic of contingencies covers potential gains and losses, not just contingencies associated with guarantees. The focus of this section will be on the noncontingent element of guarantees.

U.S. GAAP addresses the accounting for guarantees at ASC 460. ASC 460 provides for specific footnote disclosure requirements associated with guarantees. More important for the focus of this book, however, are the requirements for guarantors to record a liability for certain types of guarantees.

IFRS for guarantees is covered in IAS 39, *Financial Instruments: Recognition and Measurement*, the same standard applied in other chapters dealing with financial assets and liabilities.

Recognition—U.S. GAAP

ASC 460 provides for disclosure requirements on many guarantees, and a requirement to record a liability for some, but not all, of those guarantees. These rules apply to most, but not all, guarantees. The most common guarantees that are covered and that have important fair value considerations fall into two broad categories:

1. Contracts that require a guarantor to make payments if another party fails to perform under an agreement. The performance that is guaranteed can be in the form of making payments to another party (e.g., repaying a loan to a bank), manufacturing or delivering goods to a customer, performance of services for a customer, or many other types of performance. The payment made by the guarantor can be in the form of cash, transfer of other assets, or even the provision of services.
2. Contracts that require a guarantor to make payments based on changes in an underlying that is related to an asset, liability, or equity security. An underlying can be an interest rate, foreign exchange rate, an index, credit rating, price of a financial instrument, or some other variable. So, as an example, a change in an exchange rate could trigger a requirement for a guarantor to perform.

Commercial letters of credit and other commitments (often referred to as guarantees of funding) are excluded from the scope of ASC 460. In addition, ASC 460 provides a list of additional scope exceptions, such as certain contingent rent provisions and others.

ASC 460 requires that at the inception of a guarantee, a liability must be recognized in the financial statements of the guarantor. Generally, this liability should be measured at the fair value of the guarantee. However, if the contingent liability required to be reported under ASC 450 is greater, then that larger amount should be recognized.

There are several exceptions to the requirement to record a liability by a guarantor. Among the most important exceptions are those involving affiliated entities (parent-subsidiary and brother-sister relationships) and those that are accounted for as derivatives.

Measurement—U.S. GAAP

The fair value of a guarantee is not equal to the maximum amount that a guarantor may ultimately have to pay. Instead, it represents an assessment of the value for taking on a risk of financial or nonfinancial performance for a specified period of time, considering all market and entity-specific risks present at the time.

In many cases, the initial fair value of a guarantee is easy to determine since one party pays or promises to pay another party (the guarantor) a specified amount in exchange for their guarantee. That amount will usually represent the initial fair value of the guarantee, as it was negotiated by the two parties using all relevant and available information at the time. If the guarantee is one component of a larger transaction involving multiple components, the assessment of fair value becomes more difficult.

In addition, in some cases, consideration for entering into a guarantee contract is not necessarily in the form of cash. Instead, nonmonetary consideration is provided. In these cases, the fair value of the nonmonetary consideration received or receivable must be determined. See Chapter 7 for more on nonmonetary transactions.

ASC 460 does not prescribe any particular methods for measuring this liability subsequent to the initial measurement. Generally, a liability should remain for the duration of the guarantee, which may span several years. Three common approaches to subsequent measurement of a guarantee have emerged:

1. Retaining the liability at its original measurement until the guarantee has expired or is otherwise settled
2. Utilizing an amortization approach to systematically reduce the liability over the term of the guarantee
3. Assessing the fair value of the guarantee at the end of each fiscal year and making appropriate adjustments to the liability each year

As the liability is decreased over time, the reduction is offset by a corresponding credit to revenue of the guarantor, much like recognizing revenue that had previously been deferred.

If it becomes apparent that the guarantor may have to perform under the guarantee arrangement, the contingent liability associated with performance may then need to be recorded as a liability. The criteria for recording a liability for this contingency are covered in Chapter 9.

Recognition—IFRS

IAS 39 defines a financial guarantee contract as "a contract that requires the issuer to make specified payments to reimburse the holder for a loss it incurs because a specified debtor fails to make payment when due in accordance with the original or modified terms of a debt instrument." Financial guarantee contracts are to be initially recognized at fair value, which normally equals the consideration received in exchange for entering into the contract.

Subsequent to the initial recognition, the liability associated with financial guarantee contracts is to be measured at the greater of:

1. The amount initially recognized, less any accumulated amortization recognized to date
2. The amount that would be recognized under IAS 37

Amortization of the liability associated with a financial guarantee contract results in the recognition of revenue. Accordingly, it falls within the scope of IAS 18, *Revenue*, for purposes of determining an appropriate revenue recognition (amortization) method. Since IAS 18 states that revenue should be measured based on fair value, the amortization, and therefore the resulting balance of the liability, should be measured at fair value under this approach.

The second approach measures the liability as it would be measured under IAS 37, *Provisions, Contingent Liabilities and Contingent Assets*. IAS 37 measures liabilities associated with provisions based on the expected expenditures necessary to settle the provision. See Chapter 9 for details on IAS 37.

Based on the preceding, a typical liability would initially be established based on the consideration received, then reduced based on an appropriate method of amortization. Measuring the liability based on the principles of IAS 37 would likely be done only in cases in which it has become likely that the guarantor will have to perform and an estimate of the expected costs of settling the obligation can be made.

PENSION LIABILITIES

Some employee benefit plans are characterized as defined contribution plans, meaning that contributions to the plan are defined in the plan agreement.

Often, employers contribute a stated percentage (or a range of percentages) of eligible employees' salaries or match employee contributions up to a certain percentage. Other plans are categorized as defined benefit plans, meaning the benefit that an individual receives is clearly defined in the plan and is not necessarily tied to specific contributions. Defined contribution plans are the more common of the two. The most common defined benefit plans are certain health benefit plans and retirement plans in which retired employees receive a stated or determinable payment for the remainder of their lives.

Employee benefit plans are normally separate legal entities and many obtain their own financial statement audit. As such, the assets and liabilities of the plan normally are not also reported as assets and liabilities of the plan sponsors. However, plan sponsors are expected to make certain disclosures about their employee benefit plans.

In certain cases, however, the fair values of a plan's assets and liabilities can result in an asset or liability that must be recorded in the financial statements of the plan's sponsor, not merely a footnote disclosure. This can happen only with defined benefit plans.

The global financial crisis that began in 2008 had an impact on the financial statements of many sponsors of employee benefit plans. In some cases, the financial collapse left many retirement plans woefully underfunded. A report from the Mercer consulting firm indicated that a $60 billion surplus in U.S. corporate pension plans had turned into a $409 billion underfunded status as of the end of 2008. The values of some of these plans have recovered in whole or in part since then, while others remain underfunded.

Sources of U.S. GAAP and IFRS

An important fair value liability issue was introduced into U.S. GAAP with the implementation of SFAS 158, *Employers' Accounting for Defined Benefit Pension and Other Postretirement Plans—an amendment of FASB Statements No. 87, 88, 106, and 132(R)*. As its name suggests, SFAS 158 applies only to defined benefit plans, the most common being certain retirement and health plans. SFAS 158 was codified at ASC 715.

The IFRS guidance that corresponds to ASC 715 is found in IAS 19, *Employee Benefits*, although IAS 19 has broader application than the ASC 715 topic covered in this chapter.

Recognition and Measurement—U.S. GAAP

Under ASC 715, the sponsor of a single-employer defined benefit plan is required to recognize an asset or liability for the over- or underfunded nature of the plan. This is defined as the difference between the fair value of the plan's assets and the associated benefit obligation. In the case of an employer with multiple plans, an asset would result from the aggregation of all overfunded plans, while a liability would result from the aggregation of all underfunded plans, meaning both an asset and a liability could appear on the sponsor's financial statements.

The plan itself is generally a separate entity, which issues its own set of financial statements subject to audit by an independent auditor. The assets and liabilities of the plan are not also included in the financial statements of the plan sponsor. Only the potential over- or underfunded nature of the plan would be reported as an asset or liability of the sponsor.

The two financial reporting fraud risks here are rather straightforward. First, if the fair value of the plan's investments and other assets is overstated, then one of the following will also be present:

1. The asset reported in the plan sponsor's financial statements, representing the overfunded nature of the plan, will be overstated
2. The liability reported in the plan sponsor's financial statements, representing the underfunded nature of the plan, will be understated

Assessing whether a recognized asset is overstated or a recognized liability is understated is one thing. But, readers of the financial statements of the plan sponsor may not even notice the complete omission of a liability. Therefore, reading the financial statements carefully to determine whether a defined benefit plan exists is the first step in assessing the risk of liability omission.

The second financial reporting fraud risk pertains to the possibility of understating a plan's benefit obligation. Preparing or obtaining a faulty actuarial analysis of a plan's obligation, or making improper changes or conclusions from the analysis, is another method of overstating an asset or understating a liability in the financial statements of a plan sponsor.

A faulty actuarial analysis can result from any of the following:

- Incorrect assumptions and calculations used in an internally prepared analysis (e.g., incorrect determination of the present value of the defined benefit obligation at the end of the reporting period)
- Use of an external actuary who is not independent of the entity, and who intentionally undervalues a benefit obligation, then representing it as an independent analysis
- Making alterations to a properly prepared actuarial analysis
- Bribing an external valuation expert in order to obtain the desired (lower) measurement of a benefit obligation

- Providing false information to an external valuation expert in order to trick the expert into providing a lower measurement of a plan's benefit obligation

Auditors and investigators may be convinced that benefit obligation valuations, actuarial studies, and other reports that are used in measuring the over- or underfunded nature of an employee benefit plan are reliable simply because they appear to have come from outside experts. But these reports and studies must be tested regardless of whether they appear to have come from a reliable expert.

Recognition and Measurement—IFRS

The IFRS guidance that corresponds to ASC 715 is found in IAS 19, *Employee Benefits*. Like U.S. GAAP, IAS 19 requires that an entity that sponsors a defined benefit plan recognize a liability under certain circumstances. The liability would be equal to the present value of the defined benefit obligation at the end of the reporting period minus the fair value of plan assets, plus or minus certain other adjustments.

IAS 19 encourages, but does not require, an entity to involve a qualified actuary in the measurement of all material postemployment benefit obligations.

If the difference between the fair value of plan assets and present value of the plan obligations results in an asset, IFRS permits the recognition of an asset in the financial statements of the plan sponsor, just like U.S. GAAP. Accordingly, the fraud risks under IFRS are identical to those explained earlier under U.S. GAAP.

CONDITIONAL ASSET RETIREMENT OBLIGATIONS

Under ASC 410-20, a company must recognize the fair value of a liability for an asset retirement obligation in the period in which it is incurred if a reasonable estimate of fair value can be made. If a tangible long-lived asset with an existing asset retirement obligation is acquired, a liability for that obligation shall be recognized at the asset's acquisition date as if that obligation were incurred on that date.

The term *conditional asset retirement obligation* refers to a legal obligation to perform an asset retirement activity in which the timing and (or) method of settlement are conditional on a future event that may or may not be within the control of the entity. The obligation to perform the asset retirement activity is unconditional even though uncertainty exists about the timing and (or) method of settlement. Thus, the timing and (or) method of settlement may be conditional on a future event. Accordingly, an entity shall recognize a liability for the fair value of a conditional asset retirement obligation if the fair value of the liability can be reasonably estimated. An entity is required to recognize the fair value of a legal obligation to perform asset retirement activities when the obligation is incurred—generally upon acquisition, construction, or development, and (or) through the normal operation of the asset.

To apply these rules, an organization should identify all of its asset retirement obligations. If an organization has sufficient information to reasonably estimate the fair value of an asset retirement obligation, it must recognize a liability at the time the liability is incurred. An asset retirement obligation would be reasonably estimable if any of the following conditions are present:

- It is evident that the fair value of the obligation is embodied in the acquisition price of the asset
- An active market exists for the transfer of the obligation
- Sufficient information exists to apply an expected present value technique

If sufficient information is not available at the time the liability is incurred, a liability should be recognized initially in the period in which sufficient information becomes available to estimate its fair value. If the liability's fair value cannot be reasonably estimated, that fact and the reasons must be disclosed in the notes to the financial statements.

For amounts recognized upon the initial application of ASC 410-20, an organization must recognize the following items in its statement of financial position:

- A liability for any existing asset retirement obligation(s) adjusted for cumulative accretion to the date of adoption of ASC 410-20
- An asset retirement cost capitalized as an increase to the carrying amount of the associated long-lived asset(s)
- Accumulated depreciation on that capitalized cost

Amounts resulting from initial application of ASC 410-20 must be measured using current information (that is, as of the date of adoption of the

Interpretation), current assumptions, and current interest rates. The amount recognized as an asset retirement cost shall be measured as of the date the asset retirement obligation was incurred. Cumulative accretion and accumulated depreciation shall be recorded for the time period from the date the liability would have been recognized had the provisions of this Interpretation been in effect when the liability was incurred to the date of adoption.

PART FOUR

Other Financial Reporting Schemes

WHILE THE MAJORITY OF FRAUD SCHEMES are triggered by a desire to manipulate assets, revenues, liabilities, or expenses, there are a variety of other schemes, initiated in connection with other types of transactions. Those schemes are the subject of this part. Schemes covered in this part include:

1. Preparation of consolidated financial statements (i.e., improper inclusion or exclusion of other entities from the financial statements)
2. Business combinations (i.e., acquisitions of other companies)
3. Financial statement fraud perpetrated as a method of concealing asset misappropriations
4. Financial statement fraud perpetrated as a means of concealing illegal acts
5. Financial reporting fraud by not-for-profit organizations
6. Disclosure fraud

The third and fourth categories from this list also represent reminders that not all financial reporting frauds are motivated by an attempt to inflate a company's reported profits or financial condition.

CHAPTER ELEVEN

Consolidations and Business Combinations

FRAUDULENT REPORTING INVOLVING CONSOLIDATIONS

Many financial statements include the accounts of not just one company, but of several companies. When the accounts of multiple entities are included in a single set of financial statements, the financial statements are referred to as consolidated financial statements. The purpose of preparing consolidated financial statements is to present the results of operations and the financial position of a parent entity and its subsidiaries as if the group were a single entity with multiple branches or divisions.

The determination of which entities comprise the consolidated reporting entity, then, becomes a matter involving interpretation of accounting standards. As a result, the risk of financial reporting fraud exists in two basic forms:

1. Including entities in the consolidated financial statements that do not meet the criteria for consolidation (e.g., improperly including the accounts of a profitable and financially stable entity)
2. Excluding entities from a consolidation that should be included (e.g., improperly omitting the accounts of an unprofitable or financially unstable affiliate)

Consolidation Accounting Principles

Consolidation is addressed in U.S. GAAP at ASC 810. For IFRS, new rules impacting consolidations were issued in May 2011:

1. IFRS 10, *Consolidated Financial Statements*
2. IFRS 11, *Joint Arrangements*
3. IFRS 12, *Disclosure of Interests in Other Entities*
4. IAS 27(R), *Separate Financial Statements*
5. IAS 28(R), *Investments in Associates and Joint Ventures*

IFRS 10 and 11 replace guidance previously found in IAS 27, *Consolidated and Separate Financial Statements*, and SIC-12, *Consolidation—Special Purpose Entities*. IFRS 12 replaces disclosure guidance found in IAS 28, *Investments in Associates*. IFRS 10, 11, and 12, and the revised versions of IAS 27 and IAS 28, are effective beginning January 1, 2013. Prior to that date, the earlier standards apply.

A detailed analysis of the U.S. GAAP and IFRS rules pertaining to consolidations is beyond the scope of this book. The rules are complex and extensive, not to mention the fact that two sets of IFRS rules must be considered, depending on the year of the financial statements under consideration. However, some high-level points and comparisons can be made that will be sufficient for purposes of discussing how financial statement fraud could occur.

U.S. GAAP

U.S. GAAP utilizes a two-tiered approach to consolidations. One tier focuses on voting rights and is referred to as the voting interest model. The second focuses on a qualitative analysis of power over significant activities and exposure to potentially significant losses or benefits. This is referred to as the variable interest model.

The starting point in assessing whether consolidation is required under U.S. GAAP is to determine whether the entity involved is a variable interest entity (VIE). The reporting entity that consolidates a VIE is referred to as the primary beneficiary of that entity.

A reporting entity with a variable interest in a VIE should assess whether it has a controlling financial interest in the VIE and is, therefore, the VIE's primary beneficiary. This should include an assessment of each of the following:

1. The characteristics of the reporting entity's variable interest or interests and other involvements (including involvement of related parties and de facto agents)

2. The involvement of other variable interest holders
3. The variable interest entity's purpose and design, including the risks that the variable interest entity was designed to create and pass through to its variable interest holders

A reporting entity is deemed to have a controlling financial interest in a variable interest entity if it has both of the following characteristics:

1. The power to direct the activities of a variable interest entity that most significantly affect its economic performance
2. The obligation to absorb potentially significant losses of the variable interest entity or the right to receive potentially significant benefits from the variable interest entity

Only one entity, if any, is expected to be identified as the primary beneficiary of a variable interest entity and, therefore, consolidate the accounts of the VIE into its own financial statements.

If the entity under consideration is not a VIE, it should be evaluated for consolidation using the voting interest model. Under this model, actual voting rights are the only consideration. Control can be either direct or indirect (i.e., through another entity). If greater than 50 percent control exists, consolidation is required. Exceptions from the requirement to consolidate in cases involving greater than 50 percent control are provided for situations like legal reorganizations and bankruptcy.

Control may also exist in situations involving less than 50 percent ownership, but only when a contractual relationship creates what is referred to as effective control. All of the following requirements must be met to establish effective control over an entity (and, therefore, subject the entity to consolidation) through a contractual arrangement:

1. The contractual term between the parties must be for the remaining life of the controlled entity or a period of at least 10 years
2. The contract is not terminable by the controlled entity, except for gross negligence, fraud, other illegal acts, or bankruptcy of the controlling entity
3. The controlling party has exclusive authority of all decision making in ongoing major or central operations
4. The controlling party has exclusive authority for establishing compensation levels and hiring and firing of key personnel

5. The controlling party has a significant financial interest in the other party that it may transfer without limitation
6. The controlling party has the right to receive income, both ongoing and as proceeds from the sale of its interest, in an amount that fluctuates based on the performance of the operations of the controlled entity and change in its fair value

U.S. GAAP also provides for special rules when considering limited partnerships that are not VIEs. In these cases, a general partner is presumed to have control, regardless of the general partner's interest in the profits or losses of the partnership. This presumption can be overcome only if the limited partners possess substantive rights to remove the general partner without cause or to liquidate the partnership.

IFRS

Unlike U.S. GAAP, the IFRS approach to determining whether consolidation is appropriate does not include a variable interest entity step as its first step. Instead, IFRS goes straight to the control issue. Control is presumed to exist when an entity owns, directly or indirectly, more than 50 percent of another entity's voting power. Control may also exist at 50 percent or less if certain conditions are present, as described in IAS 27. These include the power over half the voting rights via an agreement with investors, power over financial and operating policies, power to appoint or remove a majority of the members of the governing board of directors (or comparable governing body), or the power to cast a majority of votes at meetings of the board of directors or similar governing body.

Where U.S. GAAP refers to variable interest entities, IFRS includes a discussion of special purpose entities (SPEs), defined as an entity created to accomplish a narrow and well-defined objective (e.g., a specific research and development project), which can be a corporation, trust, partnership, or unincorporated entity. SIC 12 requires consolidation when an SPE is controlled by another entity.

IFRS 10 introduces a new definition of control. Under this new concept, an entity controls another entity when it is exposed, or has rights, to variable returns from its involvement with the investee and has the ability to affect those returns through its power over the investee. Power is explained as the current ability to direct the activities that significantly influence returns, which must vary and be positive, negative, or both. This new approach aligns IFRS more closely with U.S. GAAP pertaining to VIEs, but differences between the two sets of rules continue to exist.

IFRS includes another concept that is not addressed in U.S. GAAP—the element of "de facto" control. De facto control exists when there is 50 percent or less control involving voting rights, and there is a lack of legal or contractual rights by which to control a majority of another entity's voting power or board of directors. By comparison, recall that "effective" control under U.S. GAAP exists in connection with contractual rights. IFRS 10 provides clarification regarding de facto control, stating that in assessing control, an investor should consider economic dependency, the size of its shareholding in comparison to other holdings, and voting patterns at shareholder meetings.

In other words, the existence of the de facto control consideration under IFRS provides for greater use of judgment in making consolidation decisions than that under U.S. GAAP.

IFRS goes yet one step further than U.S. GAAP in providing for opportunities for consolidation. Unlike U.S. GAAP, IFRS specifically requires that the issue of potential voting rights (e.g., exercisable or convertible financial instruments) be considered in assessing control. Prior to IFRS those rights need not even be currently exercisable. With the implementation of IFRS, potential voting rights must be considered only if they are currently exercisable.

Cases

Similar to some of the revenue-based and other schemes explained in this book, improper application of the consolidation rules can involve:

1. Noncompliance with accounting standards in relation to whether an entity should be consolidated
2. Timing differences involving consolidation-triggering transactions

In this section, an example of each type of scheme will be explained, starting with the Royal Ahold case to illustrate the first type. The Chancellor Corporation case will be used as example of a timing difference scheme.

Royal Ahold

An example of improper application of the accounting standards governing consolidations is the case of Koninklijke Ahold N.V. ("Royal Ahold"), a publicly held international supermarket operator organized in the Netherlands. Royal Ahold's history dates to 1887 with the founding of the Albert Heijn grocery store. The name "Ahold" was adopted in 1973 and stands for Albert Heijn Holdings. In addition to the fraudulent recognition of promotional allowances, Royal Ahold was charged with improperly consolidating several joint ventures, the use of which became a significant part of the company's growth strategy beginning in the 1990s. The charges came from the SEC, since Royal Ahold securities were also registered in the United States.

The improperly consolidated joint ventures included the following:

1. Jerónimo Martins Retail, a Portuguese company in which Royal Ahold acquired a 49 percent interest. The remaining 51 percent, however, was owned by one unrelated Portuguese entity that also appointed four of the joint venture's seven-person board of directors. Clearly, Royal Ahold did not control this joint venture, yet it was improperly consolidated into its financial statements beginning in 1992.
2. Bompreço S.A., a Brazilian company in which Royal Ahold acquired 50 percent of the voting shares. The remaining 50 percent was owned by an unrelated Brazilian entity and the two owners held an equal number of seats on the joint venture's board of directors. Royal Ahold began improperly consolidating Bompreço into its financial statements beginning in 1996, yet it wasn't until 2000 that Royal Ahold acquired the remaining 50 percent, leaving it fully in control and eligible for consolidation.
3. Disco Ahold International Holdings, a company organized under the laws of the Netherlands Antilles, and in which Royal Ahold acquired a 50 percent interest. The remaining 50 percent was owned by an unrelated entity organized in the Cayman Islands. The shareholders' agreement provided for equal voting rights and the same number of seats on the board of directors and all major decisions required a unanimous vote. Royal Ahold began improperly consolidating this entity into its financial statements beginning in 1998.
4. Paiz Ahold, another company organized under the laws of the Netherlands Antilles, in which Royal Ahold owned 50 percent of the shares. The other 50 percent was held by a company based in the Bahamas. The shareholders' agreement provided for each shareholder to have equal numbers of votes on the board of directors and required board decisions to be decided by majority vote, except for major decisions, which required unanimous approval. Royal Ahold began improperly consolidating Paiz Ahold into its financial statements beginning in 2000.
5. ICA Group, an enterprise in which Royal Ahold acquired a 50 percent stake. Of the remaining shares, 30 percent were held by a Swedish company and

> 20 percent were held by a Norwegian company. In spite of the fact that Royal Ahold held the largest, if not the majority, interest, the shareholders agreement provided that the other two partners would act jointly as one 50 percent partner, in essence creating a 50-50 partnership. Royal Ahold began improperly consolidating ICA Group into its financial statements beginning in 2000.

Beginning in 1998 and continuing into 2000, Royal Ahold's auditor, Deloitte Netherlands, questioned the consolidations of these five entities, stating that consolidating these joint ventures violated applicable accounting principles. Royal Ahold's financial statements were prepared using Dutch GAAP, but, as an SEC registrant, included a reconciliation to U.S. GAAP. Royal Ahold's response to the auditor's objection to consolidation was that it would modify the joint venture agreements to make consolidation acceptable. Ahold then provided the auditors with letters signed by both Ahold and the joint venture partners stating that Ahold controlled the joint ventures, supporting the position that consolidation was appropriate. However, undisclosed to the auditors, shortly after these letters were prepared, Ahold and the joint venture partners executed "rescinding letters," effectively secret side agreements that rescinded Ahold's control over the joint ventures.

Chancellor Corporation

In August 1998, Chancellor entered into a letter of intent to acquire a subsidiary, MRB, Inc. The transaction consummating the acquisition closed on January 29, 1999. However, desperate to show strong 1998 results, Chancellor included MRB's financial results in its financial statements for December 31, 1998, despite only having signed the letter of intent by that date. As of December 31, 1998, Chancellor did not have sufficient control of MRB to warrant consolidation.

To convince their auditors that Chancellor did, in fact, have control in August 1998, a phony management agreement was prepared in February 1999 and backdated to August 1, 1998. Chancellor claimed this agreement gave them sufficient control over MRB to support consolidation. After the auditors said the agreement did not give Chancellor control sufficient for consolidation, a phony "First Amendment," falsely dated August 17, 1998, was prepared. This amendment purportedly gave Chancellor control over MRB's daily operations, such that, starting in August 1998, all significant decisions of MRB required the approval of Chancellor. The two controlling shareholders of MRB never saw or approved the amendment, and the amendment's terms were inconsistent with the actual relations between the two companies between August 1998 and the January 1999 closing.

Even the phony amendment, however, failed to convince the auditors that MRB qualified for consolidation as of August 1998. So, Chancellor's management did what dishonest managers sometimes do—they fired the auditor!

Chancellor's management was able to convince a new audit firm that MRB qualified for consolidation by providing them with the same backdated management agreement and phony amendment, along with some additional fabricated documents supposedly instructing MRB officers to take certain actions on various business matters.

As a result of this timing difference scheme, Chancellor reported $29.6 million in revenue for the year ended December 31, 1998, when its actual revenue, excluding MRB, was only $10.7 million. Chancellor's actual assets of $8.2 million as of December 31, 1998, were inflated to $29.6 million as a result of this scheme.

In a separate but related matter, $3.3 million of the asset overstatement was caused by the capitalization of a consulting fee payable to Vestex Capital Corporation for services purportedly rendered in connection with Chancellor's acquisition of MRB. However, Vestex was wholly owned by Chancellor's CEO and there was no apparent basis for these fees. The consulting agreement and other supporting documentation, including a promissory note, were phony documents fabricated by Chancellor management.

BUSINESS COMBINATIONS

When one business merges with or acquires another business, the resulting accounting treatment is ripe for financial statement fraud. All of the acquired assets and assumed liabilities must be recorded on the books of the acquirer. This poses a number of accounting challenges and requires significant use of judgment and estimation. And anytime this much judgment and estimation is involved, the risk of fraud escalates.

U.S. GAAP for business combinations is covered as ASC 805. The international standard that addresses business combinations is IFRS 3, *Business Combinations*.

Under U.S. GAAP, a business combination is a transaction or other event in which an entity (the acquirer) acquires the net assets of a business, or acquires equity interests in one or more entities that are businesses and those equity interests represent a controlling financial interest. A business can also be controlled by contract alone.

The IFRS definition is similar, noting that a business combination involves an entity obtaining control of one or more businesses. IFRS 3 defines control as the power to govern the financial and operating policies of an entity so as to obtain benefits from its activities.

A business combination, then, normally results in the acquisition of assets and the assumption of liabilities. If assets acquired do not constitute a business, their acquisition should be accounted for as an asset acquisition and not a business combination.

The methods used to acquire a business can vary, from the typical transfer of cash, to transferring other types of assets, issuing stock, assuming or incurring liabilities, or some combination of multiple types of consideration.

From a legal and tax standpoint, there are also many different ways to handle an acquisition, for example:

- One business becomes a wholly owned subsidiary of another
- The assets of one business are transferred to, and become assets of, another business
- A new entity is created, into which the assets of both businesses are transferred (this technique is also sometimes called a roll-up transaction)

Normally, determining which entity is the acquirer and which is acquired is a simple step. But, sometimes it is not entirely clear, especially when several entities are involved. Both U.S. GAAP and IFRS provide guidance on determining which entity is the acquirer and which is an acquiree in situations in which it is not clear. Considerations in making this determination include the following:

- Relative voting rights in the combined entity after the transaction
- Composition of the governing body of the combined entity (or the ability to appoint or remove members of the governing body)
- Composition of senior management of the combined entity
- The power to control financial and operating policies of the combined entity

Both U.S. GAAP and IFRS prohibit the pooling-of-interests method of accounting for business combinations. Under the pooling-of-interests method, assets acquired in a combination would generally be recorded on the books of the acquirer at the same book value that they had on the acquired entity's books.

Instead, U.S. GAAP and IFRS both require that an entity that acquires the assets and liabilities of another entity in a business combination allocate the purchase price to the identifiable assets acquired and liabilities assumed based on the fair value of each underlying asset and liability. This is referred to as the acquisition (or purchase) method of accounting.

A 2008 complaint filed by the SEC charges The BISYS Group, Inc., a provider of financial products and support services, with a variety of financial reporting improprieties, including two separate but related instances of improper business combination accounting.

In July 2000, BISYS acquired Ascensus, a privately held insurance company. As part of its due diligence leading up to the consummation of the acquisition, BISYS became aware that Ascensus had inadvertently understated its accounts receivable by more than $4 million. The missing receivables pertained to bonus commission revenue for 1999 and 2000, based on Ascensus's achievement of certain insurance sales targets.

BISYS failed to include the $4 million receivable as an asset on the balance sheet of Ascensus at the date of the acquisition. Instead, BISYS improperly recorded these amounts as its own revenue when they were collected subsequent to the acquisition.

The second act of improper accounting for the acquisition of Ascensus took place almost a year after the acquisition. In June 2001, BISYS became aware that a company called Quotesmith claimed it was owed monies by Ascensus. BISYS investigated the claim over the next six months and negotiated a settlement whereby it paid Quotesmith $551,000. BISYS initially recorded this amount as an expense. In fact, $462,000 of the $551,000 pertained to policies placed after the Ascensus acquisition and were appropriately recorded as an expense of BISYS.

However, in January 2002, in an effort to meet earnings targets, BISYS recorded a journal entry improperly reclassifying the entire $551,000 from expense to goodwill associated with the Ascensus acquisition. Then, in a further desperate attempt to improve its income statement, BISYS reduced its expenses by another $256,000, with a corresponding increase to goodwill, for expenses paid to Quotesmith by Ascensus prior to the acquisition by BISYS, an entry for which there was absolutely no justification. In total, BISYS fraudulently inflated goodwill by $718,000 through this series of entries.

The acquirer in a business combination should take the following steps to properly account for the transaction:

1. Identify all assets acquired in the transaction, recognizing that some acquired assets, especially intangible assets, may not be represented as

assets on the books of the acquired business (recall from Chapter 6 that often the developer of an intangible asset is not permitted to capitalize the costs associated with developing an intangible asset, even though the asset may have value to outside parties and, indeed, helps the developer of the asset to generate revenue).
2. Identify all liabilities assumed in the transaction
3. Determine the acquisition date, which is the date that the acquiring entity obtains control over the acquiree (this is an important date, since the next step, involving fair value accounting, is to be performed as of the acquisition date)
4. Determine the fair value of each identified asset acquired and liability assumed on the acquisition date
5. Determine the purchase price associated with the transaction, which may involve items other than cash
6. Determine the extent of any goodwill resulting from the transaction, which is simply the excess of the purchase price over the net fair value of assets acquired minus the liabilities assumed in the transaction
7. Measure and recognize any noncontrolling interest in the acquiree (this step applies in cases in which an acquirer acquires a less than 100 percent interest in another entity)

Although the preceding guidance is based on U.S. GAAP, IFRS 3 identifies and describes virtually the same steps.

Occasionally, step 6 results in the identification of bargain purchase—one in which the purchase price is less than the net fair value of the assets acquired and liabilities assumed. Generally, when this happens, the acquirer should recognize a gain on the acquisition date. This gain is recognized in earnings (profit or loss).

The primary fraud risks in the allocation of the purchase price in a business combination are as follows:

1. Allocating part of the purchase price to intangible assets that do not qualify for recognition—explained further at the end of this chapter
2. Assigning too much of the purchase price to assets that are not subject to depreciation or amortization, such as:
   a. Land
   b. Intangible assets with indefinite lives (see Chapter 7)
3. Overallocating the purchase price to assets with longer useful lives than those with shorter useful lives or that will be consumed in the near term.

This enables the entity to retain a greater percentage of the purchase price as assets on the financial statements for longer periods of time. For example, overallocation of the purchase price to a building with a useful life of 40 years and underallocating to equipment with useful lives of 5 to 7 years results in stretching out the book value of assets for longer periods of time
4. Failing to recognize liabilities that were assumed in connection with a business combination
5. Intentionally failing to recognize accounts receivable of the acquiree at the acquisition date in order to improperly recognize revenue when those amounts are subsequently collected, a form of timing scheme (see the BISYS case described earlier for an example of this)
6. Improper capitalization of acquisition costs

Regarding the final item from this list, under U.S. GAAP and IFRS, most acquisition costs should be expensed as incurred. Acquisition costs include external costs such as fees for legal, accounting, valuation, and other professional services, as well as finder's fees and other advisory fees. Internal acquisition costs, such as labor and benefits associated with employees involved in the acquisition, should also be expensed as incurred.

The only exception from the requirement of expensing acquisition costs pertains to the cost of registering and issuing equity or debt securities to effect a business combination. Costs associated with registering equity securities are to be charged against paid-in-capital, while costs involved with registering debt securities should generally be deferred and amortized.

An example of item 2b from the preceding list occurred in the case of JBI, Inc. Readers may remember JBI from Chapter 7 in connection with a material asset overstatement scheme. Another JBI misstatement involved its allocation of the purchase prices paid in connection with two acquisitions. JBI acquired a company called Javaco in August 2009 and another company, Pak-It, in September 2009. JBI paid $2.65 million for Javaco and $4,615,000 for Pak-It. In recording the acquired assets and assumed liabilities of Javaco and Pak-It for its December 31, 2009 financial statements, JBI initially allocated $5,179,249 to goodwill and just $10,014 to other intangible assets. Goodwill, as noted earlier, is not subject to amortization but rather to annual impairment testing. The other intangible assets acquired by JBI were mostly subject to amortization.

JBI subsequently restated its 2009 financial statements, shifting more than $2 million from goodwill to other (amortizable) intangible assets. Separately, other intangible assets were further increased in the restatement, with a corresponding offset to a deferred income tax liability account. None of these changes in the allocation of purchase prices was mentioned in the SEC's complaint, which focused on the asset inflation scheme referred to earlier. However, they were included as part of the same restatement of JBI's 2009 financial statements.

Testing the allocation of the purchase price in a business combination is a complex process that may require the use of outside experts with a variety of valuation specialties, from real estate appraisers to industry experts and intellectual property specialists.

In a business combination, the acquirer should recognize separately from goodwill any identifiable intangible assets that have been acquired. The key word in the preceding sentence is identifiable. An intangible asset is identifiable if it has either of the following characteristics:

1. It is separable, meaning it is capable of being separated from the entity and sold, transferred, licensed, rented, or exchanged (regardless of whether the acquiring entity actually intends to do so)
2. It arises from contractual or other legal rights, regardless of whether those rights are transferable or separable from the entity or from other rights and obligations

In many cases, the identification of intangible assets is obvious, since they were an integral part of the negotiations leading up to the agreement on a purchase price. But in other cases, intangible assets are not separately considered in the negotiation phase, with the focus instead being on the acquired entity taken as a whole. In these cases, identification of intangible assets can become much more complicated and subject to manipulation.

CHAPTER TWELVE

Financial Reporting Fraud as a Concealment Tool

UP TO THIS POINT, all of the financial statement fraud schemes explained have been the primary tool in the perpetration of a fraud. But in some cases, the falsification of the financial statements is secondary to the primary fraud. In these cases, the perpetration of financial statement fraud is done in order to conceal some other fraud or illegal act.

In this chapter, the two most common applications of financial statement fraud as a concealment weapon are explained:

1. As a method of concealing asset misappropriations
2. As a method of concealing illegal acts

FINANCIAL STATEMENT FRAUD TO CONCEAL ASSET MISAPPROPRIATIONS

One reason for perpetrating financial statement fraud is the concealment of asset misappropriations. Asset misappropriations are more likely to be carried out by higher-level individuals, such as senior finance personnel or other senior managers, who may be in a position to disguise their theft in the accounting records.

Let's examine two cases to illustrate this fraud risk.

The first case involves UCI Medical Affiliates, Inc. (UCI). Between 2003 and 2008, UCI's former executive vice president and CFO embezzled $2.97 million, according to a 2009 action filed by the SEC. He carried out the asset misappropriation primarily using three methods:

1. Charging personal purchases on UCI's corporate credit card, followed by arranging for UCI to pay the credit card statement by check
2. Preparing false expense reports and submitting them for reimbursement, resulting in payment to himself since nobody other than the accounts payable supervisor reviewed these reports
3. Submitting unsupported check requests for personal credit card accounts and nonbusiness expenditures, such as construction work on his personal residence

The fraudulent financial reporting took place in his attempts to conceal these expenditures. In many instances, the expenditures were capitalized as fixed assets. The perpetrator would sometimes alter invoices from contractors performing work on his personal residence to make it appear the work was being performed on UCI's facilities. In addition, false descriptions were often provided on check request forms. The result was an overstatement of UCI's earnings for the years 2003 through 2007.

The scheme came to light in December 2008 when UCI's outside auditor raised questions about certain charitable contributions paid by UCI on behalf of the perpetrator. UCI's audit committee requested that the auditor examine all company disbursements to UCI's top three officers. This led to the discovery of the asset misappropriation.

No recent case illustrates the use of financial statement fraud to conceal an asset misappropriation better than Koss Corporation, a Wisconsin-based manufacturer and seller of stereo headphones. From 2005 to 2009, the principal accounting officer and vice president of finance, Sujata Sachdeva, stole more than $30 million from Koss. As large as this amount is, even more amazing is how material this theft was to Koss. For example, during fiscal year 2009, when $8.5 million was embezzled, Koss reported total sales of $41.7 million. More than 20 percent of its total reported sales stolen!

The methods used to steal from Koss were relatively simple. More than $15 million was in the form of unauthorized cashier's checks. Another $16 million in fraudulent wire transfers were made, all of which were to pay various personal credit card bills and other purchases made by Sachdeva. In October 2009 alone, evidencing the growing addiction to stealing from Koss, 17 wire transfers totaling more than $1.5 million were made on Sachdeva's personal credit card.

Sachdeva, with the assistance of the senior accountant, Julie Mulvaney, circumvented Koss's internal controls in the process. None of the cashier's checks or wire transfers were approved by Michael J. Koss, the CEO, or Koss's vice president of operations, as required by company policy (which required all disbursements over $5,000 to be approved by the CEO).

The massive embezzlement was hidden from the CEO and others with a series of journal entries. Once unraveled, the credits to (reductions in) cash associated with the unauthorized cashier's checks and wire transfers were offset by debits in several areas:

1. Sales (reducing net sales)
2. Cost of sales (overstating cost of sales)
3. Accounts receivable (inflating this asset)
4. Administrative expenses (overstating operating expenses)

In addition, cash was overstated due to some of the embezzled funds not being recorded anywhere in the accounting records. As a result, the cash accounts did not reconcile. When Koss restated its 2008 and 2009 financial statements after discovering the embezzlement, the net effect of the embezzlement was reported as operating expenses.

The Koss case represents a failure in internal controls in so many ways. Among the weaknesses in internal controls cited by the SEC in its civil complaint against Koss and its CEO were the following:

- The lack of documentation for journal entries (weaknesses over journal entries enabled Sachdeva and Mulvaney to conceal the fraud)
- Lack of segregation of duties over disbursements and the bank reconciliation process (all controlled by Sachdeva and Mulvaney)
- Failure to perform monthly bank reconciliations
- No review of wire transfers was required in order for a wire to be executed
- No after-the-fact review of journal entries
- A very cursory review of financial information by the CEO (e.g., no review of the trial balance, journal entries, or schedules)

- Very limited monthly analytical procedures, insufficient to detect unusual relationships or trends (such as the shrinking gross margin caused by reducing sales and increasing cost of sales to conceal the asset misappropriation)
- A very old and weak accounting system, leaving little to no audit trail, enabling post-closing entries, and other weaknesses
- Failure to change access passwords on a regular basis, along with several other information technology control deficiencies

FINANCIAL STATEMENT FRAUD TO CONCEAL ILLEGAL ACTS

Another potential incentive to engage in financial reporting fraud involves the recording of false transactions in the accounting records to cover up other illegal acts. The most likely of these acts is the payment of bribes. There are a number of laws within the United States, as well as in other countries, that make the payment of certain bribes illegal. In addition, the Foreign Corrupt Practices Act (FCPA) prohibits the payment of bribes by U.S. companies (including its non-U.S. subsidiaries, agents, and employees) to public employees of foreign countries.

When the payment of bribes is an ongoing practice that is known and tolerated by senior management, there is often an organized scheme to intentionally misclassify these payments as some other form of ordinary business expense. Whether the payments are classified and reported as "bribes" or as some other type of expense makes no difference to the net profit or loss of a company. But, misrepresenting the nature (classification) of an expense nonetheless is a form of financial statement fraud as the readers of those statements are being deceived regarding the nature of a company's expenses.

Two cases, one involving FCPA and the other involving other bribes, illustrate this fraud risk.

The first case involves bribes paid within the United States. In June 2012, the SEC charged FalconStor Software, Inc. with a variety of violations pertaining to the payment of bribes to obtain business with a subsidiary of J.P. Morgan Chase & Co. The bribes were paid between October 2007 and July 2010 at the direction of FalconStor's co-founder and then-CEO, president, and chairman, who is now deceased. The bribes evidently worked, as FalconStor secured a large multi-million dollar contract shortly after the payments began.

The bribes totaled $430,000 and consisted of FalconStor stock options and restricted stock, direct cash payments, gift cards, payment of golf club fees, and entertainment, including gambling trips. Among the SEC's charges was the allegation that FalconStor hid the bribes on its books by intentionally misclassifying the payments, thereby misleading investors. FalconStor agreed to pay a $2.9 million civil penalty to settle the case.

The second case involves bribes paid outside the U.S. In March 2012, the SEC charged Biomet, Inc. with FCPA violations in connection with Biomet's subsidiaries and agents in Argentina, Brazil, and China. Biomet agreed to pay $22 million to settle the charges. According to the SEC complaint, Biomet and four subsidiaries paid bribes from 2000 to 2008 to publicly employed doctors in order to win business for the sale of products used by orthopedic surgeons.

According to the complaint, Biomet's Argentine subsidiary paid kickbacks of 15 to 20 percent of each sale, creating fraudulent invoices to make the payments appear to be consulting fees or commissions, which is how the payments were then recorded and classified in the accounting records. Executives and internal auditors were aware of the practice, but failed to stop it.

A similar practice was carried out in Brazil, where kickbacks of 10 to 20 percent were the norm. Shockingly, disguising these payments on the books was openly discussed among employees, executives, and even the internal auditors. For example, the following internal memorandum regarding a limited audit was cited by the SEC:

> Brazilian Distributor makes payments to surgeons that may be considered as a kickback. These payments are made in cash that allows the surgeon to receive income tax free. . . . The accounting entry is to increase a prepaid expense account. In the consolidated financials sent to Biomet, these payments were reclassified to expense in the income statement.

Finally, two Chinese subsidiaries sold medical devices through a distributor in China who provided publicly employed doctors with money and travel in exchange for their purchases of Biomet products. This part of the complaint provides a good illustration of the fact that actions of agents (the unrelated Chinese distributor) will be attributed to the principal (Biomet's two Chinese subsidiaries) when bribes or kickbacks are paid on behalf of a principal.

CHAPTER THIRTEEN

Financial Statement Fraud by Not-for-Profit Organizations

SO FAR, ALL OF THE SCHEMES DESCRIBED have involved commercial businesses, all of which have a motive of generating a profit. But there is another type of entity that operates quite differently, where making a profit is not the primary goal. There are more than 1 million not-for-profit organizations in the United States, and many more throughout the world.

Not-for-profit organizations do not have owners. As a result, their operating goals and objectives differ from those of a commercial business. Instead of maximizing profits, the goal of a not-for-profit organization, particularly a charitable organization, is to achieve a mission that forms the basis for an exemption from income taxes. Examples of charitable missions include social welfare, scientific and medical, religious, healthcare, and many others. Not-for-profit organizations with noncharitable missions include trade and professional associations, chambers of commerce, labor unions, and numerous other categories.

With a different goal, one that cannot be measured in terms of net profits, the financial reporting fraud risks differ as well. This is especially true when the most important financial measures revolve around demonstrating that a significant portion of an organization's available funds are devoted to its mission (which also means demonstrating that as little as possible is devoted to administrative costs and fund-raising expenses).

In connection with this objective, one of the primary ratios that is monitored for charitable organizations is its program expense ratio. This ratio is calculated as follows:

Program expenses/Total expenses

Program expenses represent the total costs spent in delivering the goods and services that form the basis for a charity's exemption from taxes. Included are direct costs as well as a reasonable allocation of the indirect costs of an organization. The two primary categories of costs that are excluded from program costs are fund-raising costs (the costs incurred in bringing charitable contributions into an organization) and administrative costs (the core costs that are necessary to running the organization, but which do not result in the delivery of programs, such as the costs of an accounting department). As with program expenses, reported fund-raising and administrative costs should include both direct and allocated indirect costs.

The program expense ratio is used by many funding sources in evaluating charities. Grantors sometimes impose minimum program expense ratios as a qualification for funding. In addition, watchdog groups use this ratio in evaluating and assigning grades to charities and some publications even rank charitable organizations based on program expense ratios.

Although the calculation of a program expense ratio is simple, there are numerous complicated methods of intentionally distorting this important measure. Five of the most common are:

1. Inflating the value of non-cash (in-kind) contributions received that are used in delivering charitable programs
2. Improperly reporting contributions raised by an organization on behalf of, or that are earmarked for, another charity
3. Netting the results of special fund-raising events
4. Improperly allocating the costs associated with activities that jointly accomplish a program as well as a fund-raising purpose simultaneously
5. Intentional misclassification of expenses incurred for nonprogrammatic purposes as program expenses

Each of these methods results in an artificial inflation of a charity's program expense ratio.

Instead of shareholders, lenders, and investment managers being deceived by fraudulent financial statements, the victims are different when a charity is involved. The usual victims are donors and grant-making institutions, including corporate foundations. These individuals and entities are victims because they perceive a charity to be more efficient (as measured by its program expense ratio) than it really is. This increases the likelihood of them making a gift or grant to the charity.

INFLATING THE VALUE OF NON-CASH CONTRIBUTIONS

Many charities receive non-cash gifts as their primary form of support. Items such as clothing, food, furniture, supplies, equipment, automobiles, and other assets are donated to charities every day. In some cases, a charity may simply convert these items into cash by selling them shortly after receiving the contribution. In other cases, the donated articles are used in furthering the charity's mission. This may be the case when a charity distributes donated articles to needy families or somehow utilizes the donated items in carrying out a charitable endeavor (e.g., using donated medical supplies to provide medical care).

When donated articles are distributed or used in furthering a charity's mission, the net effect is that the fair value of the donated items is reported both as income and as program expenses. As a result, the program expense ratio increases as equal amounts are added to both the numerator and denominator of the fraction. An unscrupulous manager of a charity may wish to inflate the fair values of donated items so that the charity is able to report a greater portion of its overall expenditures as program-related.

Secondarily, inflating the values of non-cash contributions received simply allows an organization to appear larger than it really is. This can result in donors feeling that a charity is more financially stable and more involved in doing charitable works than it actually is.

IMPROPERLY REPORTING CONTRIBUTIONS RAISED FOR OTHERS

This technique is limited to organizations that receive contributions that have been designated for another charity. Under ASC 958-605, if a charity receives a contribution with the explicit understanding that the gift must be transferred to another entity, the amount must be recorded as a liability rather than as contribution income. Therefore, when the gift is subsequently transferred to the designated party, the liability is reduced rather than reported as a program expense.

The logic behind this accounting treatment is simple. When an organization accepts this type of earmarked gift, it has essentially entered into an agreement with a donor to pass that gift on to a specific party. As a result, even though the recipient organization may have incurred costs in the execution of the transaction, it has not earned any income (somewhat analogous to a bank accepting deposits as a trustee for the benefit of named beneficiary). And when the recipient organization transfers the funds to the named beneficiary, it is simply forwarding the donor's funds, not spending its own.

This scenario most commonly occurs with charitable organizations that raise funds on behalf of others, engaging in all of the fund-raising activities, collecting donations, tracking contributions by designated beneficiary, and then remitting the amounts to each beneficiary. Only in cases in which the recipient organization is explicitly granted variance power (the power to alter the beneficiary) can the recipient record contribution income (and, later, program expense).

This situation can also occur if a donor requests that a recipient organization take a single gift and disburse it to multiple specifically named beneficiaries. The financial reporting fraud risk is that an organization acting in such an agency capacity may record the receipt and disbursement of these contributions as income and program expense, rather than as the increase in and relief of a liability. Improperly recording these transactions as income and program expenses has the same effect as the inflation scheme explained in the preceding section—the program expense ratio is inflated and overall the organization appears larger.

NETTING THE RESULTS OF FUND-RAISING EVENTS

Some charities incur substantial costs in connection with raising the contribution income that is so vital to their mission. Other organizations are fortunate in that they have an existing and loyal donor base or they benefit from the fund-raising activities of another organization. In addition, the operation of a charity that relies on thousands of small donations is very different from a charity that relies on a smaller pool of donors who make larger gifts. As a result, the effect of fund-raising costs on a charity's program expense ratio can vary quite a bit from one organization to another. For this reason, lumping all charities together and comparing their program expense ratios is inherently unfair.

To the extent that fund-raising is an ongoing activity, the costs incurred are normally reported as fund-raising costs in the statement of activities (the not-for-profit organization's counterpart to the income statement prepared by commercial businesses). However, when fund-raising costs are incurred in connection with special events, an opportunity for financial reporting fraud emerges. Special events used to raise funds for an organization come in many different forms, from benefit concerts and performances to silent auctions, sporting events, banquets, and many others.

If the results of these activities are reported at their gross amounts, in which income and expenses are reported separately, the effect is to lower the program expense ratio (although the net profits are available to be spent on programs), since the costs of the event are normally fund-raising and other non-program expenses (there can be some instances in which a fund-raising event also involves program expenses, but most events do not—see the discussion of joint activities in the next section). If, however, the special event is reported as a single net income amount, there is no effect at all on the program expense ratio. In fact, when the net proceeds are spent, only then is the program expense ratio affected. And if the net proceeds are spent on programs, the ratio is enhanced.

But the rules laid out in ASC 958-225 limit the instances in which special events can be recorded at their net amounts. Only "incidental" or "peripheral" transactions, as well as events that are largely beyond the control of the organization, may be recorded in this manner. All others must be reflected at gross—total income less total expenses.

ASC 958-225-45 notes that the frequency of events and the significance of the gross revenues and expenses distinguish major or central events from peripheral or incidental events. Events are considered to be ongoing major and central activities (and therefore need to be reported at their gross amounts) if they are normally part of an organization's strategy and it normally carries on such activities, or if the event's gross revenues or expenses are significant in relation to the organization's annual budget. Events are peripheral or incidental if they are not an integral part of an organization's usual activities or if their gross revenues or expenses are not significant in relation to the charity's annual budget.

IMPROPER ALLOCATION OF COSTS ASSOCIATED WITH JOINT ACTIVITIES

Certain activities of not-for-profit organizations accomplish multiple purposes simultaneously. Just like in a commercial business, an allocation of expenses must then be performed. When the two concurrent purposes involve a program and fund-raising, however, the risk of improper allocation takes on increased importance. The more that is allocated to programs, the less is allocated to fund-raising. The result is an improvement in the program expense ratio.

U.S. GAAP has very specific rules at ASC 958-720 to address this situation. These rules focus primarily on determining whether or not a programmatic purpose even exists in connection with an activity that includes fund-raising. If certain criteria (known as the purpose, audience, and content criteria) are not met, the entire activity, meaning all costs, direct and indirect, must be classified as fund-raising. This lowers the program expense ratio. However, if all three criteria are met, a reasonable allocation of costs between programs and fund-raising may be performed.

The purpose criterion is the most complex of the three criteria. First, the activity must include a purpose involving the accomplishment of a program or management and general function. For joint activities that purport to have a programmatic purpose, the activity must call for specific action by the audience that will help accomplish the organization's mission. Educating an audience about an organization's causes does not represent a call for specific action. A request for contributions does not meet this test either. To be a call for specific action, the activity must address specific steps that the audience is encouraged to take.

In addition to the requirement for a call for specific action, three other factors must be considered in determining whether the purpose criterion is met:

1. Compensation
2. Comparison with other activities of the entity
3. Other evidence

These factors *must be considered in the order described here.*

The first of these three factors pertains to compensation paid by an organization. The purpose criterion is automatically *failed* if a majority of compensation or fees for any party's performance of any component of a discrete joint activity varies based on contributions raised for that joint activity. If compensation is based on some other factor, but not to exceed a specified portion of contributions raised, compensation is not considered to be based on amounts raised, unless the stated maximum percentage is met. In addition, one of the examples in the standard indicates the importance of assessing compensation solely for the discrete joint activity under consideration. If an individual receives a bonus upon total annual contributions exceeding a specified amount, the compensation test is not failed since compensation does not vary based on contributions raised for a discrete joint activity.

The compensation test is a negative test, meaning that failing it results in failing the purpose criterion. Not failing the compensation test, however, does not equate to passing the purpose criterion. Rather, the second factor must then be considered.

The second factor in the purpose criterion involves a comparison of the joint activity with other activities of the entity. Two different tests may be applied, depending upon whether the joint activity involves fund raising and program purposes or fund raising and management and general purposes:

1. **Program Purposes.** If the program content contains the call to specific action described earlier and a similar program component is conducted without the fund-raising component using the same medium and on a scale that is similar to or greater than the scale on which it is conducted with the fund raising, the purpose criterion is met. Factors to consider in determining the scale of an activity may include:
   a. Dollars spent,
   b. Size of audience, and
   c. Degree to which characteristics of the audience are similar.
2. **Management and General Purposes.** A call to specific action related to an entity's mission is not required. As long as a management and general activity that is similar to the management and general component of the joint activity is conducted without the fund-raising component using the same medium and on a scale that is similar to or greater than the scale on which it is conducted with the fund raising, the purpose criterion is met.

Unlike the compensation test, the activity comparison test is a positive test. Passing it results in meeting the purpose criterion. Not passing it, however, does not result in failing the purpose criterion. Instead, the third factor, which introduces other available evidence, must be considered.

If the compensation and activity comparison tests are not determinative of the purpose of a joint activity, other evidence must be considered. Examples of other evidence that may indicate whether a legitimate programmatic purpose exists include the degree to which the organization measures program results (as opposed to only measuring fundraising results), the qualifications and duties of the people performing the joint activities (e.g. program staff vs. fundraising personnel), minutes from board meetings, internal memoranda, and other indicators of what an organization's goals were in carrying out the activity.

The second criterion is the audience criterion. This rule includes a rebuttable presumption that the audience criterion is not met if the audience includes prior donors or is otherwise selected based on its ability or likelihood to contribute to the organization. However, this presumption can be overcome if the audience is also selected for any of the following reasons:

1. The audience's need to use or reasonable potential for use of the specific action called for by the program component of the activity,
2. The audience's ability to take specific action to assist the entity in meeting the goals of the program component of the activity, or
3. The entity is required to direct the management and general component of the joint activity to the particular audience or the audience has reasonable potential for use of the management and general component.

Audiences that simply have an interest in or affinity to a program do not meet the audience criterion.

The third and final criterion, the content criterion, is met if the joint activity supports program or management and general functions. For program functions, the content criterion is met if the joint activity calls for specific action by the recipient that will help accomplish the entity's mission. The action should benefit the recipient or society. If the need for and benefits of the action are not clearly evident, information describing the action and explaining the need for and benefits of the action should be provided.

For management and general functions, the content criterion is met if the joint activity fulfills one or more of the entity's management and general responsibilities through a component of the joint activity.

There are two financial reporting fraud risks associated with fund-raising events that purport to also accomplish a programmatic purpose:

1. Improperly claiming that the ASC 958-720 criteria have been met, thus opening the door to charging costs to programs
2. Improper allocation of costs between fund-raising and program categories in connection with activities that meet (or claim to meet) the criteria

MISCLASSIFICATION OF EXPENSES

The final method of inflating a program expense ratio is the simplest of all. If an organization intentionally misclassifies expenditures as program costs that are not associated directly or indirectly with the accomplishment of a program, the program expense ratio is fraudulently improved. The following are examples of some of the areas that are particularly prone to misclassification schemes:

- **Salaries (and employee benefit costs) of staff.** These costs are classified based on time sheets or estimates of the level of effort devoted by employees (and possibly contractors) to programs, fund-raising, or general administrative activities of a not-for-profit organization. So, if someone misrepresents what duties they performed, such as by charging time to programs that was, in fact, spent in connection with fund-raising or administrative tasks, then program expenses, and therefore the program expense ratio, will be inflated.
- **Travel costs.** Much like salaries, travel costs of employees and contractors are generally classified based on the purpose of the travel. Therefore, if a staff person misrepresents how they spent their time on a particular trip (e.g., a fund-raising trip is mischaracterized as having programmatic elements), the associated travel costs, in addition to their salary, will be misclassified.
- **Professional fees and consultants**. Another area that is ripe for misclassification is fees paid to outside service providers, especially when there is limited documentation associated with their work (e.g., no contract or one that is vaguely worded, generic invoices, etc.).

If any of the preceding costs are misclassified, there is likely an additional impact on the program expense ratio due to the allocation of indirect costs. Often, these costs (especially salaries) are used as drivers for allocating indirect (overhead) costs of an organization.

CHAPTER FOURTEEN

Disclosure Fraud

PRIOR TO READING ANY FINANCIAL STATEMENTS, readers should always consider the valuable information provided in the notes to the financial statements. The same can be said for fraud investigators—study the notes. The notes may be a source of a financial statement fraud, but they may also provide useful clues about other fraud that affects amounts reported in the financial statements.

A thorough description of the disclosure requirements, and the associated red flags of fraud, would require a voluminous text of its own. So, the approach taken in this book is to provide a framework for evaluating note disclosures and to explore only a handful of the most likely suspects in the category of disclosure fraud.

There are four general types of notes that can be found in the financial statements:

1. **Policies.** Many of the notes, usually some of the first ones following the core financial statements, provide information about the accounting policies and methods used in preparing the financial statements. These notes provide answers to some of the most important questions associated with evaluating statements for the risk of fraud. For instance,

what inventory flow model does the company utilize? For which assets has an election been made to carry at fair value? What are the ranges of useful lives used in depreciating and amortizing property and equipment and intangible assets? What methods are utilized in the recognition of revenue?

2. **Composition of accounts.** The notes often provide details of amounts that appear as a single line item in the core financial statements. For example, a line item "Investments" appearing on the balance sheet may be associated with a note disclosure listing the categories and amounts of investments held, such as equities, fixed income securities, and so on. Some accounting standards are rather specific regarding the level of detail that must be disclosed, while others provide more general guidance, such as by stating that an "appropriate" level of useful disaggregation should be disclosed in the notes. Another example of this type of disclosure is the schedule of future maturities of long-term debt.
3. **Additional information about items in the statements.** In addition to further quantitative data about items in the financial statements, the notes are also used to provide descriptive information about certain amounts. For example, a long-term debt note should also provide a description of any collateral associated with loans. An important disclosure in this category pertains to related party transactions—see Chapter 3 for further details. Another important category of disclosures in this area is for changes in accounting methods and changes in accounting estimates.
4. **Information about items not in the financial statements.** Certain disclosures are required for information that does not relate to a specific amount reported in the financial statements. This is particularly true in the case of commitments that an entity has at the end of the year. In addition, important events that occur after the balance sheet date (the last day of the entity's reporting period) but before the date of the auditor's report (which coincides with either the date the financial statements were issued or the date the statements were available to be issued) must be disclosed.

As each line item or section of the financial statements is reviewed, the corresponding sections of the notes should be read carefully. Keep in mind that the notes themselves may be fraudulent or they may provide clues as to a fraud that directly affects certain line items of the financial statements.

CATEGORIES OF DISCLOSURE FRAUD

Disclosure frauds can be classified in the following manner:

- **Omissions.** Failing to disclose information required by an accounting standard represents a departure from U.S. GAAP or IFRS. Most commonly, omissions involve some negative piece of information, such as failure to disclose pending litigation against a company, the subsequent financial troubles of a major customer, or other information that would cast an adverse light on the entity.
- **Incomplete disclosures.** Certain issues are too public or too important to avoid altogether. So, an unscrupulous company may try to soften any negative publicity by leaving out a few important details, or by leaving out a negative aspect of an otherwise positive event.
- **Misrepresentations of information presented in the notes.** Some notes to financial statements contain outright inaccurate information.
- **Confusing disclosures.** While confusing descriptions provided in the notes may not be a fraud itself, it is often a sign of some underlying fraud or of an omission of information.

A useful technique in evaluating the risk of financial statement fraud is to compare the notes in the current year financial statements with the notes of the prior year. Look for changes from one year to the next. Each of the following disclosures can provide clues regarding financial reporting fraud risks:

- Changes in accounting estimates (useful lives of depreciable assets, estimates of uncollectible accounts receivable, fair value estimates, etc.)
- Changes in accounting methods (methods of depreciation, revenue recognition, methods used in measuring fair values of assets, etc.)
- Changes in descriptions of the nature of a company's operations (e.g., disclosures of new or discontinued products, opening of new locations, etc.)
- Notes indicating acquisitions or dispositions of affiliates or lines of business

COMMON DISCLOSURE RISKS

The remainder of this chapter will be devoted to explaining some examples of disclosures that tend to be the most vulnerable to fraud. There are many disclosures required under U.S. GAAP and IFRS. A complete discussion of fraud risks associated with each required disclosure would fill a large text of its own. So, the approach in this book is to focus on some specific risks that illustrate a few of the most common disclosure frauds, starting with an example of the most common type—the omission of required disclosure data.

Loss Contingencies

The primary reason for omitting a required disclosure is that the disclosure would provide negative information to the readers of the financial statements. For example, in Chapter 9, the requirement to accrue liabilities for certain loss contingencies was explained. However, as noted, not all loss contingencies are required to be recorded as liabilities. Some contingencies that are not recorded are instead disclosed in the notes to the financial statements. There are two situations in which loss contingencies that are not required to be accrued must be disclosed in the notes:

1. Loss contingencies that have at least a reasonable possibility of occurring
2. Cases in which an exposure to loss in excess of the amount accrued exists and there is at least a reasonable possibility of this additional loss being incurred

In either of these cases, a company should disclose the nature of the loss contingency and an estimate of the possible amount of the loss, or a range of losses if that cannot be determined.

Commitments

Unlike a contingency, a commitment represents a known obligation normally associated with a future outflow required under an existing contract or lease. For example, minimum future lease obligations must be disclosed in the notes, even though this liability is not reported on the balance sheet (unless certain criteria are met, and the overall treatment of leases is currently in the process of undergoing change).

An example of a failure to disclose a commitment is included in the case involving Vivendi Universal, S.A., a French company whose financial statements were prepared in accordance with French GAAP, but also included U.S. GAAP-based disclosures. Vivendi had stock traded on the EuroNext Paris, S.A. as well as on the New York Stock Exchange during the time covered by this case, from 2000 to 2002.

Among a series of charges against Vivendi was the allegation that the company failed to disclose a major commitment. The commitment originated in February 2001, when Vivendi and the Moroccan government allegedly entered into an agreement that required Vivendi to purchase shares of Maroc Telecom, a Moroccan telecommunications operator, in February 2002 for approximately €1.1 billion. In 2000, Vivendi had acquired a 35 percent interest in Maroc Telecom. This additional commitment to acquire an another 16 percent interest was not disclosed in Vivendi's financial reports filed in 2001 and early 2002.

Related Party Transactions

As noted in other sections of this book, transactions with related parties are often susceptible to misstatement (see Chapter 3 for a definition of related party). In fact, the concern over the reporting of related party transactions has risen to the point that in February 2012, the PCAOB proposed a new auditing standard focused solely on the evaluation, accounting, and disclosure of related party transactions.

These transactions require separate disclosure in the notes to the financial statements. An exception from disclosure applies under U.S. GAAP for compensation paid to related parties. This exception does not apply under IFRS, and IAS 24 specifically requires disclosure of compensation and benefits provided to related parties.

ASC 850 requires disclosure of material related party transactions, including all of the following:

1. Nature of the relationship
2. Description of the transactions, including transactions to which no amounts or nominal amounts were ascribed, for each period for which income statements are presented
3. Such other information deemed necessary to an understanding of the effects of the transactions on the financial statements
4. Amount of the transactions for each of the periods for which income statements are presented and the effects of any change in the method of establishing the terms from that used in the preceding period
5. Amounts due from or to related parties as of the date of each balance sheet presented and, if not otherwise apparent, the terms and manner of settlement

IAS 24 requires disclosure of the nature of related party transactions, as well as amounts of the transactions and amounts of outstanding balances at year-end.

A significant majority of public companies (75 percent in a 2003 *Wall Street Journal* study) disclose the existence of related party transactions. Most of these disclosures are fully compliant with the accounting standards. So, the challenge, then, is to weed out the inaccurate disclosures. Even more challenging is the detection of omitted disclosures.

The most common disclosure fraud risk associated with related parties is the failure to disclose transactions with these parties. Secondarily, misrepresentations regarding the nature of the related party or incomplete disclosures pertaining to the nature of related party transactions are additional risks.

Two cases provide illustrations of how fraud in the form of non-disclosure is carried out.

A fascinating case involving allegations of failing to disclose related party transactions is that of the Anglo Irish Bank and loans made by the bank to the chair and another member of its board of directors. As expected, Anglo Irish Bank disclosed its "Loans to Directors" in its year-end financial statements. However, loans estimated at €87 million at the end of fiscal year ended September 30, 2008 were not disclosed. The reason—shortly before year-end, the loans were paid off, usually by transferring them to another entity. Then, immediately after year-end, the loans were transferred back onto the books of Anglo Irish Bank. This temporary removal of related party balances, which purportedly took place from 2000 to 2008, might arguably meet an exception from disclosure of the balance at year-end. But, most experts would agree that disclosure of this practice and the existence of the transactions themselves should have been made in the notes to Anglo Irish Bank's financial statements.

The scandal over Anglo Irish Bank's circular transactions and failures to disclose began with the CEO's admission in December 2008, but then progressed to nationalization of the bank in 2009 and additional investigations, including assertions that the auditors were negligent.

In May 2012, China Natural Gas, Inc. (CHNG) was charged with concealing the related party nature of two short-term loans totaling $14.3 million. CHNG is based in the People's Republic of China and is a distributor of natural gas through fueling stations owned by affiliates. In January 2010, CHNG made two loans totaling $14.3 million and reported the loans as being made to unrelated third parties. In fact, the beneficiary of both loans was a real estate company that was 90 percent owned by the son of CHNG's chairman and former CEO and 10 percent by a nephew. In one of the loans, an individual served as a sham borrower in order to conceal the true nature of the loan to the real estate company. In light of CHNG's total reported assets of just over $200 million, this failure to disclose the related party loans was considered to be a material misstatement of the financial statements. As part of the scheme, CHNG provided a fraudulent legal opinion from its legal counsel to CHNG's auditors as additional support for the assertion that the loans were to unrelated third parties when the auditors questioned the loans.

Changes in Accounting Principles

ASC 250 requires disclosure of the following in the financial statements of the period in which a change of accounting principles is made:

1. The nature of and reason for the change, including an explanation of why the newly adopted accounting principle is preferable.
2. The method of applying the change, including all of the following:
   a. A description of the prior-period information that has been retrospectively adjusted, if any.
   b. The effect of the change on income from continuing operations, net income (or other appropriate captions of changes in the applicable net assets or performance indicator), any other affected financial statement line item, and any affected per-share amounts for the current period and any prior periods retrospectively adjusted. Presentation of the effect on financial statement subtotals and totals other than income from continuing operations and net income (or other appropriate captions of changes in the applicable net assets or performance indicator) is not required.
   c. The cumulative effect of the change on retained earnings or other components of equity or net assets in the statement of financial position as of the beginning of the earliest period presented.
   d. If retrospective application to all prior periods is impracticable, disclosure of the reasons therefore, and a description of the alternative method used to report the change.
3. If indirect effects of a change in accounting principle are recognized, then both of the following shall be disclosed:
   a. A description of the indirect effects of a change in accounting principle, including the amounts that have been recognized in the current period, and the related per-share amounts, if applicable.
   b. Unless impracticable, the amount of the total recognized indirect effects of the accounting change and the related per-share amounts, if applicable, that are attributable to each prior period presented.

IFRS disclosures for changes in accounting principle are found in IAS 8 and are substantially similar to U.S. GAAP, requiring disclosure of the nature of the change, the reasons that application of the new policy provides reliable and more relevant information, and the adjustment for each financial statement line item affected for the current reporting period and each prior reporting period presented, as well as the adjustment relating to periods before those presented.

One excellent example that illustrates the difference between an omitted disclosure and a misleading one involves Raytheon. In a 2006 complaint, the SEC claimed that from 1997 through 1999, Raytheon prematurely recognized revenue on a subsidiary's sale of unfinished aircraft through improper bill and hold transactions. As a result, the company materially overstated its net sales by approximately $80 million at year-end 1997 and $110 million at year-end 1998, which led to 13 percent overstatements in the annual operating income of the subsidiary in both of these periods. The SEC noted that although "Raytheon did restate for these material errors at year-end 1999, the company misleadingly attributed the restatement to additional 'clarification' supposedly provided by 'new guidance' on revenue recognition recently issued by the Commission in Staff Accounting Bulletin No. 101 ("SAB 101") instead of the improper accounting practices that had occurred at RAC, an aircraft manufacturing subsidiary, prior to that time."

The proper disclosure by Raytheon would have been to describe the change as a correction of an error made in the previous financial statements, rather than by suggesting that it was caused by a change from one acceptable method of accounting to a new one prescribed by the SEC.

Changes in Accounting Estimates

A change in accounting estimate is defined as a change that has the effect of adjusting the carrying amount of an existing asset or liability or altering the subsequent accounting for existing or future assets or liabilities. A change in accounting estimate is a necessary consequence of the assessment of the present status and expected future benefits and obligations associated with assets and liabilities. Changes in accounting estimates result from new information. Examples of items for which estimates are necessary are uncollectible receivables, inventory obsolescence, useful lives and residual values of depreciable and amortizable assets, and warranty obligations.

ASC 250 notes that a change in a valuation technique or its application does not represent a change in accounting estimate. ASC 250 requires disclosure of changes in accounting estimates that will impact future periods.

IAS 8 requires disclosure of the following for a change in accounting estimate that has an effect on the current financial statements or that is expected to have an effect on future financial statements:

1. The nature of the change.
2. The amount of the change (or, if applicable, the fact that the amount of the effect on future periods is not disclosed because estimating it would require undue cost or effort).

Subsequent Events

Subsequent events are events that occur after the end of the reporting period but before the date that the financial statements are available to be issued (for SEC filers, subsequent events are events occurring up through the date that the financial statements are issued).

U.S. GAAP for subsequent events is found in ASC 855, while IFRS is found in IAS 10. Certain subsequent events require retroactive recognition in the financial statements (called adjusting events under IFRS). Others do not require recognition (known as nonadjusting events), but must be considered for possible disclosure in the notes to the financial statements.

Under both U.S. GAAP and IFRS, subsequent events that require retroactive recognition are those events that provide additional evidence about conditions that existed at the date of the balance sheet.

ASC 855 provides an example of an event requiring retroactive recognition in the form of a loss on an uncollectible trade account receivable resulting from a customer's deteriorating financial condition leading to bankruptcy subsequent to the balance sheet date. This event would be indicative of conditions existing at the balance sheet date, requiring adjustment of the financial statements before their issuance. On the other hand, a similar loss resulting from a customer's major casualty such as a fire or flood subsequent to the balance sheet date would not be indicative of conditions existing at the balance sheet date and adjustment of the financial statements would not be appropriate.

IAS 10 provides additional examples of adjusting events occurring after the reporting period:

- The settlement after the reporting period of a court case that confirms that the entity had an obligation at the end of the reporting period.
- The receipt of information after the reporting period indicating that an asset was impaired at the end of the reporting period, or that a previously recognized impairment loss should be adjusted.

- The determination after the reporting period of the cost of assets purchased, or the proceeds of assets sold, before the end of the reporting period.
- The discovery of fraud or errors that show the financial statements are incorrect.

Subsequent events that are not to be recognized are those events that provide evidence about conditions that did not exist as of the balance sheet date. For subsequent events that are not to be retroactively recognized, the determination of whether or not to disclose the event is based on whether the event is considered to be material. Disclosure should be made if the financial statements would be misleading if the event was not disclosed.

ASC 855 provides the following examples of nonrecognized subsequent events that require disclosure to the financial statements:

- Sale of a bond or capital stock issue
- Purchase of a business
- Settlement of litigation when the event giving rise to the claim took place subsequent to the balance sheet date
- Loss of plant or inventories as a result of fire or flood

Two important disclosures must be made in notes with respect to material subsequent events that have not been retroactively recognized in the financial statements:

1. The nature of the event
2. An estimate of the event's financial effect, or a statement that such an estimate cannot be made

PART FIVE

Detection and Investigation

UNDERSTANDING HOW FINANCIAL STATEMENT FRAUDS are perpetrated is the most important consideration in detecting these schemes. And that has been the sole focus of Parts I through IV. In this part, we turn our attention to other aspects of detection and investigation, including:

- Understanding the motives behind financial statement fraud, so that its warning signs can be recognized early
- Recognizing the red flags of financial reporting fraud
- Using a variety of ratios and other analytical tools as elements of a financial statement fraud detection program
- Other procedures that can reveal the existence of fraud
- Addressing the issue of intent—is a misstatement in the financial statements merely an honest misstate, an overly aggressive interpretation of an accounting standard, or an intentional act to commit fraud?
- Assessing (or, for the auditors, minimizing) auditor liability in situations in which financial statement fraud occurs

CHAPTER FIFTEEN

Detecting Financial Statement Fraud

THE DETECTION AND INVESTIGATION of financial statement fraud involves the following 10 steps:

1. Understanding whether the behavioral conditions are ripe for fraud, primarily by determining whether there is a strong incentive present for individuals to engage in fraudulent financial reporting
2. Identifying the presence of fraud risk indicators (red flags); these are the symptoms that exist when certain financial reporting frauds are occurring
3. Considering whether there are weaknesses in internal controls that could make it easier for financial reporting fraud to be carried out without detection in the normal course of business
4. Performing analytical procedures geared toward the identification of financial statement fraud, such as ratio and trend analysis
5. Engaging in targeted analysis of journal entries, since most financial reporting fraud is either carried out or covered up through the use of nonstandard journal entries
6. Following up on and assessing the information gathered to determine whether there are clear signs of fraudulent financial reporting

7. Assessing whether the financial statements are materially misstated as a result of noncompliance with U.S. GAAP or IFRS (or another acceptable basis of accounting)
8. Digging deeper into additional evidence to determine whether there is evidence of intentional circumvention of internal controls and intentional misstatement of financial reports
9. Determining who is involved and how long the scheme has been going on
10. Assessing whether any external parties may have willingly participated in the scheme (e.g., vendors or customers) or may otherwise have liability (e.g., the possibility that auditors failed to detect the fraud as a result of performing a substandard audit)

Whereas the first four parts of this book have explored how financial statement frauds are perpetrated and whether a scheme violates the accounting principles, this final part is devoted to the other aspects of detection and investigation.

MOTIVES FOR FINANCIAL STATEMENT FRAUD

An essential element of detection is a thorough understanding of the environment in which a perpetrator operates. Noted criminologist Donald R. Cressey (1919–1987) studied white collar criminals and concluded that three factors are normally present when fraud is perpetrated:

1. A pressure (i.e., motive, incentive) to commit the act.
2. An opportunity (real or perceived), which normally manifests itself as a weakness in the design or the operation of one or more internal controls.
3. A rationalization for the act.

These three factors became known as the fraud triangle. Initially, the fraud triangle was first applied in connection with asset misappropriations, where the motive behind the act is often an unbearable financial pressure. However, the fraud triangle also applies to financial statement fraud, where the motive behind the fraud may be one involving direct financial gain, but may also involve other factors.

Therefore, the first step in evaluating an environment is to gain an understanding of the reasons behind the perpetration of financial statement fraud. Because when these motives are present, the risk of fraud increases.

- **To meet earnings expectations.** Many of the cases studied in this book began with actual earnings or revenues lagging behind the expectations of internal management (i.e., budgets and forecasts) and external parties, such as stock analysts. Failing to meet these expectations often results in the stock price dropping, as analysts express disappointment in the financial stability of a company. But, even when a company is not publicly traded, falling short of expectations can be a strong motivator for financial statement fraud. Earnings expectations may be set by individual owners, parent companies, joint venture partners, or other parties.
- **To satisfy borrowing requirements.** Financial institutions place reliance on a company's financial statements for purposes of lending, as well as monitoring ongoing compliance with debt covenants. Financial statement fraud may be perpetrated for several loan-related reasons:
  - To qualify for a new loan or an increase in a loan limit (especially in connection with asset-based loans)
  - To qualify for a preferred (lower) rate of interest
  - To qualify for more lenient terms, such as having to pledge less collateral
  - To avoid default triggered by violating a loan covenant

  Each of these incentives is accompanied by more than just a risk of overstating the profits of a company. A variety of factors are considered by a financial institution when lending money to a company. As a result, the risk of fraudulent financial reporting can involve misstating a current or quick ratio, cash flows from operations, earnings as adjusted for certain items (such as interest, depreciation, taxes, etc.), or a variety of other financial measures.
- **To qualify for bonuses or other compensation incentives.** Senior management may be eligible for a variety of lucrative incentives by achieving certain financial targets, such as total revenue levels or profitability. Some companies have introduced various measures of cash flows into the list of factors that determine whether someone earns an incentive, thereby lowering certain financial statement fraud risks and raising others. Understanding these incentives is critical to evaluating where the risk of fraud exists.
- **To maximize a price in an acquisition.** When management considers selling the company, the risk of financial reporting fraud increases. Often the sales price is based on some element of reported profits or gross revenue. Therefore, the more financially healthy the company appears, the bigger the payoff for the current owners. This can be the case with privately held businesses as well as publicly traded companies.

- **To maximize a stock price in an initial public offering.** When a company issues stock, a primary driver in establishing its price is its recent pattern of growth and profitability. Therefore, the years leading up to such offerings are prime candidates for financial reporting fraud.
- **To appear stable.** Wild fluctuations in profits are never viewed as kindly as steady growth, whether the readers of the financial statements are investors, bankers, potential buyers, or even private owners. Showing steady growth makes a company appear well-managed. And this can lead to fraudulent financial reporting in an effort to maintain that appearance. Interestingly, this incentive also introduces the risk of understating profits. In several cases described in this book, companies were found to have hidden revenues that should have been recognized in one year by establishing reserves so that the revenue could be recognized in a future period. This risk is heightened when a company is enjoying a particularly strong year, creating an incentive to "save" some of the current year's revenue as a hedge against less than stellar performance in the future.
- **To reduce the value of a business in divorce cases.** Speaking of the risk of understating financial performance, this risk is also present in connection with divorce and certain other division of property cases, in which there may be an incentive to make a company appear less valuable than it really is.

FRAUD RISK INDICATORS

Fraud risk indicators associated with each of the major categories of financial statement fraud are provided in the Appendix. The indicators in the Appendix are scheme-specific (or category-specific). However, other fraud risk indicators are broader or entity-wide in nature. Examples include internal control risk indicators, described in the next section.

INTERNAL CONTROL INDICATORS

The most commonly applied model for designing and auditing internal controls was developed by the Committee of Sponsoring Organizations (COSO). The COSO model involves five interrelated components of internal control:

1. Control environment
2. Risk assessment

3. Control activities
4. Information and communication
5. Monitoring

These components can be considered broadly, such as on an entity-wide basis. But they can also be considered in relation to specific aspects of an entity's operations:

1. By function (e.g., human resources, information technology, etc.)
2. By location
3. By division or department
4. By subsidiary
5. By accounting cycle (e.g., payroll, purchasing, cash receipts, inventory, etc.)

There are three goals of a system of internal controls:

1. Reliability of financial reporting
2. Compliance with laws and regulations
3. Operational efficiency and effectiveness

The important goal in this book is the first one—reliability of financial reporting. Think back to Cressey's fraud triangle, which states that three conditions are normally present when fraud occurs. One of those factors is an opportunity (real or perceived) to commit a fraud and not be detected.

The focus in this section is on internal controls over financial reporting. When those internal controls are strong, the opportunity to commit and conceal financial statement fraud is lowered. Therefore, a careful consideration of the five interrelated components of internal control can refine an assessment of the risk of financial reporting fraud.

A thorough consideration of all five components of internal control is beyond the scope of this book. Instead, the focus of this section will be on highlighting some of the characteristics of internal controls that are most often found to be weak in connection with financial statement fraud cases, using the COSO model as our guide.

Control Environment

The control environment represents the overall control consciousness of an entity. The expression "tone at the top" is sometimes used in reference to certain important elements of the control environment. The control environment establishes a structure and theme for other elements of internal control. Specific control environment factors that are most relevant to financial statement fraud include the following:

- The philosophy and operating style of management and the board of directors, especially as it relates to risk-taking and aggressiveness of financial reporting positions (i.e., does management focus so heavily on profitability or revenue growth that their discussion expands from looking at ways of improving operations to looking into which accounting treatment could help to achieve objectives?).
- The operation of a trusted whistleblower system, whereby employees would feel comfortable in reporting violations of the code of conduct without fear of retaliation (it should be noted that tips reported by employees are considered the most effective tool in detecting fraud in general).
- A board of directors, audit committee, and finance committee that are independent from management, empowered with the tools necessary to discharge their duties, and properly engaged in and committed to fulfilling their oversight roles (note: as required under the Sarbanes-Oxley Act, but also advisable for companies not subject to the Act, committees should include individuals with sound knowledge of financial reporting).
- Management's respect for the functions of internal and external auditors and those charged with the responsibilities of setting accounting policies and preparing financial statements.
- Clear assignment of job duties and establishment of organizational structure (note: vague organizational structure is consistent with environments in which it is acceptable for nonfinancial personnel to have unreasonable levels of involvement in accounting and financial reporting duties)
- Human resources policies and practices that include proper background screening of employees involved in all key accounting and financial functions (note: several of the individuals involved in the cases described in this book had previous criminal convictions or other warning signs that would have been discovered in a proper background check).
- A commitment to ongoing training for all employees involved in the accounting and financial reporting functions to ensure a high level of technical competence (note: in some of the cases described in this book, an environment was present in which one or two individuals dominated an unskilled team of accountants).

Risk Assessment

Risk assessment is the process of identifying and assessing relevant risks to the achievement of an entity's objectives. As it relates to financial reporting, factors involved in risk assessment include the following:

- Proper assignment of responsibilities for the identification and assessment of risks involving financial reporting
- Identification and assessment of the applications of estimation (e.g., fair value measurements, establishment of useful lives, etc.) in the financial statements
- Identification and assessment of external factors that could impact financial reporting, such as declines in quoted stock prices, introduction of new competitors or new products of competitors, new technology, and so on
- Identification and assessment of changes in laws, regulations, or accounting standards that could impact financial reporting
- Identification and assessment of risks associated with the introduction of new personnel, including outside contractors, or information systems that affect accounting and financial reporting systems

Control Activities

Control activities are the policies and procedures applied to carry out the specific functions of an organization. This is the element of internal control that most people think of when they are asked about internal controls. Specific factors involving control activities pertaining to financial reporting include the following:

- Segregation of duties, such as the separation of functions involving the determination of fair value, the estimation of percentage of completion, inventory, and the review of financial statements
- Controls designed to make sure that management cannot override established controls (note: the circumvention of internal controls by management personnel is a common theme in many of the fraud cases profiled in this book)
- Procedures in place to implement new accounting standards issued by FASB and IASB
- Procedures in place to review significant new transactions (such as business acquisitions and mergers, joint ventures, and so on) for proper application of relevant accounting standards

- Requiring proper supporting documentation for all accounting entries, especially all nonstandard (nonrecurring) journal entries
- Periodic review of nonfinancial assets for signs of impairment
- Review and approval of the selections of methods used in the determination of fair value, as well as the application of those methods
- Information technology hardware and software controls designed to prevent unauthorized access to all systems and leave an appropriate audit trail
- Due diligence in the selection and monitoring of outside consultants and vendors used in any accounting or financial reporting capacity (e.g., third-party specialists such as appraisers)
- Verifying the independence of third-party valuation specialists used by the entity

Information and Communication

Information and communication consist of the processes utilized to record and report transactions and to maintain accountability over assets and liabilities of an entity. Important elements of information and communication include the following:

- Retention of proper supporting documentation for all transactions and journal entries
- Accurate and timely information is available to those who need it in making determinations regarding accounting estimates, such as fair value measurements, asset impairments, collectibility of receivables, percentage of completion, and so on
- Critical accounting issues (e.g., fair value accounting issues and other estimates) and their treatment are properly disclosed and explained to the finance committee, audit committee, and/or board of directors
- Adequate resources are provided for the thorough research of external data useful in accounting and financial reporting (e.g., industry benchmarks, fair value comparisons, etc.)
- Adequate channels of communication (e.g., hotlines, etc.) are provided for the reporting of allegations of accounting improprieties, such as financial reporting fraud, by whistleblowers
- Employees are properly informed regarding the information they are requested to provide to those in charge of accounting and financial reporting
- Accounting system provides for the proper collection and reporting of information needed to comply with accounting standards, including

all information necessary for disclosure in the notes to the financial statements
- Proper record retention and destruction policies and practices

Monitoring

Monitoring represents the process of assessing the quality of internal controls over time. Monitoring assesses both the design and the operation of internal controls over financial reporting. Important elements of monitoring may include the following:

- Ongoing account reconciliations and reviews of reconciliations
- Comparisons of financial results with budget
- Benchmarking of financial performance against entities with similar operations
- Ongoing ratio and trend analysis
- A robust internal audit function that assesses the performance of internal controls over financial reporting
- Proper ongoing communication with the entity's external auditors
- Periodic special studies of internal controls, especially in connection with specialized aspects of accounting, such as fair value measurements, assessment of inventory obsolescence, and so on
- Periodic special audits of procurement involving the selection of vendors used in any accounting or financial reporting function (e.g., valuation specialists)
- Periodic special audits of IT security relevant to accounting and financial reporting
- Monitoring the performance of third parties that are relied upon for accounting or financial reporting functions
- Monitoring the performance of joint ventures partners that are not consolidated or part of the entity's own internal control system

CHAPTER SIXTEEN

Financial Statement Analysis

USE OF ANALYTICAL TECHNIQUES TO DETECT FRAUD

Financial statement fraud normally leaves a trail that an alert reader can use to detect the fraud. Unfortunately, that trail is often very muddled with immense amounts of information, most of which simply represents legitimate changes in a company's operations. As noted in Chapter 15, for every fraud risk indicator, there is a possible non-fraud explanation.

The challenge for us, then, is to create a reliable set of procedures for detecting fraud in its earliest stages, starting with the use of fraud risk factors but also incorporating other techniques.

One of the most useful techniques for detecting fraudulent financial reporting is financial statement analysis, the subject of this chapter as well as Chapters 17 and 18. While financial statement analysis is also useful in detecting asset misappropriations, the focus here is on its application to detecting financial statement fraud.

HORIZONTAL ANALYSIS

Horizontal analysis involves the comparison of data across multiple time periods. In its most basic application, current results and account balances are compared to those of the prior reporting period. Comparing actual results with budgeted amounts for the same period is another form of horizontal analysis. This analysis should be performed not only for revenues and expenses, but also for asset and liability accounts.

Generally, material variances in current year balances from either prior year amounts or budgeted amounts should be investigated. More often than not, there are legitimate reasons behind such variances, such as changes in prices, the economy, or strategy. But, these variances may also be an indicator of manipulation in the accounting records. Sudden, unexplained changes in account balances from period to period are a common indicator of fraud (either an asset misappropriation or a financial reporting fraud). For example:

- Unexplained increases in property and equipment could be a sign of improper expense capitalization (especially when the increase is not associated with known growth or expansion activities)
- Large increases in sales coupled with a similarly large increase in accounts receivable could be a sign that fictitious revenue has been recorded
- An unchanged balance in intangible assets could raise the question of whether impairment losses have been ignored, especially if reported revenue associated with such assets is flat or declining (this illustrates the importance of identifying unchanging balances, not just unusual changes, as red flags of fraud)

A useful extension of horizontal analysis is to compare results over several periods, which may identify long-term trends. While some indicators become apparent by simply comparing one period to the preceding period, others are more gradual and take time to reveal themselves.

Explanations of variances between actual and budgeted amounts should be a standard element of internal control present in all entities. If this is not being performed, a material weakness in internal controls is likely present.

Another consideration in performing horizontal analysis is to determine what, if any, level of account grouping is most likely to be useful. Horizontal analysis can be done on many different grouping levels:

- On an account-by-account basis (i.e., without grouping any accounts together)

- Rolling up similar objective categories of accounts together (e.g., instead of comparing rent expense, utilities expense, facilities maintenance, and other similar costs separately, group all occupancy-related costs together)
- Grouping revenues and expenses together by division or by functional area
- Grouping revenues and expenses together by geographic location
- Grouping revenues and expenses together by manager—this can be particularly useful when individual managers have input into the development of accounting estimates

Performing horizontal analysis on a few different levels of account groupings is more likely to detect fraud than limiting the analysis to company-wide data.

VERTICAL ANALYSIS

Vertical analysis involves measuring a single account, or a group of accounts, as a percentage of some larger total. It can be used to measure the composition of a total or subtotal. Examples of vertical analysis include the following:

- Measuring office supplies expense (or any other category of expense) as a percentage of total operating expenses
- Measuring the total expenses of one division as a percentage of total expenses of an entire company
- Measuring revenue from one type of product as a percentage of total revenue

Similar to horizontal analysis, vertical analysis should be performed from different angles. It can be performed using different types of groupings:

- On a line item by line item basis, comparing each element of revenue to total revenue, each item of expense to total expenses
- Grouping accounts that have similar characteristics
- Grouping accounts by region, by division, by manager, or some other useful shared characteristic

Vertical analysis is useful for detecting changes in the composition of a group of accounts over time. This, in turn, can be useful in detecting fraud. For example:

- Changes in the composition of a company's revenue (the percentage of revenue associated with each product or service) may indicate nothing more than the increasing or decreasing popularity of certain of the company's offerings. However, if the changes involve products or services that are bundled together for sale to customers, these changes could be a sign that the company is changing its method of allocating revenue among the multiple deliverables associated with a bundled offering (see Chapter 2).

- Changes in the composition of operating expenses in a manner in which depreciation and amortization expense represents a decreasing percentage of total expenses could mean that some of a company's assets in service have reached the end of their useful lives but are still providing value, or that other types of costs have increased. But it could also mean that the company is assigning unrealistically long useful lives to its depreciable assets (see Chapter 7) or that it is improperly classifying some of its intangible assets as indefinite life assets (see Chapter 6).
- Unexplained increases in gross profit (sales minus cost of goods sold) could be a sign of several of the fraud schemes described in this book, in particular those that overstate sales (e.g., fictitious sales) or that understate cost of goods sold (e.g., inventory inflation schemes)

There is always a story behind changes in the composition of accounts as revealed through vertical analysis. Internal auditors, external auditors, and investigators must dig to find the true reasons behind these variances. As with most red flags, these variances are often explained by reasons that have nothing to do with fraud. There are many other factors that can cause a variance, such as the economy, success or failure of marketing efforts, internal efficiencies (or inefficiencies), etc. But when financial statement fraud occurs, one or more of these indicators are also normally present.

BUDGET VARIANCE ANALYSIS

A budget should serve as a reliable expectation of a company's performance. If a budget is prepared under a strong system of internal controls, it can provide a solid tool for the detection of fraud.

If a company's actual operating results differ materially from budgeted amounts, this variance should be explored. But, the exploration must be done carefully. Explanations for budget variances are most reliable when the source of the explanation is not in a position to perpetrate and conceal a fraud. An independent source is always best. For instance, if a company has budgeted a certain amount for writing inventory off the books due to obsolescence each year, based on historical patterns, and in the current year none has been written off, who is in the best position to provide the most accurate answer to this question? The person responsible for recording the journal entries or the chief financial officer could be the very individuals who are attempting to inflate the value of the company's inventory. If an inventory valuation scheme is in the works, these individuals could be involved and will, therefore, lie about the reason for the budget variance. However, a warehouse employee in charge of taking inventory and who observes inventory on a daily basis, is more apt to provide a thorough and accurate answer to an inquiry about this variance. In fact, the fraud risk associated with warehouse employees is more likely to be some form of inventory misappropriation scheme, in which case these individuals would be more prone to saying that inventory should be written off due to obsolescence. So, verification by these individuals that inventory is not obsolete may be more reliable than a representation from someone else.

One of the inherent flaws in budget analysis is that the budgets may be prepared by people in a position to perpetrate financial reporting frauds. In such cases, it is possible that the budget itself is an unreliable benchmark to which actual results should be compared. Additionally, as seen in several cases in this book, financial statement fraud often involves creating fraudulent entries in order for a company to achieve its budgeted results. In these cases, budget variances will not appear.

Finally, one additional caution in using budget variance analysis as a detection tool is that once a fraud has begun, if operating results from one year are used as a basis for establishing future budgets, a company can actually begin budgeting for fraud without this fact being apparent to individuals not involved in the fraud.

CHAPTER SEVENTEEN

Ratio Analysis

IN CHAPTER 16, BASIC FINANCIAL STATEMENT ANALYSIS was introduced in the form of vertical and horizontal analysis. In this chapter, more advanced forms of ratio and data analysis will be explained.

Use of operating ratio analysis is one of the most reliable methods of detecting financial statement fraud. These ratios are most likely to detect fraud when the fraud impacts the numerator and denominator in a proportion that differs from the normal (properly stated) ratio. For example, if the carrying amount of current investments has been overstated as a result of recording fraudulent gains in connection with nonexistent increases in fair value, the entity's current ratio (current assets divided by current liabilities) would be artificially inflated (or an expected deterioration would not occur). Of course, there are numerous other explanations for an improved current ratio, most of which do not involve fraud. But, unexplained changes in key ratios, especially when this occurs with respect to multiple important ratios, should always be investigated, as this may be the first warning sign of a financial reporting fraud.

RESEARCH ON RATIO ANALYSIS

Many books and articles have been written on the subject of ratio analysis as a tool in detecting financial reporting fraud. Most focus on basic horizontal and vertical analysis, or on some of the commonly used financial ratios. Many ratios have the potential for detecting fraud. But which ones actually have been proven to have a direct link to fraudulent financial reporting? That is the challenge.

Numerous academic studies on financial statement fraud have been conducted and were reviewed for this book. However, two of these studies have particular relevance to this chapter and have been chosen for citation in this book:

1. "Fraud Risk Factors and the Likelihood of Fraudulent Financial Reporting: Evidence from Statement on Auditing Standards No. 43 in Taiwan," by Ken Y. Chen and Randel J. Elder, December 2007, hereinafter cited as "Chen and Elder."
2. "Data Mining Techniques for the Detection of Fraudulent Financial Statements," by Efstathios Kirkos, Charalambos Spathis, and Yannis Manolopoulos, from *Expert Systems with Applications* 32 (2007), hereinafter cited as "Kirkos et al."

These studies were chosen for two reasons. First, they provide extremely relevant analysis that correlates certain ratios with financial statement fraud. In addition, each study utilizes non-U.S. data, helping to balance the U.S. data and reports of fraud used elsewhere in this book. Other studies and papers will be introduced in Chapter 18.

Chen and Elder studied the correlation of certain financial ratios to the three elements of Donald Cressey's fraud triangle:

1. Pressures or incentives
2. Opportunities
3. Rationalizations

The population used for Chen and Elder's study consisted of 97 Taiwanese companies that were subject to financial restatements mandated by the Securities and Futures Bureau between 1996 and 2006 (similar to Accounting and Auditing Enforcement Releases issued in the United States by the SEC). These 97 companies were contrasted with 467 companies in which no financial reporting fraud was reported.

Kirkos et al. studied 38 Greek manufacturing firms where there was published proof of involvement in issuing fraudulent financial statements. These 38 companies were matched with 38 firms that did not possess any characteristics of fraudulent financial reporting (i.e., there were no published reports of fraud) in order to determine the degree of correlation of certain ratios to the existence of financial statement fraud.

As with any red flag of fraud, the existence of an anomaly in connection with any ratio can often be explained with many reasons that have nothing to do with fraud, such as changes in operations, cost structures, and so on. However, when anomalies are detected, auditors and investigators should consider the risk of fraud and then proceed to consider the non-fraud reasons for each anomaly. As each non-fraud reason is considered and eliminated, the risk of fraud grows.

USE OF OPERATING RATIO ANALYSIS TO DETECT FINANCIAL STATEMENT FRAUD

The use of vertical and horizontal analysis, explained in Chapter 16, is well established as a technique for detecting financial reporting fraud. However, simple horizontal and vertical analysis is limited in their ability to detect fraud. More sophisticated ratio analysis is often much more reliable in detecting the red flags associated with financial statement fraud. Some of the most useful operating ratios for detecting are covered in this section.

Operating ratios that could be of use in detecting financial statement fraud can be classified as follows:

1. Liquidity ratios
2. Activity ratios
3. Leverage ratios
4. Profitability ratios

Liquidity Ratios

Liquidity ratios measure an entity's ability to meet its short-term obligations with its short-term assets. There are two commonly used liquidity measures—the current ratio and the quick (or acid-test) ratio.

$$\text{Current ratio} = \frac{\text{Current Assets}}{\text{Current Liabilities}}$$

The current ratio is the most commonly used liquidity measure. It assesses an entity's ability to satisfy current liabilities, which include all short-term claims of creditors, with any of the current assets held at the reporting date.

$$\text{Quick (acid-test) ratio} = \frac{\text{Cash} + \text{Cash Equivalents} + \text{Short} - \text{Term Investments} + \text{Accounts Receivable}}{\text{Current Liabilities}}$$

The quick ratio takes a slightly different view of liquidity than does the current ratio. Instead of measuring an entity's ability to pay its creditors using any of its current assets, the quick ratio assesses this ability using only the most liquid of current assets. For example, since prepaid expenses cannot be used to pay a creditor, these current assets are excluded from the numerator of the quick ratio.

Either of the liquidity measures can be useful when assessing the risk of fraud. Short-term investments, in particular, can be subject to fluctuations in fair value and are therefore a target for fraudulent reporting. Other potential current assets and current liabilities with fraudulent accounting implications are receivables, certain derivatives, inventory, current portions of debt obligations, accounts payabe, and several others described in this book.

Activity Ratios

Activity ratios, sometimes called efficiency ratios, indicate how effectively an entity utilizes its assets. Some of the more commonly used activity ratios are as follows:

$$\text{Accounts receivable turnover} = \frac{\text{Annual Net Sales}}{\text{Average Accounts Receivable}}$$

$$\text{Days outstanding in accounts receivable} = \frac{365}{\text{Average Receivable Turnover}}$$

$$\text{Inventory turnover} = \frac{\text{Cost of Goods Sold}}{\text{Average Inventory}}$$

$$\text{Average age of inventory} = \frac{365}{\text{Inventory Turnover}}$$

$$\text{Days payables outstanding} = \frac{365}{\text{Cost of Sales/Average Accounts Payable}}$$

$$\text{Total asset turnover} = \frac{\text{Net Sales}}{\text{Average Total Assets}}$$

$$\text{Fixed asset turnover} = \frac{\text{Net Sales}}{\text{Average Fixed Assets}}$$

$$\text{Intangible asset turnover} = \frac{\text{Net Sales}}{\text{Average Intangible Assets}}$$

$$\text{Related party sales ratio} = \frac{\text{Sales to Related Parties}}{\text{Total Sales}}$$

As with horizontal and vertical analysis, many of these activity ratios become even more valuable if they can be calculated not only on an entity-wide basis, but also by region, location, product line, division, manager, and so on. While all of the preceding ratios are helpful, the following have been proven to show particular correlation to financial statement fraud.

Days Receivables Outstanding

The days receivables ratio, one of the activity ratios introduced in the preceding section, measures the number of days it would take to collect the ending balance in accounts receivable at the average sales per day. This ratio is particularly useful in detecting certain types of frauds. The ratio is calculated as follows:

$$\text{Days receivables outstanding} = \frac{365}{\text{Net Sales/Average Accounts Receivable}}$$

The denominator in this ratio, referred to as accounts receivable turnover, is also a useful ratio in detecting fraud. Overall, this ratio normally remains steady even as sales volume increases or decreases, absent other changes that could affect the ratio. If a company is overstating receivables by carrying uncollectible receivables on the books, the number of days outstanding increases.

If a company is recording fictitious sales, the effect on this ratio varies depending on what part of the balance sheet is affected. If the overstatement in sales is accompanied by a corresponding inflation of accounts receivable, both the numerator and denominator of the receivables turnover ratio are increased by equal amounts. But since the numerator (sales) is a much larger figure than the denominator, the effect on the turnover ratio is to decrease it as fictitious sales are recorded. And since the turnover ratio is the denominator in the days receivables outstanding calculation, the effect of this fraud is to inflate the number of days of receivables outstanding.

If the fictitious sales are recorded elsewhere in the balance sheet (such as by increasing property and equipment), the effect is to lower the number of days of receivables outstanding.

Days Payables Outstanding

This ratio represents the liability side of the number of days in accounts receivable. The ratio is calculated as follows:

$$\frac{365}{\text{Cost of Sales/Average Accounts Payable}}$$

The denominator in this ratio is also referred to as accounts payable turnover. The ratio represents the number of days it would take to pay the ending balance in accounts payable at the average cost of goods sold per day.

It would be expected that this ratio would remain relatively steady as sales and cost of sales increase or decrease, absent some other logical explanation. Unexplained improvements (decreases) in the days payables outstanding ratio could be a sign of understating accounts payable.

Sales to Total Assets

The sales to total assets ratio (also known as asset turnover) is one of the more reliable indicators of fraud. A sudden or continuing decrease in this ratio is often associated with improper capitalization of expenses, which increase the denominator without a corresponding increase in the numerator (keep in mind that overstating sales is most often done by inflating assets, so increases in this ratio have less of a correlation with overstatement of sales than do decreases with false capitalization of costs). Kirkos et al. found that the mean asset turnover ratio in firms with fraudulent financial reporting was 0.699, while the mean for firms without fraud was 1.055, indicating a strong correlation.

WorldCom was not the only expense capitalization scheme to be evidenced by declining sales to total assets ratios. The Livent case of the late 1990s is another excellent example. In Livent's case, changes in this ratio sent a strong signal that costs that should have been reported as expenses were instead improperly capitalized as fixed assets, and that costs were also improperly shifted from asset accounts subject to upcoming expensing to asset accounts that would be carried for longer periods (i.e., deferring of costs to future periods).

The asset turnover ratio is also useful for detecting failures to write off assets (such as uncollectible accounts receivable or obsolete inventory) or failing to record impairment losses on property or intangible assets (covered further in the next subsection).

As with most high-level ratios (ratios based on significant totals and subtotals in a set of financial statements), the asset turnover ratio can be an indicator of more than one type of fraud. Drilling down a bit more into specific accounts or classes is necessary in order to determine the specifics of the fraud.

Sales to Intangible Assets

Intangible assets are assets with no physical presence, but that have value to a company. They can be internally developed (subject to rules regarding whether the costs can be capitalized), purchased separately from third parties, or acquired in connection with a merger with or acquisition of another entity. Most intangible assets are associated with the production of income, such as goodwill, trademarks, copyrights, trade secrets, customer lists, certain contracts, and many others. Some intangible assets may not be associated directly with a specific income stream, but should nonetheless only be carried as an asset if there is some basis for identifying and measuring their value.

As explained earlier, all intangible assets are carried in the financial statements in one of two manners:

1. They are amortized over an estimated useful life.
2. They are not amortized, but are tested for impairment in value every year.

In either case (and it works differently for each of the two categories), if the fair value of the asset declines below the net book value, an impairment loss should generally be recorded. Fair value of an income-producing intangible asset is normally measured using one of several versions of the income approach to valuation, in which fair value is based on the present value of a future income stream.

Thus, intangible assets should be analyzed in the following manner:

1. Increases from one year to the next should be studied:
   a. What types of intangible assets were acquired and how?
   b. Are these assets being amortized over an estimated useful life?
2. No change or a very small reduction in intangible assets from one year to the next should be scrutinized for the possibility of using overly long useful lives or for failing to record impairment losses.
3. Perform ratio analysis on intangible assets as a group and, if possible, on specific assets or categories of assets.

The ratio of sales or revenue to intangible assets provides a measure of how productive intangible assets are. Decreases in this ratio may be a strong sign that intangible assets are declining in usefulness without the required recording of an impairment loss.

Disclosures associated with intangible assets can provide much insight into whether this type of fraud is occurring. Readers of financial statements should expect to see disclosures for all of the following:

- Amounts of intangible assets subject to amortization and amounts not subject to amortization.
- Methods and periods used for amortization.
- Descriptions of major classes of intangibles.
- Estimated amortization expense to be recognized in each of the five years after year-end.
- If an impairment loss has been recognized, the amount of the loss, a description of the impaired asset and the facts and circumstances leading to its impairment, and a description of the method used to determine fair value of the asset.

These disclosure requirements are based on U.S. GAAP, but IFRS rules are very similar in this area.

Of course, missing from these disclosure requirements, and for obvious reasons, is an explanation of why an impairment loss has *not* been recorded. Management and the external auditor are required to analyze this issue. But a careful analysis of the financial statements may identify a failure to record an impairment loss.

Related Party Sales to Total Assets

While the asset turnover ratio may be an indicator of fraud when it decreases inexplicably, one specific category of sales should be monitored for unexplained increases. The ratio of sales to related parties (affiliates, parent companies, subsidiaries, etc.) was found by Chen and Elder to have a strong correlation to fraudulent financial reporting. In their study, the mean ratio of related party sales to total assets was 0.1285 for companies without fraudulent financial reporting, but jumped to 0.1816 (a 50% increase) with firms that were found to have fraudulent financial statements. Sudden or ongoing increases in this ratio could mean that a company is generating revenue from transactions with affiliated entities, and this revenue could be intentionally overstated due to the close relationship the reporting entity has with these companies.

A useful variation on this ratio is calculated simply by dividing sales to related parties by total sales. This ratio, while not the specific one used by Chen and Elder, measures the proportion of a company's sales that are to related parties. Significant increases in this ratio should be scrutinized carefully as this could be a sign of fraud.

Disclosures pertaining to related party transactions should be closely scrutinized. Requirements for these disclosures were explained in Chapter 14. Incomplete, vague, or confusing note disclosures about related party transactions can be a sign that these transactions are being used to somehow hide a problem or create an image of financial strength when such strength does not exist.

Revenue Composition Analysis

Determining whether revenue has been inflated can be difficult if a company generates revenue from many different types of products and services. Rarely is each category of revenue inflated by the same percentage. Therefore, breaking revenue into various categories and comparing the composition of revenue from period to period is an essential step. Sudden shifts in the composition of revenue can be a sign of fraud.

This is particularly true when a company "bundles" some of its products and services together in transactions in which certain portions of a transaction represent current period income while others must be deferred for recognition in future periods. These multiple-deliverable arrangements have been abused for fraudulent financial reporting purposes on several occasions. For example, the SEC determined that Xerox recognized more than $3 billion in revenue too early between 1997 and 2000 in connection with certain multiple-deliverable arrangements. In the Xerox case, a single lease transaction with a customer would result in three types of revenue: revenue from the equipment itself, revenue from servicing the equipment over the lease term, and financing revenue. Manipulating the allocation of revenue among the three elements resulted in early recognition.

The red flags associated with premature revenue recognition in connection with these multiple-deliverable arrangements include the following:

- Decreases in revenue associated with elements of revenue that are to be recognized in future periods, coupled with increases in revenue associated with revenue elements that are to be deferred and recognized in later periods

- Changes in the description of the revenue recognition methods applied to multiple-deliverable arrangements as explained in the notes to the financial statements

Careful review of the notes is one of the keys to detecting certain methods of fraudulently inflating revenue. In connection with multiple-deliverables, a description of the arrangement and the methods of recognizing each component should be included in the notes.

Leverage Ratios

Leverage ratios provide a measure of solvency of an entity. Strong leverage ratios indicate that an entity is well-prepared for surviving an economic downturn.

$$\text{Debt to equity ratio} = \frac{\text{Total Debt(long-term and short-term)}}{\text{Total Equity}}$$

$$\text{Long-term debt to equity} = \frac{\text{Long-Term Debt}}{\text{Total Equity}}$$

$$\text{Debt to assets} = \frac{\text{Total Debt}}{\text{Total Assets}}$$

$$\text{Equity to assets ratio} = \frac{\text{Total Equity}}{\text{Average Assets}}$$

$$\text{Times interest earned} = \frac{\text{Net Income before Interest and Taxes}}{\text{Interest Expense}}$$

Leverage ratios, while they are very useful tools for analysts, are probably the least valuable of the four categories of operating ratios as a financial statement fraud detection tool. Their use is limited primarily to the detection of fraudulent valuations of debt obligations.

However, two of these ratios have been shown to have a correlation to financial statement fraud:

1. The debt to equity ratio
2. The debt to total assets ratio

Unlike some of the other ratios explained here, neither of these ratios directly predicts a specific type of fraud. However, excessive reliance on debt clearly suggests a company with potentially extreme financial pressures, creating a high expectation of solid earnings and financial health, leading to financial reporting fraud.

Kirkos et al. determined that the median debt to equity ratio of companies with financial statement fraud was 2.706, while non-fraud companies had a median ratio of only 1.075. Likewise, companies with financial statement fraud had a median debt to total assets ratio of 0.629, while this ratio was just 0.437 for companies without fraud.

Profitability Ratios

Profitability ratios measure an entity's record of producing profits for shareholders. Some of the most useful profitability ratios include:

$$\text{Gross profit margin} = \frac{\text{Net Sales} - \text{Cost of Goods Sold}}{\text{Net Sales}}$$

$$\text{Operating profit margin} = \frac{\text{Net Income before Interest and Taxes}}{\text{Net Sales}}$$

$$\text{Net income ratio} = \frac{\text{Net Income}}{\text{Net Sales}}$$

$$\text{Return on equity} = \frac{\text{Net Income}}{\text{Average Stockholders' Equity}}$$

$$\text{Return on assets} = \frac{\text{Net Income} + \text{Interest Expense}(1 - \text{Tax Rate})}{\text{Average Total Assets}}$$

$$\text{Return on investment} = \frac{\text{Net Income} + \text{Interest Expense }(1 - \text{Tax Rate})}{\text{Average}(\text{Stockholders' Equity} + \text{Long-Term Debt})}$$

As with many of the other ratios explained in this chapter, profitability ratios can be even more valuable as a fraud detection technique if they are calculated on the basis of product line, division, region, or other useful subcategory in addition to a company-wide basis.

ANOTHER USEFUL MEASURE: WORKING CAPITAL TO TOTAL ASSETS

The ratio of working capital to total assets has been found to have a correlation to financial statement fraud. Since actual liquid assets are rarely produced as financial statement fraud progresses, the fraud often sits on the balance sheet in the form of other assets. As such, the ratio of working capital to total assets declines.

Kirkos et al. found that the mean working capital to total assets ratio in companies without any financial statement fraud was 0.253. However, in companies reported to have engaged in fraudulent financial reporting, the mean was only 0.054. Sudden or continuing decreases in this ratio should be investigated.

CHAPTER EIGHTEEN

Other Detection Procedures

ANALYSIS UTILIZING MULTIPLE RATIOS

Using single ratios as an indicator of fraud can be valuable. There is some evidence, however, that using a blend of several ratios can be an even more reliable method of detecting fraud than any single ratio alone.

The M-Score

In his 1999 article, "The Detection of Earnings Manipulation," Messod Beneish describes a blended formula, called the M-Score, that may be useful in detecting financial statement fraud. The formula was based on an evaluation of the financial statements of a sample of companies that had engaged in earnings manipulation. In particular, the financial statements of the first period in which earnings manipulation occurred were compared to the preceding year's financial statements.

The M-Score described by Beneish is a weighted blend of eight different indexes, each measuring the change in a ratio from one year to the next. The eight indexes utilized in the M-Score are as follows:

1. **DSRI = Days' Sales in Receivables Index.** This is the ratio of the current year's days' sales in receivables to that of the prior year, expressed as the following formula, where CY stands for current year and PY stands for prior year:

$$\text{DSRI} = \frac{\text{CY Receivables/CY Sales}}{\text{PY Receivables/PY Sales}}$$

2. **GMI = Gross Margin Index.** This is the ratio of the prior year's gross margin to that of the current year, where an index of less than 1 means that margins have declined.

$$\text{GMI} = \frac{\text{(PY Sales} - \text{PY Cost of Goods Sold)/PY Sales}}{\text{(CY Sales} - \text{CY Cost of Goods Sold)/CY Sales}}$$

3. **AQI = Asset Quality Index.** This is the ratio of the current year's noncurrent assets other than property and equipment to total assets to that of the prior year.

$$\text{AQI} = \frac{\text{(CY Total Assets} - \text{CY Current Assets} - \text{CY PP\&E)/CY Total Assets}}{\text{(PY Total Assets} - \text{PY Current Assets} - \text{PY PP\&E)/PY Total Assets}}$$

4. **SGI = Sales Growth Index.** This is the ratio of the current year's sales to that of the prior year.

$$\text{SGI} = \frac{\text{CY Sales}}{\text{PY Sales}}$$

5. **DEPI = Depreciation Index.** This is the ratio of the rate of depreciation expense for the prior year to that of the current year.

$$\text{DEPI} = \frac{\text{PY Depreciation/(PY Depreciation} + \text{PY PP\&E)}}{\text{CY Depreciation/(CY Depreciation} + \text{CY PP\&E)}}$$

6. **SGAI = Sales, General, and Administrative Expenses Index.** This is the ratio of current year's sales, general, and administrative expenses to that of the prior year.

$$\text{SGAI} = \frac{\text{CY SG\&A Expense/CY Sales}}{\text{PY SG\&A Expense/PY Sales}}$$

7. **LVGI = Leverage Index.** This is the ratio of total debt to total assets for the current year to the same ratio of the prior year.

$$\text{LVGI} = \frac{(\text{CY LTD} + \text{CY Current Liabilities})/\text{CY Total Assets}}{(\text{PY LTD} + \text{PY Current Liabilities})/\text{PY Total Assets}}$$

8. **TATA = Total Accruals to Total Assets.** This is the ratio of total accruals (defined as the change in working capital accounts other than cash, less depreciation) to total assets.

$$\text{TATA} = \frac{\Delta\text{Working Capital} - \Delta\text{Cash} - \Delta\text{Income Taxes Payable} - \text{CY Depreciation and Amortization}}{\text{CY Total Assets}}$$

The eight-factor M-Score is calculated as follows:

$$M = -4.84 + 0.920{*}\text{DSRI} + 0.528{*}\text{GMI} + 0.404{*}\text{AQI} + 0.892{*}\text{SGI} + 0.115{*}\text{DEPI} - 0.172{*}\text{SGAI} + 4.679{*}\text{TATA} - 0.327{*}\text{LVGI}$$

An M-Score of greater than –2.22 (i.e., a less negative score, such as –1.50) indicates a strong likelihood of financial statement fraud.

There is also a five-factor version of the M-Score. This version, developed after further research, excludes SGAI, DEPI, and LVGI based on the conclusion that these three indexes were less significant than the other five. The five-factor M-Score is calculated as follows:

$$M = -6.065 + 0.823{*}\text{DSRI} + 0.906{*}\text{GMI} + 0.593{*}\text{AQI} + 0.717{*}\text{SGI} + 0.107{*}\text{DEP}$$

In the paper, "Financial Statement Fraud Detection Using Ratio and Digital Analysis," Maria L. Roxas put the five-factor and eight-factor versions of the Beneish model to the test using more current data, focusing solely on revenue recognition frauds disclosed in SEC AAERs issued between December 1999 and June 2008. 116 such AAERs were identified for this study, which concluded that the five-factor version of the M-Score (with a benchmark of greater than –2.76) was a more reliable predictor of revenue recognition earnings manipulation than the eight-factor version (with a benchmark of greater than –2.22).

The F-Score

In their article, "Predicting Material Accounting Misstatements," Dechow, Ge, Larson, and Sloan present another model that utilizes multiple financial statement variables as a basis for predicting misstatements (not necessarily those caused by fraud, but misstatements in general). The authors studied 2,190 SEC AAERs issued from 1982 to 2005. The variables used were classified as follows:

1. Accruals quality related variables (nine variables, including change in receivables, percentage soft assets, etc.)
2. Performance variables (five variables, such as change in return on assets and others)
3. Nonfinancial variables (two variables: abnormal change in employees and abnormal change in order backlog)
4. Off-balance-sheet variables (four variables, including existence of operating leases, expected return on pension plan assets, etc.)
5. Market-related incentives (eight variables, including leverage, earnings-to-price, and others)

The 28 variables were studied for misstating firms and the authors made several conclusions:

1. Companies with misstatements appear to engage in off-balance sheet financing through leases with greater frequency than firms without misstatements.
2. A greater percentage of firms with misstatements have high percentages of their assets in the form of soft assets, which are subject to a greater risk of manipulation.
3. Stock performance of misstating companies tends to be high and these companies are often issuing equity and raising financing around the time of their misstatements.
4. Companies with misstatements tend to have high accruals followed by significant declines in the return on assets ratio during years of misstatements.

Altman Z-Score

The Altman Z-Score, first published in 1968 by Edward I. Altman, has been reliably used as a predictor of bankruptcy. It has also been used as a broader measure of deteriorating financial health by auditors and others involved with financial statements.

The original Altman Z-Score, which focused solely on publicly held manufacturing companies, is calculated by summing the following five elements:

0.012 × (Working Capital/Total Assets)
0.014 × (Retained Earnings/Total Assets)
0.033 × (Earnings before Interest and Taxes/Total Assets)
0.006 × (Market Value of Equity/Book Value of Total Liabilities)
0.999 × (Sales/Total Assets)

Notice that two of the ratios that comprise the Altman Z-Score (the first and fifth ones) are also strongly correlated to fraud as stand-alone ratios. Altman found that the average score for bankrupt companies was −0.25, while the score for the non-bankrupt group averaged +4.48.

Alternate factors for each of the five ratios were developed for other sectors of the economy. For instance, for private companies, the five ratios would be multiplied by 0.717, 0.847, 3.107, 0.420, and 0.998, respectively.

The Altman Z-Score was found by Kirkos et al. (see Chapter 17) to have a correlation with financial statement fraud. This should be expected, as many companies involved in financial reporting fraud are doing so to stave off financial deterioration. Kirkos et al. found the mean Z-Score for Greek manufacturers not involved in fraudulent financial reporting to be 1.990. The mean Z-Score for companies found to have engaged in fraudulent financial reporting was 0.778.

RATIOS INVOLVING NONFINANCIAL DATA

The ratios described so far all involve amounts from the financial statements. Another extremely valuable method of detecting fraud is through the use of ratios that involve nonfinancial data. Pairing financial amounts with relevant nonfinancial data often reveals clear signs of fraud. For example, analysis may involve dividing annual sales or revenue by any or all of the following factors:

- Number of employees
- Square footage of a store or warehouse
- Quantities of items sold
- Number of customers
- Number of sales transactions

Likewise, analyzing cost of goods sold or other categories of expense using these nonfinancial statistics can be quite revealing.

Part of the value of analyzing ratios involving nonfinancial data is that perpetrators of fraud normally either do not have the ability to falsify the nonfinancial data or they do not think to do so. The difficulty in using this type of analysis is that access to relevant nonfinancial data may be limited.

The key to successful use of this technique is to identify appropriate nonfinancial measures that should be expected to have a predictable relationship with a financial amount. What makes these ratios so valuable is that rarely does the perpetrator of a financial reporting fraud have the ability (or the awareness) to manipulate both the financial statements and the nonfinancial statistics in equal proportions.

For example, let's say we are evaluating whether a fair value accounting fraud has been perpetrated in connection with a particular intangible asset. The potential fraud involves a failure to record an impairment loss on the intangible asset. Depending on the type of intangible asset, potentially useful ratios to consider include the following:

- Book value of the asset/Revenue derived from the asset
- Book value of the asset/Units of production derived from the asset
- Amortization expense/Units of production derived from the asset

Much like any of the ratios described in this chapter, customized ratios do not prove that a fair value accounting fraud has occurred. These ratios, when properly designed and compared over time, merely indicate that something unexpected has occurred. But that something just might be your first clue that you are on the trail of a major fraud involving the misapplication of fair value accounting. If you miss that clue, the opportunity to detect the fraud may be missed.

OTHER INFORMATION AND DISCLOSURES IN FINANCIAL STATEMENTS

In the preceding sections, select ratios, as well as some of the related note disclosures, were examined. There are, however, certain additional disclosures in the financial statements, those that are not associated with any of the specific ratios covered thus far, which can also provide valuable insight into whether a financial statement fraud exists.

Who Performed the Audit?

The first disclosure found in an audit report is not the footnote disclosures to the financial statements. It is the name of the auditor, an important piece of information. Turnover in the independent firm that audits a company's financial statements has been associated with financial reporting fraud. Chen and Elder found a mean number of changes in external auditor of 0.1900 in the 97 companies with financial statement fraud, compared to a mean of 0.0150 in the 467 companies without fraud. This indicates that the risk of financial reporting fraud appears to be much higher in the year of auditor changes, perhaps due to one of the following reasons:

1. The new firm was not as familiar with all of the systems, internal controls, and accounting treatments in its first year of working with a new client.
2. Disagreements over accounting treatment with a predecessor firm led to the switch to a new firm that was more likely to agree with management (i.e., opinion shopping).

Indications of disagreements with auditors or shopping around for an auditor who appears more likely to agree with accounting positions taken by a company should be viewed as suspicious.

Cash Flows from Operating Activities

Another disclosure that can help to identify financial statement fraud can be found on the statement of cash flows, which classifies a company's cash flows into three categories: operations, investing, and financing. When cash flows from operations are significantly lower than income from operations reported on the income statement, readers should immediately analyze the statements carefully, as this has been an indicator of fraud in many cases.

Of course, as with almost all red flags of fraud, there can be many non-fraud reasons for this indicator. A company may have borrowed money to fund an expanding operation, it may have prepaid certain future expenses, it may have loosened its policies for granting credit to customers, or any of dozens of other reasons. But a significant difference in operating cash flows from operating income, or a string of several periods in a row with cash flow lagging behind operating income, can be a sign of either overstatement of revenue or understatement of expenses.

In their study, Chen and Elder found a strong correlation between negative cash flows from operations and financial statement fraud. In financial statements without fraud, negative cash flows from operations was reported 11 percent of the time. In the financial statements containing fraud, that figure jumped to 25 percent.

Fair Value Disclosures

The increased use of fair value accounting concepts has been filled with controversy. As a result of this controversy, the standard-setters have increased the level of note disclosures required when fair value accounting is applied. Generally, disclosures that should be expected when assets or liabilities have been measured at fair value include the following:

- Description of the valuation methods used in measuring assets or liabilities at fair value
- Identification of the nature of the inputs used in performing fair value measurement calculations
- A ranking of these inputs using a standard hierarchy (this hierarchy is designed to inform readers about the reliability of inputs used by applying a classification system described in the accounting standards)
- Total gains or losses recognized during the period based on the application of fair value accounting measurements

Additional disclosure requirements, too voluminous to list here, may also apply. These disclosures should be read carefully, as fair value measurements can require extensive judgment. And wherever significant judgment is exercised, the risk of financial reporting fraud increases. If these disclosures are vague or confusing, fair value accounting fraud may be present.

UNDERSTANDABILITY OF FINANCIAL STATEMENT DISCLOSURES

One of the underlying assumptions made when an auditor issues an unqualified opinion on the financial statements is that the financial statements are understandable. But anyone who has read a set of financial statements knows that clarity is not always the first word that comes to mind.

Several studies have focused on use of the Gunning Fog Index to measure the readability of the notes to the financial statements, or the management discussion and analysis (MD&A) section in the financial reports of publicly traded companies. The index can be applied to any sample of writing in English. The formula for the Gunning Fog Index is as follows:

$$0.4 \times ((\text{total words}/\text{number of sentences}) + 100(\text{complex words}/\text{total words}))$$

Complex words are defined as those with three or more syllables, not counting proper nouns, compound words, or common suffixes such as –es.

While this formula appears to be quite simple, it has been well-respected as a reliable measure of readability since its development in 1952. The index generally corresponds to the grade level required to understand it. For example, a Fog index of 12 means it has the reading level equivalent of a high school senior in the United States. Many general audience newspapers and publications have a Fog Index of about 8, while others that aim at a more educated audience, such as the *Wall Street Journal*, have an index of around 12.

In remarks made in March 2007, U.S. SEC Chairman Christopher Cox noted that when the Gunning Fog Index was applied to the then-new Compensation Disclosure and Analysis sections of the reports submitted to the SEC, the average Index was 16.45!

A 2006 study of SEC filings by Feng Li of the Stephen M. Ross School of Business at the University of Michigan (published in the working paper, "Annual Report Readability, Current Earnings, and Earnings Persistence"), found that the median Fog Index of the notes to audited financial statements ranged from 18.65 to 18.95 during the 11 years from 1994 to 2004. This means that the notes would not likely be understood fully by someone possessing even a college degree or perhaps a graduate degree.

There are a number of websites that will calculate the Fog Index by simply cutting and pasting blocks of text. Whether a formal calculation of a Fog Index is performed or not, when notes to the financial statements are confusing or vague, this could be a sign of deceptive financial reporting.

TESTING OF JOURNAL ENTRIES

As noted in many of the cases described in this book, financial statement fraud is often perpetrated by recording journal entries, rather than through improper recording of cash transactions and other activities in the normal course of business.

The challenge, however, is to develop a reliable technique for identifying the fraudulent journal entries out of a population that can number into the tens or hundreds of thousands of journal entries made by companies. One theory that may help in this cause is Benford's Law.

According to Benford's Law, the following list reflects the frequency with which each digit appears as the first digit of a number:

1 = 30.1%
2 = 17.6%
3 = 12.5%
4 = 9.7%
5 = 7.9%
6 = 6.7%
7 = 5.8%
8 = 5.1%
9 = 4.6%

Thus, the digit "1" can be expected to be the first digit of a number 30.1 percent of the time.

Benford's Law can be useful in the detection of financial statement fraud (it can also be quite useful in detecting certain types of asset misappropriation schemes, but that type of fraud is not the focus here). In their 2009 paper, "Data Mining Journal Entries for Fraud Detection: A Pilot Study," Roger Debreceny and Glen Gray studied the journal entries of 29 entities and found a high correlation between Benford's Law and the first digits of the amounts in journal entries. Only a handful of anomalies were found, suggesting further investigation would be necessary to determine whether fraud was involved. (Note: Debreceny and Gray do not indicate what types of entities were included in their data, and the anomalies identified, such as one company having a higher than normal percentage of journal entry amounts starting with a 5, were not subject to further investigation.) Therefore, Benford's Law may have useful applications in detecting financial statement fraud.

However, Benford's Law by itself may not narrow the list of possible fraudulent journal entries down to a manageable size. For instance, if there is an unusually large quantity of journal entries starting with a particular digit, there may be thousands of entries identified for analysis. Some possible next steps might be to examine the following characteristics of the pool of entries that have been identified using Benford's Law:

1. The general ledger account numbers involved
2. The person preparing the journal entries
3. The department affected by the entries
4. The location affected by the entries
5. The date within the month or month within the year of the entries
6. The level at which the journal entries were made (i.e., were they top-side entries made at the corporate level or were they made at the operating level)

Finding a correlation between the suspect pool of journal entries and one or more of these characteristics can help to narrow the list of entries requiring further investigation down to a reasonable quantity.

The recording of journal entries to perpetrate a financial statement fraud almost always involves some form of circumvention of internal controls. These entries are often made at the highest level (i.e., top-side level entries or at the consolidation level). And they are normally associated with limited or a complete lack of proper supporting documentation, and may lack the reviews and approvals required by a company's policies.

CHAPTER NINETEEN

Fraud or Honest Mistake?

WHEN A RESTATEMENT OF A COMPANY'S financial statements is necessary, it is understood that the previously issued statements were not prepared in accordance with the accounting principles that the company claimed it used. But what is it that distinguishes a restatement from a fraud case?

When confronted with an accusation of financial statement fraud, a common response on the part of the perpetrator is that he or she was merely being aggressive in the interpretation of the applicable accounting principles in an effort to present the company's financial statements in the best light possible. There's nothing wrong with that, right?

One of the challenges presented to the fraud investigator is to prove that the material misstatement in the financial statements was caused not by an honest but overaggressive interpretation of the accounting standards, but by a deliberate misstatement designed to deceive readers.

THE "SMOKING GUN"

If the investigator is lucky, the white-collar crime equivalent of a smoking gun is found. There are two key elements of a smoking gun:

- The perpetrator is aware that the accounting treatment does not conform to applicable accounting principles.
- The perpetrator initiates the activity that violates the accounting principle (e.g., the individual makes or requests a journal entry that executes the fraud).

The smoking gun must be in the form of some record that can be traced to the individual. An e-mail message, for instance, wherein the perpetrator acknowledges these facts, is an excellent piece of information that can be used to show that the individual intended to commit financial reporting fraud (e.g., "I don't care what that silly accounting standard says, just record it this way!"). Other written memos can also be used for this purpose.

WITNESSES

For obvious reasons, simply having a witness testify that they heard the perpetrator make these statements is not quite as strong as documentation from the perpetrator. However, witnesses who have heard the perpetrator make statements that involve the two elements introduced in the preceding section can be powerful evidence, especially when multiple witnesses have heard the same or similar things.

The best example of this might come from an individual who was somehow involved in the scheme. An accounting clerk who was ordered to make an entry that was acknowledged to be in conflict with accounting principles can provide strong support for an assertion that the perpetrator knew that their actions were fraudulent. Sometimes, the individuals who are in the best position to make these statements may have some liability themselves. They may have willingly participated or may have been coerced by an influential or domineering supervisor or co-worker. But, they can have tremendous value as witnesses if managed properly.

Other individuals who can serve as useful witnesses may have simply been in the room when the perpetrator made statements that demonstrate an intent to commit financial reporting fraud. Investigators can find useful witnesses by determining which individuals sat on certain internal committees or would otherwise have reason to be in attendance at meetings in which the perpetrator may have discussed the fraudulent financial reporting.

ALTERED DOCUMENTS

Another strong piece of evidence that can be used to demonstrate a willful act of deceit is an altered document, especially if it can be traced back to the suspect. A correction to erroneous documentation is one thing, but when the "correction" turns an accurate document into one that supports improper accounting treatment, the investigator has discovered valuable evidence. Examples of altered documents that have proven useful in fraud cases include the following:

- Shipping documents (e.g., making it appear that a shipment took place earlier than it really did)
- Inventory records (e.g., altering count sheets to inflate the quantity on hand during a physical inventory)
- Contracts (e.g., altering dates or other key terms of a contract to support a fraudulent accounting treatment)
- Appraisals and valuation reports (e.g., altering the fair value assigned to certain assets that are carried on the balance sheet, or to avoid recognition of an impairment loss)

Of course, proving that a document has been altered is not always easy. Physical evidence may be present in the form of correction fluid, correction tape, and so on. In some cases, documentation that appears to be a photocopy when an original was at one time present, or would be expected to be present, should be a sign that further investigation is necessary. The original document may have been altered and then scanned or copied in order to conceal evidence of the alteration. Sometimes, this can be proven through careful analysis of the document.

Alterations of electronic records are also possible to detect. Some software leaves a distinct trail that can tell an investigator who altered a document and when the alteration took place. In other cases, outside experts can be called upon to analyze electronic files for signs of alteration.

Harder still is proving *who* altered a document, especially physical documents (electronic documents often provide an indication of who has accessed the document). Once again, an eyewitness who observed or participated in the alteration is best. But, sometimes using the process of elimination can be helpful. Proving that no one other than the suspect had access to, or any reason to access the document can provide some degree of useful support for an assertion that the individual altered the document.

MULTIPLE RECORDS

The number of reasons for maintaining two or more sets of accounting records is very limited. In some cases, a tax-basis set of records may be a legitimate second record that differs from those prepared in accordance with applicable accounting principles. But these cases are few and far between.

Normally, when a fraud scheme involves the creation and maintenance of a second set of records, this represents strong evidence that the misstatement in the financial statements was no honest mistake. Why would a company maintain two accounts receivable subsidiary ledgers (as was done in the case of Del Global Technologies Corp.—see Chapter 20) other than to keep track of the real receivables separately from the inflated receivables? Likewise with a second set of inventory records.

Proving that there is no legitimate need for a second set of accounting records is strong evidence of someone's intent to present false information, especially when the false information is used to prepare the financial statements.

DESTRUCTION OF EVIDENCE

Many readers of this book will recall one instance in which an overzealous shredder cost a company dearly. Destruction of evidence can be an important indicator of intent on the part of a suspect.

Companies destroy documents and records all the time. Every company should have a policy regarding record retention and destruction. Many companies also have strictly enforced policies governing retention of e-mail messages and other electronic files.

Accordingly, an important part of an investigation is to determine what a company's record retention and destruction policies and procedures were at the time of the misstatement in the company's financial statements. Signs that are consistent with deliberate, willful misstatements include the following:

- The suspect violates the company's policies in destroying records that could be used to prove a financial reporting fraud.
- Selective compliance with the company's policies (i.e., technically, the records that were destroyed were eligible for destruction under the company's policies, but the policy was only practiced in connection with the records most valuable to the investigation, while all other records eligible for destruction remain intact).
- The destruction of records technically complies with company policy, but the timing of the destruction is suspicious (e.g., immediately after a whistleblower complaint surfaces, or notification of an audit is received).

Once a suspect has been notified of an investigation, or is otherwise aware of a pending investigation, destruction of pertinent records, even those records otherwise eligible for destruction, may violate company policy and definitely violates certain provisions of the Sarbanes-Oxley Act if the investigation pertains to a violation of U.S. law.

ACTIONS THAT CONTRADICT RECOMMENDATIONS

Another sign that an individual may have deliberately misstated a company's financial statements exists when the individual acts in a manner that contradicts recommendations received from others, such as from internal or external auditors. Examples of such contradictory actions include the following:

- Failing to take action in response to reported weaknesses in internal controls, especially controls that, left unaddressed, could allow for the perpetration and/or concealment of a financial reporting fraud (e.g., poor controls for the recording of journal entries).
- Not following an auditor's recommended accounting treatment for a certain transaction or category of transactions.

Contradicting an auditor's recommended accounting treatment should always be considered suspicious. If it becomes apparent that management has sought out the opinions of other accountants and auditors, this is yet another indication that fraud may be occurring. Opinion shopping, as it is known, takes place when management looks around for auditors who they can convince to go along with their preferred accounting treatment. This should always be viewed as suspicious behavior.

PATTERNS OF BEHAVIOR

Speaking of behavior, repeatedly engaging in an activity that the suspect knows, or should have known, was wrong also is a strong indicator of an intent to engage in that behavior. In other words, doing something once or twice is easier to justify as an honest mistake. Engaging in the same act over and over again is more consistent with the behavior of someone who knew exactly what they were doing and intended to continue doing it.

PERSONAL GAIN

While not directly associated with proving whether someone perpetrated a fraud scheme, showing that the individual personally benefited can help in proving intent. Examples of personal gain that best support attempts to prove intent are increases in stock price that correspond with the suspect's sale of stock at the higher price, bonuses (especially if directly tied to financial performance of the company), salary increases, and any other benefit that is provided in response to the reported financial results of the company.

Personal gain may also be established less directly. For example, someone may have received a promotion or elevation in title (with or without any adjustments in compensation), an excellent performance evaluation, or some nonfinancial benefit. In some cases, simply keeping one's job is the benefit that an individual receives, when loss of employment would have been the alternative.

THERE'S NO OTHER EXPLANATION FOR IT

Finally, another way to prove that an individual intended to commit a dishonest act is to show, through process of elimination, that there was no honest reason for their actions. This process is sometimes referred to as reverse proof. It involves seeking out and disproving every legitimate explanation for the evidence at hand, leading to the only remaining conclusion—that fraud has occurred.

As it pertains to financial statement fraud, this can be a difficult task. One of the common assertions made by individuals who have committed financial statement fraud is that they thought that their accounting estimates, methods, and positions taken all complied with GAAP or IFRS, even if their actions represent aggressive interpretations of the rules.

CHAPTER TWENTY

Assessing (or Minimizing) Auditor Liability

ONCE IT HAS BEEN DETERMINED that the financial statements contain a material misstatement, two important questions must be asked:

1. Was the misstatement an intentional act of one or more individuals in management (as discussed in Chapter 19), thereby making a case for fraud?
2. Do the auditors of the financial statements have liability for failing to detect the misstatement in connection with their audit?

In this chapter, the issue of assessing auditor liability in financial statement fraud cases is addressed. The goals of this chapter are as follows:

- Provide guidance to auditors to help them minimize the risk of successful auditor liability claims by performing better audits
- Provide guidance to investigators in assessing whether auditors have failed to perform an audit that fulfills professional responsibilities

Auditors are required to exercise professional skepticism in performing an audit. This is described as having a questioning mind and a critical assessment of audit evidence. As it relates to the potential for fraud, auditors are instructed to neither assume that management is dishonest nor to assume unquestioned honesty.

LITIGATION AGAINST AUDITORS

Potential plaintiffs in litigation involving cases in which auditors failed to detect a material misstatement in the audited financial statements include the following:

- Initial and subsequent purchasers and sellers of stock (either in cases involving publicly traded companies or closely held private companies).
- The company that was audited (the client of the auditor)
- Third-party primary beneficiaries (parties specifically identified to the auditor, beneficiaries of the auditor's services)
- Other third parties (parties not specifically identified, but that are known, such as creditors, as well as others who may have a reasonable need for relying on the audited financial statements)

The potential liabilities that an auditor might face include breach of contract and tort. Under breach of contract, the most likely assertion is that the auditor violated the auditing standards that were contractually agreed to under the terms of the audit engagement letter. As a tort, the likely charges are for ordinary or gross negligence. In each of these cases, a failure to follow auditing standards is also asserted. Under ordinary negligence, it is asserted that there was a lack of reasonable care in performing the audit. Under gross negligence, the claim is that the auditor engaged in reckless departure from the auditing standards, demonstrating a lack of even minimum care in performing the audit.

In each case, the outcome hinges upon the answers to the following questions:

1. Were the financial statements materially misstated (i.e., did the financial statements contain a material departure from the accounting principles in conformity with which they purport to be prepared, such as U.S. GAAP or IFRS)?

2. Did the auditor fail to comply with the auditing standards that are required to be followed, and to which the auditor claims compliance in the auditor's report?

The burden of proof in most cases is generally on the plaintiff, who must demonstrate that the auditors failed to comply with auditing standards or were otherwise negligent. However, this book is not designed to explain the burden of proof in detail, which can vary somewhat from one jurisdiction to another. Instead, the focus here is on the auditing standards and how auditors may or may not fulfill the requirements of those standards. In particular, the focus will be on those areas of an audit that appear to be most prone to negligence assertions or under-auditing.

There is the additional possibility that an auditor may be directly involved in a fraud through intentional concealment. But this chapter focuses solely on the issue of auditor liability associated with failing to follow auditing standards and the resultant failure to detect a material misstatement in the financial statements.

CONCEALMENT FROM THE AUDITORS

The biggest challenge to auditors is the intentional nature of a financial statement fraud. Unlike unintentional errors and deliberately aggressive accounting treatment of transactions, financial statement fraud involves attempts to conceal schemes from the auditors—be they internal or external auditors. In some cases, the efforts to trick the auditors were quite elaborate. Consider the following examples from fraud cases described earlier in this book:

- **Del Global Technologies Corp., Inc.** This case involved a variety of schemes, as well as multiple subsidiary companies. At least four of these subsidiaries maintained two sets of accounting records—one for the auditors and one correct set. The records maintained for the auditors even included bogus sales invoices, product testing documents, and shipping records in support of a premature revenue recognition scheme in which quarters were held open after the end of the quarter, premature shipments were made to third-party warehouses, and sales were recorded for products that hadn't even been manufactured yet. In connection with improperly capitalized costs, phony vendor invoices were created that supported capitalization.

- **Sterling Financial Corp.** This case involved the overstatement of a loan portfolio, including the hiding of delinquent loans at one of Sterling's subsidiaries, Equipment Finance, LLC (see Chapter 7). Senior management hid the delinquent and bogus loans from the internal and external auditors using a variety of techniques:
  - The removal of fraudulent loan information from the loan system in advance of audits, preventing internal and external auditors from discovering the scheme, followed by reentering the fraudulent information back into the system once the audits were completed.
  - Insertion of fake work references, summary approvals, and credit reports into loan files, in some cases simply using correction fluid on photocopied credit reports to alter dates and alter or conceal other information.
  - After the auditors selected loan customers for confirmation, customer addresses were changed to ensure that the confirmations went undelivered or were delivered to others involved in the scheme.
- **Koninklijke Ahold N.V. (Royal Ahold).** This case involved the improper consolidation of certain joint ventures associated with a subsidiary of this company based in the Netherlands. To support the consolidation of joint ventures, Ahold provided its auditors with letters signed by both Ahold and the joint venture partners stating that Ahold controlled the joint ventures. These letters were critical to consolidation, since the joint venture agreements did not demonstrate control on the part of Ahold, which held 50 percent or less ownership interests in each of the joint ventures. However, undisclosed to the auditors, shortly after these letters were prepared, Ahold and the joint venture partners executed "rescinding letters," effectively secret side agreements that rescinded Ahold's control over the joint ventures. This practice was carried out at least four times, until the head of Ahold's internal audit department became aware of the existence of the rescinding letters. Shortly thereafter, an internal investigation commenced.

  This element of concealment makes detection by auditors much more complicated. As an auditor assesses the risk of fraud, the risk of concealment must be factored equally into the planned audit procedures.

AUDITING STANDARDS

In the United States, auditing standards for audits of publicly traded companies are promulgated by the Public Company Accounting Oversight Board

(PCAOB), while the auditing standards for audits of all other entities (referred to as "non-issuers") have as their source the American Institute of Certified Public Accountants (AICPA). The PCAOB follows all standards issued by the AICPA through April 16, 2003, and has subsequently issued standards of its own. These additional standards mostly mirror those issued by the AICPA, but with certain differences and provisions that are unique to audits of public companies. The AICPA auditing standards are issued as individual standards (e.g., Statement on Auditing Standards No. 115), but are then codified using a standardized referencing system, referred to in this book using their AU Section number (e.g., AU Section 316).

Internationally, auditing standards are issued as International Standards on Auditing (e.g., ISA 540). These standards are issued by the International Federation of Accountants through the International Auditing and Assurance Standards Board.

The auditor's opinion on the financial statements provides reasonable assurance that the financial statements are free of material misstatement. The concept of "reasonable" is explained as being a high level of assurance, but is not meant to be absolute assurance. This correlates to an expectation that an auditor obtain sufficient evidence such that audit risk (the risk that the auditor issues an unqualified opinion on financial statements that contain a material misstatement) is kept to a low level.

The concept of "material" refers mostly to a quantitative measure. However, auditors are instructed to consider qualitative elements of materiality as well. For instance, certain misstatements, while small in amount, may have a profound effect on a reader of the financial statements. A small misstatement that allows an entity to barely meet a current ratio loan covenant could be considered material due to the effect that the misstatement has.

Audits are not expected to uncover all misstatements. But auditors are expected to detect material ones. And a material misstatement can be caused by either an unintentional act (an error) or an intentional one (fraud).

CONSIDERATION OF THE RISKS OF MATERIAL MISSTATEMENT

The first area in which the potential for auditor liability emerges is in the planning stages of the audit. Under AU Section 314 and ISA 315, auditors must identify and assess the risk that the financial statements they are about to audit contain a material misstatement. Part of that identification requires that the auditor gain an understanding of all of the following factors that can have an impact on the risk of material misstatement:

1. The client's industry in which it operates, including regulatory and other external factors
2. The nature of the audit client (i.e., its operations, ownership, organizational structure, etc.)
3. The client's objectives and strategies and the related business risks
4. The measurement and review of the entity's financial performance
5. The client's internal controls, including how the entity selects and applies accounting policies

All of these considerations should be documented in the auditor's work papers.

From this list, the first and last are areas in which auditors are most prone to falling short of expectations. The first factor is misinterpreted by some auditors to mean simply understanding what industry a client is in. But auditors should have a knowledge of the industry sufficient to understand the risks and industry developments relevant to their client, in order to plan appropriate audit procedures.

One sure sign that an auditor may not possess a sufficient understanding of an industry is that the auditor claims expertise in too many industries, as evidenced by a client list that spans multiple and diverse industries. Not only do accounting standards vary from one industry to another, but the regulatory environment, competitive forces, and numerous other factors vary, leading to very different audit risks. Good auditors tend to specialize in very few industries and are well-immersed in those industries, evidenced by subscribing to industry journals, attending industry-specific continuing professional education, and working with numerous clients in an industry.

This deficiency has been observed more commonly in smaller firms, where the same audit partner and audit team serve clients in several dissimilar industries, making it difficult to demonstrate expertise across all industries. Larger firms have generally been able to avoid assertions of this deficiency for the simple reason that with so many people, their personnel tend to be able to specialize in one industry or in fewer areas.

The fifth item from the list, the requirement that an auditor obtain an understanding of an entity's internal controls sufficient to enable the auditor to plan appropriate auditing procedures, is not new at all. This requirement has been a cornerstone of auditing for many years. However, it nonetheless represents a common area of auditor exposure if the auditor takes shortcuts in gaining and documenting internal controls. How does this happen? Usually, a failure to gain a proper understanding of internal controls occurs under one of two circumstances:

1. The auditor has already determined the specific auditing procedures that are planned for the audit (regardless of the results of gaining an understanding of internal controls), so the process of looking into internal controls is done very quickly, with an eye toward simply getting this part done so that the auditor can move on to the predetermined audit steps.
2. The task of gaining and documenting the understanding of internal controls is delegated to a very inexperienced auditor without adequate supervision and guidance from someone who understands how to make proper inquiries and observations that are more likely to turn up deficiencies in the design of internal controls.

In PCAOB Release No. 105-2010-006, the PCAOB revoked the registration of one small audit practice based on conducting substandard audits of a public company from 2006 to 2008. Among the many deficiencies cited by PCAOB was the auditor's failure to test internal controls during any of the three years, without including any documentation for "how that determination was reached or how the assessment of internal controls impacted the planning of the audit to determine the nature, timing, and extent of the tests to be performed."

The deficiencies in this case reached almost comic proportions. The auditor admitted to relying heavily on the previous audits and only inquiring of management about balance sheet accounts that changed by 10 percent or more from year to year. When asked about this approach, coupled with a few very basic procedures, the auditor replied, ". . . other than that, I did nothing."

Material misstatements can be put into two basic categories: those that result from unintentional errors (including honest misinterpretations of accounting standards) and those that result from fraud, which is an intentional act. Due to the unique characteristics of fraud, the auditing literature contains special provisions associated with detecting misstatements caused by fraud.

Consideration of fraud in an audit is covered in AU Section 316 and ISA 240. Under these sections of the auditing standards, auditors are directed to perform certain procedures, the most important of which are listed as follows:

1. Identify specific risks of fraud (asset misappropriations or financial statement fraud) that could result in a material misstatement.
2. Assess each identified risk (i.e., evaluate an entity's programs and internal controls in terms of its ability to address fraud risks)
3. Respond to the fraud risks by designing appropriate audit procedures, some of which may be overall responses and others that might be a response to a very specific risk

Audit failures can occur in any of these three critical steps. And, of course, the audit work papers must document what the auditor did with respect to each.

Perhaps even worse than failing to identify a fraud risk is an auditor's failure to do anything about a risk once one has been identified. This appears to be what happened in PCAOB Release No. 105-2010-007, which addressed the 2006 audit of a company in which 92 percent of its reported assets consisted of capitalized internal-use software (accounting for internal-use software is covered in Chapter 6). The auditor properly identified capitalized software as not only a significant audit area, but one that was classified as a risk of financial reporting fraud. Specifically, the auditor's work papers identified "overstating the valuation of capitalized software" as a fraud risk. However, the PCAOB concluded that the auditor "failed to perform sufficient procedures to determine (a) whether software costs were appropriately capitalized, and (b) whether capitalized software was fairly valued."

In essence, the PCAOB identified two separate deficiencies associated with auditing the application of two separate accounting rules. Not only did the auditor fail to test whether the initial software costs met the criteria for capitalization, but the auditor also failed to assess whether the capitalized software (even assuming its costs were initially eligible for capitalization) incurred an impairment loss as a result of its value being lower than its book value. With the impairment loss issue, the auditor once again left itself open to liability by identifying the risk, in the form of communicating to management the possibility of impairment, but then doing nothing about it.

Much guidance is available for auditors in assessing the risk of material misstatement due to fraud. Included in this guidance is coverage of Cressey's Fraud Triangle, which notes that three conditions are normally present when fraud occurs:

1. Incentive or pressure
2. Opportunity for the fraud to be perpetrated
3. Rationalization by the perpetrator

Auditors are instructed to consider each of these three elements in assessing the risk of fraud in an audit.

Another example of an audit firm being accused of failing to perform adequate procedures in response to its risk assessment is the Adelphia Communications case. This is the case, explained in Chapter 10, in which Adelphia underreported its debt obligations by shifting them to affiliated entities, all under the control of a few individuals. In AAER 2237, the SEC noted that in their work papers, the auditors identified all of the following fraud risk factors:

1. Management is concentrated in a small group or dominated by one strong personality without compensating controls.
2. Management appears willing to accept unusually high levels of risk.
3. Management tends to interpret accounting standards aggressively.
4. The organizational and/or reporting structures are unduly complex.
5. There is substantial debt from unusual sources (e.g., related parties) or on unusual terms.
6. There are significant affiliated entities or other related parties that the audit firm will not audit and with whom significant transactions might have occurred.
7. The company engages in unique, highly complex, and material transactions that pose difficult "substance over form" questions.
8. The company is under significant pressure to obtain additional capital necessary to stay competitive, and is growing near the limit of its financial resources.
9. There have been frequent disputes with the auditor on accounting, auditing, or reporting matters.

These issues would serve as a good list of fraud risk factors for any auditor in assessing a client's environment and motives for engaging in fraudulent financial reporting.

One final aspect of audit planning should be considered. Based on the extent and nature of the fraud risks identified, an audit firm should consider how to best staff an audit. The assignment of professional staff to an audit should be done according to which staff possesses the knowledge, skills, and experience necessary to properly execute the audit plan. Audit firms should document how they assigned staff to an audit engagement, and how this staffing varied according to the extent and types of fraud risks identified.

IMPROPER OR INADEQUATE USE OF ANALYTICAL PROCEDURES

Analytical procedures are described in AU Section 329 and ISA 520. Analytical procedures may be used by auditors in three stages of the audit:

1. In the planning stages of the audit, to assist in determining the nature, timing, and extent of auditing procedures to be applied.
2. During audit fieldwork, as a substantive procedure to obtain audit evidence about particular account balances or classes of transactions.
3. In the final review stages of an audit, as part of an overall review of the financial information and audit evidence gathered during the audit.

Use of analytical procedures in the planning and final review stages is required. Their use as a substantive procedure, though not required, is a common practice.

Auditor liability associated with planning-stage analytical procedures arises from either of the following failures:

1. Failure to identify a risk of material misstatement even though planning-stage analytical procedures indicated an unexplained variance from expectations.
2. Identification of a risk based on analytical procedures, but a failure to properly follow up by designing appropriate additional audit procedures to address the risk.

Using analytical procedures as a substantive tool for auditing a particular account or category of accounts is rather common. For example, an auditor may use an analytical procedure as a method of auditing a particular revenue account by multiplying a reliable statistic associated with the revenue-producing activity by an average price charged for the item or service (e.g., number of items delivered times the price per unit). This particular example may be useful for assessing either the completeness of revenue (i.e., whether someone has been skimming revenue intended for the organization) or for determining whether revenue is inflated by management.

When an analytical procedure produces an expected result that materially differs from the actual recorded amount, the auditor must evaluate the difference. One approach to investigating these differences, and a very common first step, is to make an inquiry of management. Management is often in a position to quickly assess why the variance might exist and can point the auditor in the right direction for verification. For instance, there may be a flaw in the assumptions used by the auditor in calculating an expected result, or there are changes in operations that management is aware of that explain the variance. However, regardless of how believable a management response might be, auditors must perform follow-up work. As it is stated in AU Section 329, "management responses . . . should ordinarily be corroborated with other audit evidence." Blind acceptance of management explanations of variances, or failure to gather appropriate additional audit evidence, has been the cause of numerous auditor failures.

Another cause of audit failures in using analytical procedures as a substantive procedure is the use of unreliable data on which an expectation is based. Using unreliable data to develop an expectation, in particular data that has been provided by a perpetrator of fraud, can lead to a false conclusion that an account balance or class of transactions is fairly stated when in fact, it is materially misstated. Auditors should consider the source of information that is relied upon for analytical procedures, keeping in mind that if fraud exists, it may be more than the account balances that are misstated. The data that could lead to detecting the fraud may be misstated as well.

A simple example of this scenario involves the comparison of a recorded balance with the same account's balance in a prior period. If the prior period balance is misstated, and the current year's balance is comparable to the prior balance, a false conclusion that the current year balance is fairly stated could result. Another example involves developing an expectation of recorded revenue by multiplying the number of items sold or units of service provided by an average price. Flaws in any of these data elements could lead to an erroneous calculation of expected revenue.

An example of a specific audit deficiency of this type is found in the following excerpt from a 2011 PCAOB inspection report of a large international audit firm:

> The Firm failed to perform sufficient procedures to test the existence of the issuer's inventory. The Firm performed physical inventory observations at approximately one half of one percent of the issuer's locations during the first half of the year, and used a substantive analytical procedure to test the year-end inventory balance. To develop its expectation of the year-end inventory balance, the Firm used the inventory balances from the small number of locations at which it had performed inventory observations during the first half of the year to predict the

> inventory balances for all the locations at the end of the year. The Firm, however, did not obtain evidence that the inventory balances at the issuer's retail locations were similar. In fact, there was considerable variation, approximately 15 percent, in the inventory balances at the three retail stores where physical inventories were observed. In addition, the Firm did not have evidence that the inventory balances in the first half of the year could be expected to be predictive of the balances at year end.

Reliance on analytical procedures as a substantive audit procedure is quite common in the audit revenue. Some examples of deficiencies in the application of analytical procedures to revenue are provided later, in the section on revenue recognition risks. However, one example is noteworthy here, in that it illustrates one additional issue that auditors may fail to recognize. The following is from a November 2011 PCAOB inspection report on one of the world's largest audit firms:

> The Firm failed to test the completeness and accuracy of the data it used to establish its expectations. In addition, when establishing thresholds for investigation of significant differences, the Firm failed to consider the possibility that a combination of misstatements could aggregate to an unacceptable amount. As a result, the Firm failed to investigate differences that, in combination, exceeded the Firm's established materiality level by a significant amount. Further, the Firm failed to obtain corroboration for certain of management's explanations of significant unexpected differences between expected and actual revenues.

Of particular importance in this finding is the possibility that multiple variances, each of which is not considered to be material, may accumulate to a large variance when considered together.

This finding also illustrates the importance of corroborating explanations for variances provided by management.

The final phase of the audit in which analytical procedures are used is in the final review stage. At this point, all adjustments resulting from the audit (if there are any) have been identified and recorded, and a draft set of financial statements has been prepared reflecting those adjustments. The final review should consider whether the final amounts and disclosures make sense and whether all unexpected balances or relationships have been identified and explained. Once again, conclusions about unexpected variances must be supported with proper audit evidence.

AUDITING ACCOUNTING ESTIMATES AND FAIR VALUES

Auditing accounting estimates is addressed in AU Section 342 and ISA 540. Additional guidance on auditing fair value measurements and disclosures is provided in AU Section 328 (this topic is included within ISA 540 for international auditing purposes).

Examples of accounting estimates include all of the following:

1. Assessment of the collectibility of receivables
2. Determination of whether inventory is obsolete
3. Determination of useful lives of depreciable and amortizable assets
4. Estimation of the percentage of completion associated with contracts (which impacts revenue recognition)
5. Establishment of revenue recognition criteria and timelines
6. Actuarial assumptions used in determining pension liabilities
7. Assessing the probability and amount of losses associated with litigation

All estimates that are material to the financial statements must be identified and audited. Auditing standards describe three approaches to auditing the accounting estimates developed by management:

1. Review and test the process used by management to develop the estimate.
2. Develop an independent expectation of the estimate and compare it to the estimate developed by management.
3. Review subsequent events (events occurring after the end of the year, but prior to the conclusion of the audit).

Auditors are required to utilize one or more of these procedures when auditing estimates that are material to the financial statements.

The first approach is essentially the equivalent of gaining a detailed understanding of internal controls and testing those internal controls. However, in addition to specific processes used by management, this understanding may also involve the assessment of assumptions used by management in developing an estimate. In this respect, the process is different than processes utilized in other accounting cycles, such as payroll, disbursements, and receipts.

As a result, audit failures when using the first approach tend to result from one or more of the following:

1. Failing to gain a complete understanding of the process used by management.
2. Gaining an understanding of the process, but not properly testing the application of the process.
3. Relying on the false assumption that an outside specialist hired by a client is independent, and failing to understand and test the specialist's processes.

This last oversight is particularly common with certain fair value measurements, which are explained more fully later in this section.

The second approach, developing an independent expectation, requires that the auditor re-perform the development of the estimate, using either the same methodology as that used by management or, perhaps, a different approach. The goal is to independently arrive at an estimate similar to the one developed by management. Analytical procedures may be used to develop this independent expectation. But, as pointed out in the preceding section, there are two common mistakes when taking an analytical approach:

1. Using unreliable data to develop the expectation.
2. Identifying a deviation from expectations, but not properly following up on the explanation for the deviation (e.g., taking management's explanation for the deviation at face value, without corroborating the explanation with other evidence).

The third approach, using subsequent events as evidence that an estimate is fairly stated, is useful only in certain situations. For example, subsequent events may provide evidence about the reliability of the estimate regarding collectibility of accounts receivable, by observing subsequent collections. It may also provide useful information about the fair value measurements of certain assets held at year-end, if those assets were sold shortly after the end of the year.

Intentionally omitted from the list of accounting estimates is the development of fair value measurements. The omission is due to the fact that these are a very special brand of estimate, one that is so specialized and ripe for misstatement that specialized audit guidance has been developed to address this risky area.

Many assets and liabilities are recorded at fair value under accounting principles generally accepted in the U.S., as well as under IFRS. For instance, most investments are carried at fair value. The determination of fair value can range from fairly simple, such as with certain actively traded securities, to very complex, as with many alternative investments.

AU Section 328 and ISA 540 provide guidance on auditing fair value measurements. However, the requirements are quite similar to those already described in this chapter. The auditor must gain an understanding of an entity's process for determining fair value measurements and then determine an appropriate method for auditing those measurements. The methods used mirror those used in auditing other accounting estimates, as explained earlier.

An entity's process for determining fair value measurements can be quite complex. Some of the characteristics of these processes that are particularly prone to fraud (and therefore susceptible to auditor oversight) include the following:

- Significant assumptions made by management in the development of fair values (e.g., estimated future cash flows associated with an asset, determination of discount rates used in present value calculations, etc.).
- The selection of methods used to calculate fair values (e.g., present value calculations, etc.).
- The documentation maintained in connection with management's fair value measurements.
- The extent to which information technology is utilized in the process.
- Segregation of duties and other key internal controls over the measurement process.
- Controls over the consistency and reliability of data used in the measurements.
- The extent to which reliance is placed on an outside service organization for the determination of fair value measurements (e.g., fair values provided by an investment management firm).
- The extent to which an entity utilizes outside experts to perform or assist in performing fair value measurements (e.g., appraisers and valuation specialists hired by the company).

In some cases, an audit firm may employ specialists who possess the technical skills necessary to audit complicated fair value measurements. However, many firms, smaller ones in particular, should consider temporarily employing the services of outside specialists to aid in the performance of specific audit procedures aimed at fair value measurements. And under no circumstances should an auditor rely on the outside expert used by a client as the sole evidence that fair value measurements were audited, regardless of how well-regarded the expert may be. The use of outside experts by an audit client constitutes an element of the client's internal controls. Regardless of how strong those internal controls might be, the auditor must nonetheless perform sufficient audit work on the measurements themselves if they are material to the financial statements.

One of the acceptable approaches to auditing estimates and fair values described earlier is to examine and test management's process for developing the estimate. PCAOB Release No. 105-2009-001 describes how this approach, when improperly applied, can lead to audit failures. This case dealt with the 2003, 2004, and 2005 audits of a U.S. registered company based in Beijing, China. During the period covered by the audits, the company had acquired one or more other entities. As explained in Chapter 11, the cost of such acquisitions must be allocated to the acquired assets and assumed liabilities based on the underlying fair values of such assets and liabilities. The company recorded acquired assets and liabilities at the book values at which they were carried in the accounting records of the acquired entities. Management asserted to the auditor that this was done because the acquirees' book values reasonably approximated estimated fair value. However, the auditor performed no audit procedures to verify this assertion.

This is a good example of how explanations that may make complete sense in many ways must nonetheless be audited. Simply accepting management's assertion is not an audit procedure by itself.

A review of audit firm inspection reports prepared by the PCAOB provides excellent examples of some of the fair value accounting issues that are susceptible to under-auditing. For example, in Chapter 8, the issue of evaluating fair value measurements prepared by a third-party specialist for an auditee was explained. In one 2010 inspection report for a large U.S. auditing firm, the PCAOB noted the following deficiencies:

> The issuer used a service organization to account for its investments and mortgage-backed securities and engaged a pricing specialist to validate values received from the service organization. The Firm failed to perform sufficient procedures concerning the valuation of the issuer's investments and mortgage-backed securities. Specifically:
>
> - The Firm failed to obtain an understanding of the methods and to evaluate the reasonableness of the assumptions used by either the service organization or the pricing specialist to value the issuer's investments and mortgage-backed securities.
> - For the valuation assertion, the Firm relied on controls in place at the service organization to support its control risk assessment

> of low even though the service auditor's report covered only one month of the issuer's fiscal year. Other than obtaining a representation from the service organization that there were no changes to controls during the remaining eleven-month period, the Firm failed to obtain evidence regarding whether the controls were operating effectively during the eleven-month period not covered by the service auditor's report.

In another report, the PCAOB identified deficiencies in the audit of fair values prepared by an auditee of certain equity and debt investments it held:

> The issuer valued the equity investments using an enterprise valuation method computed as a multiple of the corresponding investee's earnings before interest, taxes, depreciation, and amortization ("EBITDA") based on the unaudited financial statements of the investee. The issuer valued the debt investments using a yield approach in which the fair value of the debt was determined based on the present value of the principal and interest payments. The discount rate used in the present value calculation took into consideration the stated interest rate on the debt and the financial position and credit risk of each investee. The Firm failed to perform sufficient procedures to test the underlying data and assumptions used in the issuer's valuation models to calculate the fair value of the debt and equity investments. Specifically:
>
> - The Firm failed to apply (or to request that the issuer arrange with the investees to have other auditors apply) appropriate auditing procedures to the investees' financial statements from which the EBITDAs used to determine fair value were derived.
> - The Firm failed to sufficiently evaluate the reasonableness of the multiples that the issuer applied to the investees' EBITDA to calculate the value of the equity investments, including whether the multiples reflected, or were not inconsistent with, market information. The Firm first compared the multiples to ranges of multiples that the issuer had obtained from an outside source, but the Firm did not test these ranges. Then, for those multiples that fell outside of the issuer-provided range, the Firm compared the multiple to a multiple that the Firm obtained from an outside source. For those multiples for which the multiple it obtained from this outside source did not provide corroboration, the Firm's procedures were limited to inquiries of management.

- The Firm failed to sufficiently evaluate the reasonableness of the discount rates applied by the issuer to calculate the value of the debt investments, including whether they reflected, or were not inconsistent with, market information. Specifically, for investments for which the discount rate fell outside a range determined by the Firm's valuation group for similar companies, the Firm's procedures were limited to inquiry of management.

Similar deficiencies were found in the evaluations of audit procedures applied to impairment testing associated with goodwill (see Chapter 7). In a PCAOB inspection report released in December 2011 on one of the world's largest audit firms, the following deficiency was noted:

> The Firm failed to sufficiently evaluate the assumptions the issuer used in its revenue and expense projections, as the Firm limited its procedures to comparing current-year interim data to unaudited financial statements and verifying the mathematical accuracy of the projections. In addition, there was no evidence in the audit documentation, and no persuasive other evidence, that the Firm had evaluated the reasonableness of the risk premium that the issuer used to calculate the weighted average cost of capital, which was a significant assumption in the issuer's goodwill impairment analysis.

And, just like with the measurement of fair values of investments, companies frequently utilize outside specialists to evaluate impairment of goodwill and other intangible assets. In the PCAOB inspection report of the same audit firm (though with respect to a different audit than the one cited above), the following deficiency was included:

> As part of its impairment analysis for goodwill, the issuer obtained from its external valuation specialist two estimates of the fair value of one of its reporting units; one estimate was based on a market approach, which was weighted 60 percent, and the other on an income approach, which was the higher amount and was weighted 40 percent. The Firm did not determine the reasons for the significant difference between the two estimates in order to evaluate whether one of the individual approaches or the weighted average was the best indicator of fair value. Further, the Firm failed to sufficiently evaluate the reasonableness of the revenue growth assumptions that were used in the income approach and that were significantly higher than the issuer's historical revenue growth rates. Specifically, the Firm's evaluation

was limited to inquiry of management, review of certain long-term industry outlook reports that did not address the short-term growth rates used in the analyses, review of a few recent requests for proposals and long-term supply contracts that covered an insignificant portion of the projected revenue, and a comparison of the assumptions to those management used for other purposes.

REVENUE RECOGNITION RISKS

Auditing standards associated with the detection of fraud make an assumption that revenue recognition will always be a fraud risk factor that should be addressed. If an auditor is to claim that revenue recognition is not a fraud risk, the reasoning behind such a conclusion must be documented in the audit work papers. And acknowledging that revenue recognition is a fraud risk requires the auditor to document a response to that risk.

The fraud risk in this area is ordinarily the risk that revenue has been inflated by management in order to make the entity appear to be more successful than it really is (though there can be instances in which management is motivated to understate revenue). In some cases, management goes to great lengths to falsify revenue in order to meet outsiders' expectations of profitability. However, in one part of AU Section 316, auditors are reminded that "fraudulent financial reporting need not be the result of a grand plan or conspiracy. It may be that management representatives rationalize the appropriateness of a material misstatement, for example, as an aggressive rather than indefensible interpretation of complex accounting rules, or as a temporary misstatement of financial statements, including interim statements, expected to be corrected later when operational results improve."

The preceding statement illustrates some of the difficulty in fraud cases—proving intent. However, in pursuing the auditors, proof of management intent is not the central issue. Rather, showing that the financial statements were misstated and that the auditor failed to follow the auditing standards in failing to detect the misstatement is the central issue.

Revenue recognition can be one of the most complicated areas of an audit. Not only can the determination of an appropriate revenue recognition method be complex, but there can be numerous estimates involved in applying a revenue recognition methodology. As the business world has gotten more sophisticated, the many different practices for selling goods and services has led to numerous complex methods for recognizing revenue. Nowhere is the need for auditors to understand the details of accounting principles more pronounced than in the area of revenue recognition. Likewise, solid understanding of industry practices is essential in this area, as certain industries have developed practices based on the industry's interpretation of how a particular accounting principle should be applied, absent specific wording in the accounting principle.

A review of PCAOB inspection reports released in 2010 and 2011 provides the following examples of deficiencies found in the audits of revenue recognition by some of the largest audit firms in the world:

1. The Firm failed to perform sufficient procedures to test the issuer's recognition of revenue from contracts accounted for under the percentage-of-completion method. Specifically, the Firm failed to test costs incurred to date, including indirect cost allocations, beyond comparing certain costs to reports that were not tested. The Firm also failed to sufficiently test the estimated costs to complete, because the Firm's procedures were limited to inquiries of management.
2. The Firm failed to perform sufficient procedures to test the appropriateness of the issuer's recognition of revenue:
   a. Most of the issuer's sales to its dealers were financed by lending institutions that had repurchase agreements with the issuer in the event of the dealer's default. The Firm failed to evaluate whether the ultimate collectibility of these sales to dealers was reasonably assured.
   b. The Firm failed to consider whether a portion of the sales proceeds representing the fair value of the repurchase agreements should have been allocated to deferred revenue.
   c. The Firm failed to adequately evaluate the issuer's conclusion that sales to the issuer's largest dealer met the criteria for revenue recognition. Specifically, the Firm failed to include in its evaluation certain key facts, such as an exclusivity agreement between the dealer and the issuer that required the dealer to purchase a significant portion of its overall product requirements from the issuer; loans made by the issuer to the owner of the dealer during the year with a requirement that the proceeds be contributed as additional capital to the dealer, with half of the proceeds being used to purchase product from the issuer; and guarantees that the issuer provided to the dealer's lenders.

Many of the deficiencies found by the PCAOB in connection with audits of revenue relate to improper analytical procedures (explained earlier), as it is common for auditors to place moderate to significant reliance on analytical procedures in the audit of revenue. For example, the following deficiencies associated with analytical procedures applied to revenue were found in PCAOB inspection reports from 2010 and 2011:

1. The Firm's planned approach for auditing revenue included the performance of substantive analytical procedures. For purposes of these procedures, the Firm established its expectation for current-year revenue based on the results of certain of the issuer's competitors. The Firm, however, failed to determine that the use of the average of the historical results of certain of the issuer's competitors for its expectation was predictive of the issuer's revenue. In addition, other than by reading certain reports that management had provided to the issuer's Board of Directors, the Firm failed to obtain corroboration of management's explanations for approximately half of the significant unexpected difference between the Firm's expectation and the issuer's recorded revenue. Further, the Firm failed to investigate the remaining half of the significant unexpected difference.
2. The Firm established an expectation that the sales by each customer and product as a percentage of overall sales would be consistent with the corresponding percentage for the prior year, but failed to evaluate whether such an expectation was predictive of revenue for the current year. In addition, the Firm did not test certain of the current year and prior year data used in establishing its expectations. Further, the Firm failed to obtain corroboration of management's explanations of significant unexpected differences between expected and actual revenue for one of the reporting units. As a result of these failures, the analytical procedures provided little to no substantive assurance.
3. When performing analytical procedures to test revenue for all three segments, the Firm developed certain of its expectations based on the issuer's budget. There was no evidence in the audit documentation, and no persuasive other evidence, that the Firm had tested management's process for developing and updating the budget. In addition, the Firm failed to develop sufficiently precise expectations for certain of its analytical procedures, as it used ranges (for example, a decrease in revenue of 5 to 10 percent) for these expectations that were in excess of the Firm's established materiality levels. Further, the Firm failed to obtain corroboration of management's explanations of significant unexpected differences between expected and actual revenues.

INSUFFICIENT CONSIDERATION OF RELATED PARTY TRANSACTIONS

As explained throughout this book, transactions with related parties are particularly prone to fraudulent reporting. As such, the AICPA has placed emphasis on this area and has provided auditors with additional guidance designed to aid with identifying and analyzing related party transactions.

In their 2006 paper, "The Role of Related Party Transactions in Fraudulent Financial Reporting," Henry, Gordon, Reed, and Louwers studied 48 SEC enforcement actions in which both fraud and related party transactions were involved. In 31 of those cases, actions against the auditor were identified by the authors. In just 6 of the 31 cases did the auditor fail to identify related party transactions. Rather, the majority of cases against auditors involve some sort of failure associated with auditing the transactions.

Of the 31 cases, 16 involved deficiencies in the audit work performed regarding identified related party transactions. Nine of these cases pertained to valuing assets obtained in related party transactions and receivables from related parties. One of those nine cases involved Great American Financial, Inc., the company described in Chapter 7 that acquired a fictitious patent and a purported racehorse, each at inflated amounts. The SEC criticized the auditor in this case for overreliance on the management representation letter about the values of these assets. The remaining seven cases involved other deficiencies in audit procedures involving identified transactions.

Six of the 31 cases against auditors pertained to a failure to properly disclose related party transactions that had been identified during the audit. As explained in Chapter 14, identified transactions are subject to certain disclosure requirements.

AUDITING DISCLOSURES IN THE FINANCIAL STATEMENTS

Misstatements can occur in the basic financial statements as well as in the notes to the financial statements. Indeed, the disclosures made in the notes to the financial statements are prime candidates for fraud through the omission of required disclosures or the misstatement of information included in a disclosure. As with the basic financial statements themselves, however, auditor liability is based primarily on whether the disclosures contain a material misstatement and whether the auditor failed to follow the auditing standards in failing to detect the misstatement.

Disclosure requirements are found in the accounting standards addressing each specific area of the financial statements. As a result, auditors must be familiar not only with the required accounting treatment of relevant assets, liabilities, revenues, and expenses, but also with the disclosure requirements associated with each.

There is very little in the way of published guidance on how to audit disclosures. Instead, the auditing standards simply remind auditors of the importance of making sure that disclosures are complete and accurate. Unfortunately, some auditors have taken an approach that places little effort on these disclosures.

OVERRELIANCE ON THE MANAGEMENT REPRESENTATION LETTER

At the conclusion of an audit, the auditor must obtain a management representation letter. This letter represents management's understanding that the financial statements and disclosures are primarily the responsibility of management. The letter addresses all matters that are potentially material to the financial statements. As a result, the letter does represent a form of audit evidence. However, as noted in ISA 580, "Although written representations provide necessary audit evidence, they do not provide sufficient appropriate evidence on their own about any of the matters with which they deal." In other words, the management representation is similar to management responses to unexpected variances found in connection with analytical procedures—they must be corroborated with other audit evidence and cannot stand on their own.

There have been numerous cases in which auditors were found to be liable for failing to detect material misstatements where the auditor erroneously placed reliance on a management representation letter as the only form of audit evidence. Audit work papers should provide a clear trail of additional audit evidence that supports representations about material matters that are included in such letters.

APPENDIX

Financial Statement Fraud Indicators

WHEN FINANCIAL STATEMENT fraud takes place, it virtually always leaves a trail. The fraud indicators listed in this appendix represent characteristics that are often present when financial statement fraud occurs. Just like other red flags, their presence is not a guarantee that fraud is occurring. There are many reasons for their occurrence that have nothing to do with fraud. However, when fraud is occurring, these may be some of the signs that are observed. When these indicators are present, an explanation should be obtained in an attempt to rule out financial statement fraud. If fraud cannot be ruled out, keep investigating!

The indicators are organized by broad category of financial statement fraud—revenue-based schemes, asset-based schemes, and expense/liability-based schemes. Since many of the indicators could be consistent with a variety of schemes in each category, further investigation will be necessary to narrow the list of possible frauds down to a more manageable quantity.

Revenue-Based Schemes

- Cash flows from operations are negative or lag significantly behind reported net income.

- Rapid growth in sales in comparison with competitors or in light of current economic conditions.
- Growth in revenue from one location or division is unusually high in comparison with other locations or divisions.
- Unexplained increases in sales to specific customers.
- Changes in revenue recognition policies allowing for earlier recognition.
- Unexplained increases or decreases in reserve (liability) accounts.
- Changes in key assumptions used in revenue recognition, especially those impacting the timing of when revenue is recognized.
- Unexplained increases in accounts receivable (billed or unbilled), such as when receivables are growing at a faster rate than sales (i.e., fluctuations in the number of days' sales in receivables).
- Sales recognized are supported by documentation that indicates delivery to or acceptance by customers may have occurred after the end of the period.
- Sales supported by documentation that shows signs of having been altered, particularly with respect to dates of delivery, customer acceptance, or other information that triggers recognition of revenue.
- Supporting documentation, such as contracts, shipping documents, and sales orders, appear to be copies, rather than original documents (another sign that the originals have been altered, then copied).
- Sales invoice dates that are significantly later than the documented shipping date (which coincides with revenue recognition), perhaps indicating that the customer did not request the shipment until the later date.
- Changes in credit terms offered to customers, especially terms that are excessively lenient.
- The introduction of new incentives offered to customers.
- The introduction of highly complex sales arrangements with customers.
- An absence of a valid business purpose behind certain transactions.
- Unusually large sales to certain customers with no history of such large sales.
- Unusually large sales to certain customers at the end of the accounting period.
- A significant portion of a company's sales are recognized at the end of a quarter or year (especially if the portion of a quarter's sales that are recognized at the end of the quarter shows an increasing trend over recent quarters or if the significant recognition of sales enables the company to achieve its stated goals for the period).

- Sales arrangements that are not supported with a written agreement when such an agreement would ordinarily be expected.
- Discovery of side letters, verbal agreements, or e-mails that alter the standard terms of a sale.
- Contracts or other agreements that indicate that a customer is not required to pay for products delivered to the customer until the customer has sold the products to an end user.
- Sales at the end of one accounting period followed by returns from the same customer(s) early in the subsequent accounting period.
- Inconsistencies between information on a customer order and the shipping documentation (e.g., product numbers ordered appear to be different than those shipped), especially for orders processed right before the end of an accounting period.
- Customers listed in the sales/accounts receivable master file have incomplete information (e.g., purported customers that have no telephone numbers, street addresses, etc.).
- Multiple customers listed in the sales/accounts receivable master file with the same street address.
- Unexplained increases in sales to related parties, joint venture partners, or affiliates.
- Evidence exists of products provided to customers on a "trial basis" or under "loaner" programs under which the customer may not have an obligation to pay for the products.
- Material journal entries at the end of an accounting period (or after the end of the period), especially those resulting in the entity's meeting revenue goals for the period.
- Top-side journal entries to revenue or sales accounts that are not supported with entries to subsidiary ledgers or other records that should match.
- Changes in how revenue is allocated among the units of a multiple-element revenue arrangement.
- Changing from the cost approach to a more subjective approach to estimate the progress on contracts accounted for under the percentage of completion method of accounting.
- Unexplained fluctuations in ratios associated with revenue recognition (see Chapters 17 and 18).
- Discovery of new reserve accounts that lack apparent business justification.
- Pending acquisition or initial public offering.

Asset-Based Schemes

- Cash flow from operations is negative or lags significantly behind reported net income.
- New products have recently been introduced or have been announced, indicating the potential for research and development costs, which should be expensed as incurred.
- Asset capitalization costs appear to have been paid to related parties.
- Unexplained changes in valuation methods used in measuring the fair values of assets or liabilities.
- Unexplained changes in the assumptions used in applying valuation methods used in measuring the fair values of assets or liabilities.
- Expenditures recorded as expenses of the subsequent period are supported by documentation that indicates that the goods or services may have been received by the company in the prior period.
- Unusual increases in the number of days' purchases in inventory from one year to the next.
- The write-down rate associated with obsolete inventory declines inexplicably from one year to the next.
- Unsupported increase in the useful lives assigned to depreciable or amortizable assets.
- Changes in inventory flow or pricing assumptions.
- Inadequate internal controls associated with physical counts of inventory.
- Indications of subsequent alteration of inventory count documents.
- Unsupported changes in indirect cost (overhead) allocation policies and procedures.
- Unexplained increases or decreases in contra-asset reserve accounts.
- Significant assets resulting from transactions with related parties, affiliates, or joint venture partners.
- Changes in capitalization policies.
- Lack of documentation for management's assessment of the impairment of intangible assets or other indications that required impairment testing was not performed.
- Intangible assets being carried on the books that do not appear to be associated with the generation of revenue or other value.
- Material journal entries at the end of an accounting period (or after the end of the period), especially those that change carrying amounts of asset accounts or that reclassify costs from expense accounts to asset accounts.

- Top-side journal entries to asset accounts that are not supported with entries to subsidiary ledgers or other records that should match (e.g., inventory, accounts receivable, etc.).
- Unexplained fluctuations in ratios associated with expense capitalization or asset carrying values (see Chapters 17 and 18).
- Pending acquisition or initial public offering.

Expense/Liability-Based Schemes

- Cash flow from operations is negative or lags significantly behind reported net income.
- Unexplained increases in property and equipment accounts.
- Unexplained decreases in accounts payable, accrued expenses, and other liabilities.
- Lower than expected expenses.
- Significant use of estimates in measuring reserves and certain liability accounts.
- Significant expenditures shortly after the end of the period that were not accrued as liabilities.
- Discovery of liabilities that were transferred to unconsolidated affiliates prior to the end of the period.
- Discovery of correspondence indicating side deals with vendors or special arrangements with unconsolidated affiliates.
- Discovery of correspondence, or internal memoranda, indicating that the company is involved in litigation or may have other contingent liabilities.
- Significant purchases from related parties.
- Material journal entries at the end of an accounting period (or after the end of the period), especially those that change carrying amounts of liability accounts or that reclassify costs from expense accounts to asset accounts.
- Top-side journal entries to asset accounts that are not supported with entries to subsidiary ledgers or other records that should match (e.g., accounts payable).
- Unexplained fluctuations in ratios associated with expense capitalization or liability accounts (see Chapters 17 and 18).
- Pending acquisition or initial public offering.

Bibliography

Association of Certified Fraud Examiners. *Report to the Nations on Occupational Fraud and Abuse: 2012 Global Fraud Study*. Austin, TX: ACFE, 2012.

Association of Certified Fraud Examiners. *2010 Report to the Nations on Occupational Fraud and Abuse*. Austin, TX: ACFE, 2010.

Beasley, Mark S., Joseph V. Carcello, Dana R. Hermanson, and Terry L. Neal. *Fraudulent Financial Reporting 1998–2007, An Analysis of U.S. Public Companies.* The Committee of Sponsoring Organizations of the Treadway Commission, 2010.

Beneish, Messod D. "The Detection of Earnings Manipulation." *Financial Analysts Journal.* (Sept-Oct. 1999): 24–36.

Brennan, Niamh, and Mary McGrath. "Financial Statement Fraud: Some Lessons from US and European Case Studies." *Australian Accounting Review* 17, no. 42 (July 2007): 49–61.

Chen, Ken Y., and Randal L.Elder. *Fraud Risk Factors and the Likelihood of Fraudulent Financial Reporting: Evidence from Statement on Auditing Standards No. 43 in Taiwan*, 2007.

Debreceny, Roger S., and Glen L. Gray. "Data Mining Journal Entries for Fraud Detection: A Pilot Study." *International Journal of Accounting Information Systems* 11, no. 3 (2009): 157–181.

Dechow, Patricia M., Weili Ge, Chad R. Larson, and Richard G. Sloan. "Predicting Material Accounting Misstatements." *Contemporary Accounting Research* 28, no. 1 (Spring 2011): 17–82.

Emshwiller, John R. "Many Companies Report Transactions with Top Officers," *Wall Street Journal*, December 29, 2003, A1.

Henry, Elaine, Elizabeth A. Gordon, Brad Reed, and Tim Louwers. *The Role of Related Party Transactions in Fraudulent Financial Reporting,* 2006.

Hitchner, James R. *Financial Valuation: Applications and Methods*, Second Edition. Hoboken, NJ: John Wiley & Sons, 2006.

Kirkos, Efstathios, Charalambos Spathis, and Yannis Manolopoulos. *Data Mining Techniques for the Detection of Fraudulent Financial Statements*, 2007.

Li, Feng. *Annual Report Readability, Current Earnings, and Earnings Persistence.* Ann Arbor: University of Michigan, Ross School of Business Paper 1028, 2006.

MacKenzie, Bruce, Tapiwa Njikizana, Danie Coetsee, Raymond Chamboko, Blaise Colyvas, and Brandon Hanekom. *2012 Interpretation and Application of International Financial Reporting Standards.* Hoboken, NJ: John Wiley & Sons, 2012.

PwC, PricewaterhouseCoopers LLP. *IFRS and U.S. GAAP: Similarities and Differences,* October 2011.

Roxas, Maria L. "Financial Statement Fraud Detection Using Ratio and Digital Analysis." *Journal of Leadership, Accountability and Ethics* 8, no. 4 (2011): 56–66.

Tillman, Robert, and Michael Indergaard. *Control Overrides in Financial Statement Fraud, A Report to the Institute for Fraud Prevention.* Institute for Fraud Prevention, 2007.

Zack, Gerard M. *Fair Value Accounting Fraud: New Global Risks and Detection Techniques.* Hoboken, NJ: John Wiley & Sons, 2009.

About the Author

GERARD M. ZACK, CFE, CPA, CIA, CCEP, has provided forensic accounting, fraud investigation, expert witness testimony, fraud prevention, external and internal audit, internal control advisory, and training services for more than 30 years. He is the president of Zack, P.C., located in Rockville, Maryland. Mr. Zack has provided antifraud services for entities throughout North America and Europe.

Mr. Zack is the author of two previous books published by John Wiley & Sons:

- *Fair Value Accounting Fraud: New Global Risks and Detection Techniques*
- *Fraud and Abuse in Nonprofit Organizations: A Guide to Prevention and Detection*

In addition to his extensive antifraud and audit experience, Mr. Zack is also the author of numerous articles, papers, and self-published training manuals and guides. Mr. Zack is a frequent speaker at conferences, including those sponsored by the Association of Certified Fraud Examiners (ACFE) and the American Institute of Certified Public Accountants (AICPA), and has provided customized internal training for more than 50 CPA firms.

Mr. Zack serves on the faculty of the ACFE, providing training on a wide variety of fraud-related topics, and is the 2009 winner of the ACFE's James Baker Speaker of the Year Award.

For additional information about Gerry Zack and Zack, P.C., visit the Zack, P.C. website at www.zackpc.com, where there is a link to Mr. Zack's blog. He can be reached at Gerry@zackpc.com.

About the Website

THIS BOOK INCLUDES a companion website that can be accessed at www.wiley.com/go/financialstatementfraud.

The website contains copies of public documents associated with the majority of the cases cited in this book. While the book focuses on certain specific aspects of each case to illustrate a specific fraud risk, the materials on the site often provide many additional details about each.

Many of the materials are copies of the SEC AAERs described in the book, or of complaints filed by the SEC in connection with legal actions taken against companies and/or individuals. In some cases, the documents represent copies of class-action suits filed on behalf of stockholders or other public documents.

In many of the documents, explicit assertions of fraud are made. In others, the focus is more on the claim that the financial statements are materially misstated, without necessarily asserting fraud. Either way, these cases serve as excellent illustrations of the risks of financial statement fraud.

The password to enter this site is: Zack.

Index

Index to Cases

Printed and bound by CPI Group (UK) Ltd, Croydon, CR0 4YY
16/04/2025
14658444-0002